U.S. COAST SURVEY
VS.
NAVAL HYDROGRAPHIC OFFICE

History of American Science and Technology Series

General Editor, LESTER D. STEPHENS

U.S. COAST SURVEY vs. NAVAL HYDROGRAPHIC OFFICE

A 19th-Century Rivalry in Science and Politics

THOMAS G. MANNING

The University of Alabama Press
Tuscaloosa and London

Copyright © 1988 by
The University of Alabama Press
Tuscaloosa, Alabama 35487
All rights reserved
Manufactured in the United States of America

Library of Congress Cataloging-in-Publication Data
Manning, Thomas G.
  U.S. Coast Survey vs. Naval Hydrographic
Office.
   Bibliography: p.
   Includes index.
   1. U.S. Coast and Geodetic Survey—History—
19th century. 2. United States. Hydrographic
Office—History—19th century. I. Title. II. Title:
U.S. Coast Survey vs. Naval Hydrographic Office.
VK597.U6M36   1988   526.9′9′0973   87-25524
ISBN 0-8173-0390-1 (alk. paper)

British Library Cataloguing-in-Publication Data is
available.

For my five sisters:
Ellen, Margaret, Carolyn,
Gretchen, and Sue

Contents

viii   *Contents*

Acknowledgments

I should like to begin with the two places which I frequented the most while writing the book. First, there was the Library of Congress and its reference division, which is adjacent to the main reading room and rotunda. I received many courtesies and services from some fifteen persons of this reference division, whom I would like to thank through the two librarians who headed up the division: Bruce Martin and John Kimball. At the National Archives, my second major location, I received help from Albert Blair, Arthur Hecht (deceased), Dr. Sharon Gibbs Thibodeau, and James Paulaskas.

I extend my thanks to five other institutions where my research was considerably advanced: to the American Institute of Physics, and Charles Weiner and Joan Warnow; to the Department of History, Texas Tech University, and Alwyn Barr, George Flynn, Bill Johnson, Ben Newcomb, Ronald Rainger, and Dave Vigness (deceased), and to Clifford M. Parrish of the Civil Engineering faculty at Tech; to the U.S. Geological Survey and William T. Pecora (deceased), Mary C. Rabbitt, and Ellis Yochelson; to the National Geodetic Survey (NOAA) and Commander Jim Collins, Ed McKay, and Barney Pulitzer; and, finally, to the University Press of Kentucky and editor Jerome Crouch.

I am grateful to a number of libraries across the nation. I stayed only briefly with them, but the return was substantial. I mean the Bancroft Library at the University of California, Berkeley, the Houghton Library, Harvard University, the House and Senate libraries on Capitol Hill, the Library and Information Services Division, NOAA, the library of the U.S. Naval Oceanographic Office, now at Bay St. Louis, Mississippi, the New York State library at Albany, the Sterling Memorial Library, Yale University, the Texas Tech library at Lubbock, and the University of Washington library at Seattle.

I commend thirteen other persons, whose statements and commentary measurably improved my work: Lester D. Stephens of the University of Georgia, Kendall Birr of the New York State University at Albany, Ralph H. Gabriel (deceased), William H. Goetzman of the University of Texas, Austin, William F. King of Mount San Antonio College, California, Betty Littlejohn of the Library and Information Services Division, NOAA, Bob Montgomery of the Congressional Research Service (whose course on oceanography I attended), Hyman Orlin of the committee of geodesy of the National Academy of Sciences, Nate Reingold, senior historian, National Museum of American History, Murray Rogofsky of the U.S. Naval Oceanographic Office (when at Suitland, Maryland), Bob Seidel of the Bradbury Science Museum at Los Alamos, New Mexico, George Treasure of Washington, D.C., and Donald R. Whitnah of the University of Northern Iowa.

I cite four typists who carried me through successive drafts of this history. The first of these was Mrs. Bob Parker of Lubbock, Texas. In Washington, D.C., Theresa Seidel and Sidney C. McGaughey did typing for me. Also in Washington, D.C., Barbara Katz, proprietoress of Alternative Business Systems, typed the last two drafts of the manuscript. Stow Persons, Professor Emeritus of the University of Iowa, kindly read the fifth and final draft of the manuscript. Bill Ahern, a nephew, worked with me on reciprocal proofreading of the manuscript, the surest way I know for catching errors. Ed Lurie and Robert V. Bruce read page proof for the project.

Preface

Properly, this statement is written upon completion of the study, which examines a crucial phase of the relations of science and politics in the post–Civil War period. The topic chosen for exposition in the narrative mode is the long rivalry between the Coast Survey and the Hydrographic Office. The purpose of the statement is to sum up the meaning and lessons of the story.

The maintenance of quality science was a paramount objective of the Coast Survey in its rivalry with the Hydrographic Office, and the favorable outcome for the civilian bureau meant the preservation of this quality. The history also reaffirms the substantial amount of original and theoretical research done by Americans; any thesis proposing a lack of basic research during the nineteenth century is unacceptable. The experience with Congress and the Executive branch confirms what the other major scientific bureau, the Geological Survey, was facing concurrently: research in pure science was vulnerable to political reaction, and a generous amount of applied science made the best protection for the pure science.

From the governmental course of the Coast Survey, administrators of scientific bureaus can take the counsel that not only is good science necessary but, also, respectable, disciplined scientists. Disreputable or irresponsible scientists can only result in loss of reputation and political harm. If, out of necessity, a bureau compromises and admits unsavory appointees, close supervision of such personnel is obligatory.

One of the political discoveries is the clear and strong presence in national politics of the issue of economy in government, worthy to be compared in its importance to the railroad, tariff, money, trust, and land questions in the late nineteenth century. Republicans and Democrats divided over the question of money for science, with the Republicans showing liberality toward natural knowledge and the Democrats wishing to curb that knowledge in the name of economy.

The study also develops the theme of the conflict between civilians and the military—in this case, over the control of public science. Often cited as a tradition in American history, the supremacy of the civilian element is not so often illustrated in the actual happenings of peacetime America.

Finally, the results challenge a major legend of American history: that Representative Cannon of Illinois never gave his name to any constructive legislation during his long tenure in Congress. His performance in this story shows otherwise.

U.S. COAST SURVEY
VS.
NAVAL HYDROGRAPHIC OFFICE

The Expansion of the Coast Survey after the Civil War

Although founded in 1807, the United States Coast Survey, with Ferdinand R. Hassler as superintendent, did not become an ongoing operation until the 1830s. Introducing the best European practice in surveying, Hassler forged a union of applied and theoretical science through a precise measurement of lines and angles and a rigorous search for errors. He was solicitous about training his "assistants" (their formal designation) so that there would be a uniform practice in mapmaking, and he initiated studies in such affiliated subjects as tides, currents, and magnetism.

Upon becoming superintendent in 1844, Alexander D. Bache kept up the exact work of Hassler, and encouraged technical innovation in steam vessels, the self-registering tide gauge, and the electric telegraph for determining longitude. Descended from old Philadelphia families (including Franklin's) and a graduate of West Point, Bache was more genial and flexible than Hassler; he knew better how to fit the applied science of the Coast Survey into the political situation. He organized multiple centers along the East Coast, and was quick to follow the expansion of the American government into the Pacific West. He made the tripartite division of the Coast Survey into army, navy, and civilian forces an effective instrument for mapping, his relations with several naval officers being very close and friendly. Rather than engaging, like

I

Hassler, in futile quarrels with the bookkeepers of the Treasury, or talking endlessly about his health, Bache developed a rationale for the Coast Survey. Where shipping suffered damage and loss far beyond the cost of the Coast Survey, there was the bureau, charting dangerous shoals and rocks, and broadcasting its information. He disarmed suspicion of the Coast Survey as a bureaucratic government by declaring it a temporary organization, which only wanted more money so that it could finish the job and disappear.

Under Bache, the Coast Survey survived the crisis of the Civil War, and even improved its situation. During the first two years of the conflict there was talk in Congress of abandoning coastal science to concentrate on insurrection and economy; and early in 1862 the House of Representatives actually voted, in Committee of the Whole, to eliminate all bureau funds. Were not the army and navy gone from the coastal survey, and the vessels, too, which did the surveying? asked Representative Isaac N. Arnold of Illinois.[1] His proposed excision never came to pass, primarily because the superintendent responded effectively with information about the military demand for coastal charts and the meritorious presence of some seventy-five Coast Survey civilians on the staffs of generals or aboard naval flagships. No doubt Bache was helped in his defense by the feeling in Congress that it would be impolitic to disband government departments during the rebellion.

The pressure eased on Bache and the Coast Survey as the war wore on and the army and navy moved south, guided by peacetime charts and wartime supplements. For both branches, the civilian surveyors triangulated and sounded the rivers which the Union forces used in advancing into the Confederacy. During the Peninsular Campaign, four Coast Survey parties worked in McClellan's army corps. A longtime member led the Union navy into Port Royal, South Carolina, and afterward buoyed and lighted in the dark a channel into Charleston Harbor. Probably the most remarkable contribution came at the entrance to the Mississippi in 1862, where federal gunboats were anchored under Survey auspices to fire on Fort Jackson. Commander David D. Porter wrote to Bache to congratulate him and his bureau, after observing the damage done by the accurate mortar fire. Moreover, the superintendent used the letter in his struggle with Congress. At Vicksburg, a hydrographer sounded shallow water hard by the beleaguered city, and at Chattanooga a topographer sketched in on a plane table the rifle pits and fortifications of the enemy. Nearer home during Lee's invasions, Bache and his associates planned defenses around Washington, Baltimore, and Philadelphia. As the victorious Union armies pressed south in the last year of the war, Survey scientists worked for Grant at Cold Harbor and for Sheridan in the Shenandoah Valley at the battle of Winchester.

Threatened with extinction at the beginning of the war, by its end the Coast Survey had gained steadfast respect from the military that proved a stabilizing element even into the troubles of the eighties and nineties.[2]

Benjamin Peirce, the Harvard mathematician who succeeded Bache in 1867, continued the policies of his predecessor. He had Bache's statement of the duties of a good superintendent reprinted in the annual report and made the pledge to follow in the "footsteps" of his friend.[3]

A burst of optimism and activity was Peirce's contribution to the postbellum situation. The country was alive, he said, with "original thought" in technology, agriculture, commerce, and mining; its progress could not be stopped by "the fetters of . . . prejudice" or by the "darkness of . . . mystery." He saw the "energy of our people . . . constantly seeking" for every point and channel along the coast for development. And Peirce meant to help along this activity with topographical sheets of the shoreline, wherever railroads reached the sea from Cape May to Puget Sound.[4] Another of the new Americans looking for Coast Survey knowledge was the summer vacationer or yachtsman, who needed to know the coastal topography, the convenient harbors, and the views and approaches from the sea at New England resorts. Republicans and Democrats alike demonstrated on the floor of the House, in February 1868, for more mapping. Watchful representatives from both East and West demanded more surveying in California and on Puget Sound; they sought and received assurances that the East Coast would not get the lion's share of the money in the new budget. On the eve of acquiring Alaska, with even more coastline than the continental United States, Secretary of State Seward summoned the assistant in charge of the Washington office and ordered him to secure information about the northern country. On Capitol Hill, Senator Edmunds of Vermont legislated the Coast Survey onto Lake Champlain, not knowing that this freshwater body, as a Northern or Northwestern lake, was in the jurisdiction of the Corps of Engineers.[5]

Peirce's reaction to all these pressures was to ask for more money, and to stop talking about the early demise of the Coast Survey. The annual budget increased from $450,000 to $800,000, aided by the liberality of the Forty-first Congress (1869–71), which sponsored railroads and science with equal fervor. Concurrently, the second generation of government science came to the fore in geology, ethnology, weather forecasting, and fisheries. "So now comes the deluge," one of the assistants exclaimed, while writing to Peirce, who continued to reside in Cambridge.[6]

The field workers of the Coast Survey in this post–Civil War period were members of a self-conscious, confident group of some sixty persons within three grades, most of them holding the highest grade of assistant. Graduates of colleges, technical institutes, or superior high schools, these assistants had spent, on the average, twenty-five years with the Coast Survey and were making, on the average, twenty-five hundred dollars a year.[7] They were skilled draftsmen, they used and improved surveying instruments, and they located their major activity outdoors.

For these assistants the preeminent science was geodesy, which meant surveying or triangulation, whereby a portion of the earth's surface was divided into a number of triangles of varying size. Survey geodesists carefully measured an initial side of the first triangle, called the baseline, then determined the direction or azimuth of this baseline relative to a true north and south line. They secured altitude through leveling, or by observing vertical angles. Assistants also sought the geographical coordinates of one end of the baseline, a task which led them to practice astronomy with all the precision that the times allowed. For determining latitude, they used the method of Andrew Talcott, the American military and civil engineer, who with a telescope observed two stars as they culminated on his meridian, one a little north and the other a little south of his zenith. Upon measuring the slight departure of each star from the zenith, and given by catalogue the distance of each of the two stars from the celestial equator, Talcott found latitude. For longitude, the Coast Survey had been quick to incorporate the electric telegraph into its astronomy to create a network of determined points within the United States for use in the trigonometric survey; and also to connect this network with European observations. Astronomers considered the determination of longitude by previous methods accurate only to one thousand feet; errors shrank to one hundred feet when the telegraph came into use.

Occupying field stations at both ends of the baseline with a heavy instrument called a theodolite, geodesists sighted across an eighteen-inch circle or limb to a third point or target, selected as the vertex of the triangle and marked by cloth signals or by cones which reflected sunlight. Reading off angles or directions from the sighting, they computed the length of the two sides. With one of the computed sides taken as the base of another triangle, horizontal angles or directions were observed from both ends to a second vertex, and the two sides of the second triangle were computed. Latitude, longitude, and azimuth entered into the continuing computation, and the total process carried through a long chain of triangles.

The division of the land into a system of measured or computed lines, observed angles and directions, and computed or astronomically determined geographical points and directions constituted the science of geodetic surveying, and underlay the topographical and hydrographical work of the Coast Survey on the Atlantic, Gulf, and Pacific coasts. Initially, the large or primary triangulations ran fifty miles inland from the Atlantic, with the smaller, secondary work extending along the coast proper. After the Civil War, the primary triangles reached along the high ground toward the Appalachians, while a good deal of the secondary or tertiary triangulation filled the intervening watersheds.

In triangulation, an assumed figure of the earth was indispensable for doing computations. The sphere seemed the obvious mathematical model here, but the actual shape of the earth is "pearlike," with a bulge in the Southern Hemisphere, as scientists of the twentieth century have discovered. Not a party to this future understanding, nineteenth-century geodesists worked with a geometrical figure for the earth, called a spheroid or ellipsoid, which closely resembled a sphere but was flatter at the poles and bulging at the equator. And they competed with each other to find the best spheroid to represent the assumed figure of the earth.

This search and rivalry about the shape and size of man's home in the universe constituted the highest activity of geodesy. "The very first duty of the geodesist," wrote Assistant Charles S. Peirce, son of the superintendent, "is the study of the figure of the earth." The activity involved theorizing, yet it was also relevant to the practical business of surveying. So it seemed to another important assistant, when he urged "some Maecenas" to connect "his name with the history of the human race" by sustaining this kind of geodetic work. The contribution of Benjamin Peirce was to move the Coast Survey toward "a full geodetic survey of the country" and more data on the figure of the earth. This he accomplished in 1871 by asking permission from the Forty-first Congress to spend money on a continental project in triangulation, and Congress responded with $15,000 to make "a geodetic connection" between the Atlantic and Pacific coasts.[8]

In the beginning, the Coast Survey borrowed the spheroid for reference and projection from F. W. Bessel, the German mathematician and astronomer. By 1870 and Peirce's time, the bureau had accumulated enough spread of triangulation that it could begin to contribute independently to the knowledge of the assumed figure of the earth. The method for finding the earth's size and shape through triangulation was arc measurement, and the leadership in this kind of measuring came from Charles A. Schott, assistant in the Washington office, head of the computing division, critic and judge of all the geodetic work in the Survey, a prolific scholar, and a man who was to serve fifty years with the government.

Schott had to find, through triangulation, the length of long arcs or lines along meridians. He also needed the angular and linear measure of a degree of latitude within such meridional arcs, for then he could write equations which expressed functions of the observed latitude and incorporate corrections to the spheroid which the earth was assumed to be. The solution of these equations provided one number for the size of the earth, called its equatorial radius or semi-major axis, and another number which expressed the flattening or ellipticity of the earth as a relationship of the equatorial radius or semi-major axis to the polar radius or semi-minor axis. In 1868 Schott reported on the first arc measurement by the Coast Survey, a meridian line of some 3 degrees between Maine and Nantucket. In 1877 he measured another arc, this time of 11 degrees between middle Chesapeake Bay and Pamlico, North Carolina. In the same report of 1877, Schott combined the findings from these two U.S. arcs with the results from the measurement of a Peruvian arc by French scientists in the eighteenth century, to arrive at a Coast Survey "determination of the figure of the earth from American measures."[9] This determination gave quantities for the semi-major axis, the ellipticity, and other specifications for a spheroid modeled after the earth.

Concurrently, Schott submitted a critique of the Bessel spheroid, based upon the two kinds of latitudes used by the Coast Survey in its Eastern triangulation. When the geodetic latitudes were computed southward into North Carolina and there matched with Southern geodetic latitudes carried north from Georgia and South Carolina, a discrepancy appeared of almost 4 seconds of arc between the two chains. Or, as Schott reported, the triangulations, coming from opposite directions, overlapped, which suggested that this triangulation had been projected upon a spheroid too small for the earth's actual size in the vicinity of the surveying.[10] Further evidence that the Bessel spheroid was imperfect as a working model for the Coast Survey came to hand after completion of the primary triangulation between Maine and Virginia in the 1870s, for Schott discovered that the observed and computed latitudes within this span of the Eastern territory differed considerably. An obvious explanation for this divergence lay in the instrument of the surveyor for observing heavenly bodies to get the observed latitudes. That is to say, the plumb bob for accurate siting of the instrument was deflected from a vertical pointing downward by local gravitational forces, and this deflection caused the finding of latitude by instrument to differ from the latitude secured by computation. Schott saw, however, that this divergence between astronomic and geodetic latitude was not completely a shifting figure, as it would have been if the only element in its makeup had originated with local forces of attraction and repulsion within the expanding network of triangles. There was a constant in the amount of distortion, which Schott ascribed to a "defective spheroid of development."[11]

After a decade of arc measurement and discussion of results, Schott was ready, early in 1878, to propose a larger spheroid as "the fundamental surface upon which to develop the triangulations of the Coast Survey."[12] Choosing the model of the English geodesist A. R. Clarke, he forwarded his recommendation to the superintendent, who made the Clarke spheroid official in February 1880. A change also occurred in the wording for the Coast Survey on the title page of the annual report, which henceforth read, "U.S. Coast and Geodetic Survey." At the same time, Congress added to the heading for the annual appropriation, so that it now appeared as "Coast and Geodetic Survey." Early in the twentieth century the Survey arrived at its own independent values for the equatorial radius and the flattening of the earth. These Coast Survey values differed only slightly from those of the International Geodetic Association and, according to Assistant John F. Hayford, fell between the specifications for the Bessel and Clarke spheroids.

The attention given to theories of measurement and computation was another development within nineteenth-century geodesy, and also within the Coast Survey. Though marveling at the progress of their science, members took a nonpositivistic or pragmatic attitude toward their numerical findings. Mansfield Merriman, a professor of civil engineering at Lehigh College, who worked offseasons for the Coast Survey, denied that the geodesist obtained "absolutely true values of the observed quantities." He secured, wrote Merriman, only "accepted and used values," which he combined or adjusted to realize relative precision or accuracy.[13] Charles S. Peirce, who measured the length of pendulums for the Survey and the intervals of their swing, agreed with Merriman when he

(Peirce) wrote that "observation never gives us to know a *number* expressing the value of the unknown quantity." The knowledge obtained from observations, Peirce continued, "consists of nothing but average numbers."[14] He was asserting that in multiple measurements the accepted value of the results was their average amount; he was also saying that the truth about numbers in surveying only emerges from observations or practice in the field and earnest discussion afterward of the findings.

Correlative to the doctrine that no measurement or observation could be absolutely or exactly determined was the axiom that every such operation inevitably contained errors. So Survey geodesists labored incessantly with their observations to reduce errors and secure maximum precision. Of course they checked their work for egregious errors or blunders and, upon discovery, repeated the defective observations. Then there was the long search for errors arising out of heat, cold, and other natural forces, as well as the errors which went with instruments imperfectly constructed or adjusted, and the additional errors because each person's reflexes affected scientific performance differently. These natural, instrumental, and personal errors were systematic, and Mansfield Merriman had them in mind when he wrote that "the first duty of an observer after taking his measurements, is to discuss them and apply as far as possible the computed corrections to remove the constant errors."[15] Hayford was thinking of these kinds of errors when he warned the "inexperienced observer" against "taking extraordinary precautions" concerning "some small and unimportant class of errors while at the same time failing to realize that he is leaving the way open for the entrance of much larger errors of some other class."[16]

Another category of error particularly intrigued nineteenth-century geodesists, because they believed they had made considerable progress in handling it in the most advantageous way. This was the accidental or random error, which followed no regularities in man or nature and, therefore, was not amenable to the treatment accorded systematic errors. At the same time, geodesists knew they could do something about this kind of error, because, given their method of repeating observations, they had a degree of freedom in accepting some observations and discarding others. As both Schott and Benjamin Peirce said, however, they wanted to be sure that doubtful observations were not rejected through an "arbitrary choice" or by a "biassed judgment."[17] Gradually, these scientists came to realize that this kind of error was subject to objective manipulation. In France, P. S. Laplace was the first to discover the connection between random error and the theory of probability, saying that this category of error conformed to mathematical principles of probability, which could be expressed numerically or graphically. Accidental errors, Laplace wrote, were likely to be small, rather than large; they were positive or negative with equal frequency; and large errors were less probable. K. F. Gauss, of Germany, advanced the understanding of the connection proposed by Laplace when he announced the principle that the most probable value arising from the repetition of observations was the arithmetical mean of the measurements. Bessel concluded this discussion in 1841, shortly after the Coast Survey began to move, by proposing a method of comparing the accuracy of observations in terms of their probable errors. The most probable values of observations, he said, were those that minimized the sum of the squares of the residual or accidental errors. Thereafter, geodesists were busy writing and solving equations through the method of least squares, which gave them the most probable values of an unknown quantity.[18]

Perhaps the most prominent field geodesist and assistant of the Coast Survey was George Davidson, whom Superintendent Peirce dispatched to the West Coast after the Civil War. Davidson had already worked there, in the 1850s, and shown himself to be a zealous investigator and a public-spirited citizen. Right from the start out West, he was the Survey's astronomer and leading triangulator. He established the longitude of San Francisco by exchanging signals at his own observatory in the city with one at Cambridge, Massachusetts. He did or directed triangulation up and down the coast, first at the strategic places where commerce was heavy and then by projection eastward toward the Sierra Nevada, through large quadrilaterals named after him. Unlike some of his colleagues, he was not a perfectionist about his science, being willing to make-do with rapid reconnaissance, to return later for more refined mapping. Like most of the other assistants, he was mechanical minded: not only did he invent a device to allow the leveling rod to be moved up and down more slowly, but he incorporated a clamp for securing the rod when its proper extension had been realized. Furthermore, Davidson constructed a meridian instrument to observe stars crossing the meridian—horizontal motion required—and to measure their angular distance from the observer's zenith, which was instrumental movement with a vertical dimension. On the Pacific Coast, Davidson compiled a full-length directory for the information of all Pacific navigators. His passion for knowledge of shallow waters was famous; whenever a steamer struck a hidden rock, Davidson was certain to be on the scene shortly to locate the obstacle. He informed the superintendent in 1888 that he had discovered seven of the eight great dangers along the Pacific Coast. He was willing to do research in the documents to find magnetic observations, and he read in the writings of four languages to find out about Indian place names. Davidson was also a public figure who served as regent of the state university, who became an expert on irrigation, who named for himself an extraordinary current, not then understood (which he discovered north of San Francisco, where it was pushing ships ashore), and who wrote about the Alaskan boundary at a time when nationalistic Californians were showing great sensitivity about their rights in contested territory. He was a man of many talents and interests in an age when scientists were becoming increasingly specialized.

Davidson's eagerness for power and prominence frequently put him at cross purposes with the superintendent, other assistants, and officers of the navy. He sought continually to add to his authority on the West Coast. For three years in the 1860s, he tried to persuade Peirce to give him the title "inspector general," or "acting superintendent," or "assistant in charge." Peirce was not willing to award such titular prominence to any subordinate, and denied that he had ever promised any such thing. He said that Davidson could have general supervision of the scientific work there; that he could submit programs, which the superintendent would write up and pass on to the other assistants with Davidson; and he could be the channel of official communication with the superintendent. "You go to the Western Coast," he wrote Davidson in 1868, "with my best wishes for your success and with full confidence in your ability and the rectitude of your intentions."[19]

Davidson attempted the same power play with his associates in California, who were just as stubborn as Peirce about their integrity. Assistant William D. Dall, explorer and naturalist, would not let Davidson make the decision by himself about the seaworthiness of the *Humboldt,* the ship to take Dall to Alaska. Dall thought that Davidson acted only in an advisory role toward him, except in the transmission of official documents to the office. No one but the superintendent gave orders, he insisted. The relations with Dall were tense, in any event, because the latter did not hesitate to criticize Davidson's hurried preparation of materials about Alaska for the annual report of 1867 and for a publication in 1869 on the coast of that territory. Davidson, Dall said, tended to follow V. P. Tebenkov's charts when the earlier J. F. La Pérouse charts were better.

Davidson was no more successful in his aggressive tactics with Philip C. Johnson, the naval commander of the Survey steamer *Hassler.* "Now my dear Davidson," began Johnson, "your idea of our official relations does not accord with mine."[20] By rank and service Johnson asserted the right to independent hydrographic command. It was proper to confer with Davidson but improper to submit reports and expenditure lists to him. After referring to our "friendship which has been strengthened by years," Johnson wrote that he admired Davidson's talent, ability, and energy; that he desired advice and would be grateful for it; but he declared he was not expected or instructed to place himself under Davidson's direction.

Similarly, William Eimbeck, one of the founders of the Cosmos Club, refused to take orders from Davidson in the geodetic work, for this recently promoted assistant did not think he would get credit for any work done under Davidson.

Davidson was all for charting the coastline from San Diego to Panama, even if such operations meant ignoring the rights of the navy there. The area south of the Mexican border was not U.S. coastline and, therefore, was beyond the jurisdiction of the Coast Survey. As foreign territory, it became the mapping responsibility of the navy. Nevertheless, Davidson wanted the *Hassler,* under Johnson, to develop this foreign coastline, for the obvious reason that the harvest of knowledge was likely to be very popular with Californians concerned about the safety of the sea route to Panama. On the best of charts the coastline was fifteen to thirty miles west of the true position. Peirce seriously considered Davidson's proposal, but in the end decided against any such sweeping challenge to the navy's position in the established order of American mapping, particularly after the Hydrographic Office had sent the USS *Narragansett* and the USS *Portsmouth* to survey the Mexican coast. To Davidson, the prospect of duplication seemed an ideal opportunity to compare the Coast Survey to the Hydrographic Office in their mapping methods.

Topography was the other half of scientific surveying by the assistants. In the post–Civil War period, topographers worked in Maine, along the Gulf from Florida to Texas, and on the West Coast into southeastern Alaska. The ultimate goal was a finished chart which set forth the undersea ground and the natural features of the coastline above water, whether rock, sand, swamp, high or low land, forest or open land, and the man-made features. By the end of the century, Coast Survey scientists had constructed in field and office some five hundred of these charts, favoring the two scales 1/10000 (six inches to the mile) or 1/20000. They also made special surveys on the much larger scale of 1/1200, or one hundred feet to the inch. Publication occurred on a reduced scale, from 1/50000 to 1/60000, which was slightly above one inch for every mile.

Field work, according to the Coast Survey, was both a science and an art. The science lay first in the trigonometric or true positions on the sheets previously prepared in field and office by the geodesists of the Survey. It also lay in the use by the topographers of the plane table (introduced by Hassler), whereby many subordinate positions were added to the sheets from the office. The to-

pographers pinned the provided sheets to the plane tables, each of
which carried a sighting instrument. They then sighted across the
plane table on visible objects and plotted them for direction, distance, and height in relation to the given trigonometric points.
"Artistic skill and intuition" came into play when the topographers began filling in on the plane-table sheets the natural and social detail between the determined positions. The central task was
the "faithful representation of the hills," upon which the ultimate
value of the maps depended. Using visual means alone, the topographers drew in horizontal lines from position to position of
equal elevation. These were the contour curves, which were dis-
tanced on the Coast Survey charts to represent changing heights
every twenty feet.[21]

The most celebrated product of Survey topography in this period was the map of the harbor and city of New Haven by Richard
M. Bache.[22] Field topographers called it their best for its accuracy,
beauty, and detail; engineers and geologists admired and used it.
Bache's father Hartman Bache had been a prominent topographer
and leader in the Corps of Engineers before the Civil War. Like his
father, the son was a talented topographer, who served forty-five
years with the Survey and wrote novels on the side.

In 1870, President Noah Porter of Yale College, geologist James
D. Dana, and other members of the faculty petitioned the Survey
for a map of the city of New Haven and its environs. Bache came
amid mutual misunderstanding about the financing of the job: the
Coast Survey thought that Yale was to provide the money while
Yale believed that the Coast Survey would. What saved and transformed this muddled situation was the intervention by the mayor
of New Haven, who, after consulting with Bache, wrote to Peirce
that the city needed a hydrographic and topographic survey of the
harbor and waterfront, and would share in the expense of making
one. To his scientific work Bache now added the job of coordinat-
ing the efforts of the Coast Survey, Yale College, and the city of
New Haven. He discussed with the mayor his scientific moves,
occupied a room in City Hall, talked and lectured to committees
of the municipality, showed the Yale faculty how his instruments
worked, and began sounding the harbor with several aides and a

boat and policeman provided by New Haven. When he could, he used seniors from Yale College as his aides.

By 1876 Bache and the parties with him at New Haven had determined forty-three points in triangulation to add to the few recovered from antebellum times. On the plane table, they had drawn contour lines at intervals of three feet to cover some nine hundred acres of topography on a fringe of shoreline along half of the harbor (including wharves), as well as a large area along the inland waterways. In the end, Bache and his aides had thirteen sheets to show, each three feet square on a scale of 1/1200, and one larger sheet, incorporating the whole effort on a scale of 1/2400. Bache called the latter "the handsomest piece of topography extant on a single sheet" and "the most accurate survey ever made." It would, he thought, give the Coast Survey "great influence, not only in New Haven, but in the State."[23]

The return in topographical knowledge grew impressively in the 1870s with the publication of a new Survey series, called the *Atlantic Coast Pilots,* which were, like Davidson's directories, compendious digests of nautical information and advice. President Eliot of Harvard University reviewed the second volume of this *Atlantic Coast Pilot* (Boston Bay to New York) for the *Boston Daily Advertiser,* Survey topographer John S. Bradford having made the compilation. "Illustrated with beautifully engraved charts," this volume described coastline, harbors, and thoroughfares. Bradford warned of dangers and obstructions, and gave directions for coasting, approaching, and entering harbors, along with views and charts of major harbors. He also communicated the geographical position of all lighthouses and information about fogs, signals, tides, and currents. As an example of accurate, precise, and exhaustive work, Eliot cited Bradford's description of Boston Harbor, which included heights of landmarks, compass bearings, ranges, and the color, size, and shape of houses, beacons, and buoys. Eliot also liked the different type sizes for the descriptions of shorelines, dangers, and sailing directions, and praised the proofreading in a book where an error in typography might cause a wreck. He advised masters of vessels to become acquainted with the volume, and told insurance companies to require coasters to carry it with them. Eliot declared that this *Coast Pilot* bore to any previous work "the relation of a finished, accurate, life-like picture to a rough sketch."[24]

Another leading topographer was Augustus F. Rodgers, one of Davidson's colleagues on the West Coast. Rodgers mapped the San Francisco Bay Area, San Diego, and other major points in California. Knowing where his product would do the most good, he provided tracings of his maps for the Corps of Engineers when they were locating harbor defense batteries around San Francisco and San Diego. Like Davidson, he served on commissions to deal with encroachments on the natural lines of harbors by railroads, lumber companies, and steamboats, whose wharves, thrusting into the current, led to dead water and shoaling banks of mud. While resurveying San Diego and its bay in the 1880s, Rodgers hoped that the new charts would illustrate such encroachments and alert the citizenry to the fact that private enterprise did not look beyond the occasion or the emergency. He was arguing for the interest of the national government in deep harbors and their protection for the public good.

Rodgers was also an aggressive adviser to senators from California about dangers to navigation in the state and in the territory of Alaska. His survey of the peninsula of San Francisco (in the decade before the New Haven work) was considered by army engineers in the vicinity "the most complete ever seen." He told the superintendent that "the pilots and masters of steamboats engaged in towing deep draught ships up and down [the Columbia River], place great reliance on the Coast Survey charts upon which they are easily able to follow and trace the changes occasioned by the annual freshets."[25]

Rodgers dispatched both criticism and praise to the national office. He disliked the bureau's communication of its product, believing that the sale and distribution of charts was "imperfect and unsettled" and that the discovery of new, hidden rocks should be publicized more quickly, as the local branch of the navy's Hydrographic Office was urging. He also advised the superintendent that British Admiralty charts were popular with mariners because of their Mercator projection and their convenience for laying down courses. No doubt he raised morale in the national office with the information that the map of San Francisco had "figured in numerous lawsuits," with the saving of millions of dollars to those in the right by the "admitted impartial representation of facts." One citizen thanked him warmly for the "accurate and official data," furnished without fee, which preserved a piece of property to its rightful owner, who had paid for it in full and would have suffered hardship if its threatened loss had occurred. Rodgers was less emotional than Davidson, and citizens of the Bay Area seemed to get along well with him.[26]

Research in the physical history of the Atlantic seaboard was another innovation of the Coast Survey under Peirce, who chose Henry Mitchell of Nantucket, brother of astronomer Maria Mitchell, to be the Survey's expert in physical hydrography. The science of Mitchell's reports was his knowledge of tidal, coastal, and river currents. As early as 1858 he knew about undercurrents at the mouth of the Hudson, where an incoming tide at the bottom could be salt while the seaward surface flow was fresh.[27] Mitchell codified his science in diagrams, which gave transverse curves of velocity and a profile of water movement from top to bottom. Width, depth, velocity, volume, and perimeter of current were his fundamental data. Constants of velocity and coefficients of scour also entered into his calculations. At Sandy Hook and in Martha's Vineyard Sound, where seagoing or coastal vessels passed in great numbers, he studied the movement of sand impelled by the ocean. And in harbor areas, going beyond Rodgers, he sought knowledge of tidal currents to understand their effect on man-made structures.

For the annual report of the Coast Survey in 1886, he did his most famous study, an article with the title "On the Circulation of the Sea through New York Harbor." Mitchell's objective here was the province of the East River in the movement of water through New York Harbor, and he began with the obvious fact that the river was a conduit for tidal currents from Long Island Sound moving toward Upper New York Harbor—and then, conversely, a conduit for water flowing from the Upper Bay toward Long Island Sound. From his statistics, he drew the important conclusion that in the ebb and flow through New York Harbor there was "a net gain" of water discharge in the westerly direction from Long Island Sound through the Upper and Lower Bays into the ocean past Sandy Hook.[28] The predominance of current west and south assured him and the commercial interests of New York that Sandy Hook would never block the city, as the tidal scour worked in the outward direction.

Mitchell also held a membership in the National Academy of Sciences and sat on harbor commissions from Portland, Maine, to the Delaware.

The outdoor work tested the physical and mental endurance of the assistants. In camp, they performed such extraordinary chores as liming tents to prevent mildew, setting traps to catch possums and skunks, and building brush fences to keep out cattle. In the field, each kind of country offered its special brand of obstacle or discomfort. Lowlands along the Gulf Coast and the Mississippi River were marshy or wet, forcing topographers to wade continually in mud or water. In wooded country, the climbing of trees, sometimes near two hundred feet high, required skilled hands and cool heads. In the mountains, there was the breaking of trails over ragged rock and climbing up and down on hands and knees with heavy packs. In Maine during July, according to Charles H. Boyd, the woods were "uninhabitable from the black-fly pest."[29] Ordinary people, going into the forest, could use tar and oil for protection, but not the Survey assistants, who must handle instruments and notebooks. In the Midwest, one scientist noticed the approach of a dirty yellow and green storm cloud, which soon carried away eight tent flies. Next morning the camp area was found strewn with broken chairs, articles of clothing, tin pans, and bedding; some items were found half a mile away. In southern Texas, it seemed to another worker that every tree and bush was covered with thorns, and the sand was filled with millions of ants.[30] After long and troublesome labor in preparation for sightings, fog, smoke, or clouds often made the taking of observations impossible.

Danger of grave physical harm was the ultimate threat outdoors.

In California, Rodgers feared rattlesnakes, who enjoyed a warm blanket as much as any scientist occupying a station, but lacking a cot to sleep on. According to Boyd, illness was the worst feature of camp life, for the reason that the party was frequently so situated that no physician could be called for quickly. In the mountains, lightning was a terrifying experience. Eimbeck suffered the continual apprehension of "instant destruction," which he found a tremendous drain on his nervous system. He had yet to meet the person who bore up tranquilly under the strain; only men of exceptional nerve and devotion could stand the sound of the crackling electricity, he wrote. One party of signal sighters at Jeff Davis Mountain in Nevada was "so . . . frightened out of their wits as never to stop fleeing until they reached their homes near Pioche." In the scenery, Eimbeck found compensation for his fright. At the apex of Mount Ouray in Colorado, "upon the very axis of the great 'Continental Divide,'" he enjoyed a magnificent prospect—"a perfect tumult of bold and cragged mountain peaks," he exulted.[31]

A specific account of an outdoor event vividly communicates the harsh experience of Survey scientists. In the late spring of 1887, assistants John F. Pratt and Fremont Morse made eight preliminary topographical sheets of the coastline between Gray's Harbor and Cape Flattery in the territory of Washington. Pratt, in command, was a graduate of Dartmouth College in 1871, and had been on the West Coast since the mid-seventies, where he was well on his way to participation in every class of Survey work. On their feet twelve hours a day, the two men waded cold streams, climbed ravines and cliffs, and slept on the ground. "I have roughed it a good deal," wrote Pratt, "but my entire experience has been nothing compared to it." Bad weather prevented him from taking many astronomic sightings; time and latitude were found with the sextant. The assistants did their measuring of length with steel wire and, when feasible, made point angles with the theodolite. Morse took the wire measurements on the beach while someone else recorded for him. After Pratt raised range poles and selected terminal points, Morse ran the plane table over the country. Pratt lost fourteen pounds in five weeks, and both men suffered aching limbs and rheumatic pains for a fortnight after their return to Seattle. Of course, the topographical sheets improved locations of capes, ports, and islands—up to two miles.[32]

Jasper S. Bilby, foreman and signalman, was the ideal member of the Survey force in the field. In this period he dominated the building of the signal towers, by which the triangulation was carried forward. Bilby often traveled eight hundred or one thousand miles a month, scarcely giving himself "opportunity for rest or meals," as he opened lines of sight, posted or reposted the cones which flashed sunlight to other stations, and wished for signal-builders who were good both aground and aloft. Five of the assistants were so impressed with Bilby that they wanted to bestow on him the special title "Artificer to the Coast Survey." These level-headed surveyors saw him as someone "who could stand the wear and tear of outdoor life," who made "no mistakes" in "details or accounts," and was "the most generally useful and entirely reliable man . . . in the service."[33] Bilby never disappointed the faith of his admirers in his genius. Early in the twentieth century he invented a steel tower, which named after him, and assembled and dismantled at site after site, replaced in the Coast Survey the trees or wooden structures traditionally relied upon by surveyors.

The scientific momentum of the Coast Survey continued into the eighties, under the superintendency of Julius Erasmus Hilgard, who was as capable a scientist as the bureau ever had. A photograph shows him to have been a good-looking man, with a large, well-proportioned face, mildly bearded, and altogether presenting an intelligent, courtly appearance. Fifty-six years old when he came to the headship, after twenty years in charge of the Washington office, and in effect superintendent during Bache's illness and Peirce's absence, Hilgard was talented and versatile. He possessed intimate knowledge of surveying instruments of precision, for he wrote many articles in the annual reports on testing them and discussing their errors.

He left Washington one summer to relate the longitude of the American continent to Europe and England, a task which required him to unite at Brest, in France, signals from America, Greenwich, and Paris. On another occasion, he gave twenty lectures at

Johns Hopkins University on surveying. For many years he directed the business of weights and measures for the Coast Survey, comparing the British and American standard yards, writing on the length of the nautical mile for the U.S. Naval Institute, and preparing metric standards for the states. He was in charge of the Coast Survey eclipse party at Des Moines, Iowa, in 1869; his main job there was to work with the spectroscope. During the seventies, Hilgard was president of the American Association for the Advancement of Science, secretary of the National Academy of Sciences, and a judge of scientific apparatus at the Centennial Exhibition. Also, he had the refusal of the directorship of the new International Bureau of Weights and Measures in Paris. Like Sigsbee, he won a gold medal in 1883, at the London Fisheries Exhibition, for inventing a densimeter to measure the specific gravity of ocean water.[34]

Given Hilgard's experience and accomplishments, it should cause no surprise that under his leadership the science of the Coast Survey continued to be productive, inspiring healthy demand and praise. The hydrographic and topographic parties continued on the Maine coast; they surveyed Long Island Sound and Delaware River and Bay, and advanced toward completion of the charts for the American shores of the Gulf of Mexico. A new area for surveying on the Pacific Coast was Puget Sound and the Straits of San Juan de Fuca. Even more, Hilgard revived the Alaskan work, suspended since the severe budget reductions of the late seventies. Commercial and fishing interests, centered in San Francisco, were insisting that interior passages of southeastern Alaska, like Wrangell Strait, needed more mapping to uncover their hidden dangers. The outstanding feature of Hilgard's initiative was his success in persuading Congress to appropriate $100,000 in 1883 to build a bark-rigged wooden steamer for the Alaskan surveying. Launched in 1884, this steamer was named the *Patterson* after Hilgard's predecessor, who had designed the vessel. He also secured from Congress small raises for the great majority of the assistants of the Coast Survey.

A strong advance in tidal observation and theory occurred under Hilgard. William Ferrel, a noted meteorologist, theorized in the modern spirit when he wrote in a Coast Survey publication of

1874, entitled *Tidal Researches,* that tides did not materialize because of a worldwide wave originating in the ocean south of the continents (William Whewell and G. B. Airy of England were divided here). On the contrary, tides were regional or local phenomena; in the Atlantic Ocean of the North American continent, they resulted from periodic oscillations within the basin of the North Atlantic, and were not affected by tides in other localities, however large. Ferrel also practiced Scotsman William Thomson's method for obtaining a complete tide table. Two figures were needed: the height of the tide, often designated its amplitude, and the interval until high water after the moon's passage, called the epoch of the tide. Given these two tidal constants over a nineteen-year period, the mathematician or tidal expert could construct tables of prediction for all future tides at any tide-measuring station.

Thomson and Ferrel's method of tide computation was analytical: they broke down the actual, complex tide, incorporating the irregular positions and unequal motions of the sun, moon, and earth into a large number of simple tides. Then they computed the amplitude and epoch of each of these simple tides by assuming a score of ideal moons and suns as the tide-producing forces. One such ideal satellite, according to Ferrel, was the mean moon, moving uniformly in the plane of the equator and always at the same distance from the earth. This mean moon gave rise to the large and important semi-diurnal tide. There were two ideal satellites for the diurnal components of the moon tides and, of course, a series of satellites, variously positioned, to express the tide-producing force of the sun. The sum total of the constants in amplitude and epoch for the simple tidal constants constituted the tidal constants for the actual tide. To solve for these actual tidal constants, the expert needed the period of each ideal satellite (determined by theory) and a year's observations of actual tide for height and time.

Ferrel, like Thomson, invented a tide-predicting machine to go with the analysis of tidal observations and save the labor of many human computers. Ferrel submitted the theory and plan in 1880. George N. Saegmuller, the foreman of the instrument division, supervised the construction of the machine by a Washington firm, and in three years the machine was being used to predict the tides for the year 1885. Ferrel's machine predicted time and height of high and low water for any coastal station of the Survey. It incorporated nineteen of the larger tidal constants into the machinery through settings for nineteen axles, cranks, and pulleys. On the face of the machine, dials indicated the times and heights of the predicted tides. The machine was operated by a handle, which was turned manually until two hands, moving over the face of the machine, came together. When the convergence of the dial hands signaled to the operator that a high or low water was being recorded, he stopped cranking the handle and read from the dials the time and height of the tide.[35]

For all the qualities and successes of Hilgard and his assistants, the Survey was vulnerable to reforming zeal or partisan attack because of the superintendent. During his long tenure in the government, Hilgard had become a schemer and manipulator, and was recognized as such by those around him. Peirce, learning to expect and dislike lack of sincerity in Hilgard, delayed his ascension to the superintendency by installing Hydrographic Inspector C. P. Patterson as chief, for the middle and late seventies. When assigning a temporary and easy job of surveying in some pleasant community, Hilgard frequently betrayed his cynical attitude by implying that this kind of a job was exactly what the "lucky" recipient wanted. One of the rare occasions when the Allison Commission, an important investigatory body in this history, showed irritation came after Hilgard's departure from the government. The Commission had asked the superintendent to submit salary schedules, and Hilgard had provided a listing of line items from the budget. Later, the Commission discovered, to its annoyance, that Hilgard had not told them of the substantial income of Coast Survey scientists from other items in the Coast Survey budget.

Two incidents in Coast Survey affairs a year before the crisis in 1885 show how Hilgard operated.[36] When in January 1884 the wooden steamer *Patterson* was launched at Brooklyn for Alaskan duty, a collation, including champagne, was served for sixty guests, and the vessel was christened with some of the same champagne by one of the daughters of the late superintendent. Shortly

after the christening, Lieutenant Albion V. Wadhams of the Coast
Survey hydrographic force presented a voucher to the disbursing
agent of the Coast Survey, along with subvouchers from trades-
people in Brooklyn, which certified the expenditure of $99 at the
christening of the *Patterson*. The disbursing agent, William B.
Morgan, disallowed the voucher. In the middle of February, another voucher to cover the festivities was submitted, by Commander Colby M. Chester, the Hydrographic Inspector of the
Coast Survey, and was approved by Hilgard. Again, Morgan refused payment.

But Hilgard was a resourceful bureaucrat, and his third attempt
to secure public money for the launching ceremony succeeded.
Prior to the event he had obtained two checks, one for $100 and
the other for $120, at the disbursing office of the Coast Survey,
drawn on the Treasurer of the United States and payable to the
order of Hilgard. With these two checks the superintendent not
only met the social expenses at the Brooklyn shipyard, amounting
to $99, but also the travel bill ($120) of the two Patterson daughters, who came from Washington to be present at the christening.
Upon the delivery of the two checks to Hilgard, an account in his
name, to the amount of $220, was recorded in the disbursing of-
fice, and after several months Morgan asked the superintendent to
settle this account. Hilgard responded by handing over a voucher
signed by Julius Bien & Company, photolithographers of New
York City, which bore the information that the company had engraved on stone three illustrations of the plans of the surveying
steamer *Patterson* at a cost of $220, one dollar more than Hilgard's
indebtedness at the disbursing office. The Bien voucher was
charged to the congressional appropriation for the building of the
steamer *Patterson,* and the date of the voucher was made to correspond with the dates of the two checks that amounted to $220 and
were issued to Hilgard before the launching.

Thus, through the complicity of a New York photoengraving
company, Hilgard covered his unauthorized expenditure of public
money. Bien & Company actually did the three engravings on
stone and delivered them to the Coast Survey. What was omitted
was payment for the work, the company having agreed with Hil-

gard beforehand that the engravings would constitute a "courteous gratuity" extended by the company because of its large printing business in Coast Survey charts.

The same year, 1884, Hilgard exploited the good will of a second supplier of the Coast Survey, Edward Kübel, a local instrumentmaker. Hilgard went to Kübel, told him that the Coast Survey office was in a financial squeeze, and said that he could help by signing two blank vouchers. Kübel signed and Hilgard immediately filled in the vouchers with the information that two optical densimeters, worth $192, had been made for the Coast Survey. The superintendent then gave checks to Kübel for the amount, who went off to cash them. Bringing the money to the Coast Survey building, he stopped in the waiting room adjacent to Hilgard's office. In a classic maneuver for passing money secretively, Hilgard led Kübel down a corridor into a washroom, where the superintendent took the $192, counted it, and put it in his pocket. Kübel neither built nor sold densimeters on this occasion; he simply provided a signature, thereby allowing Hilgard to lay his hands on public money.

Perhaps these financial manipulations would never have come to light had not Hilgard allowed internal discipline to relax in flagrant ways. Political appointments were an obvious cause of poor or unruly performance within government departments, and Hilgard, like other heads of scientific bureaus in Washington at this time, had to bow to the inevitable. He failed, however, to do as well as his scientific colleagues in curbing the harmful effect of these political appointments. Several times the superintendent put persons on the payroll at the request of members of Congress, then required no work from them. Having allowed political partisans to join the Coast Survey, Hilgard did not prevent these partisans from identifying the Coast Survey with their political activity. In 1882, a Portland (Maine) newspaper carried a story from Washington that a congressional assessment committee and the Garfield Memorial Fund had been using Coast Survey envelopes. And two years later, in 1884, a janitor of the Coast Survey building shook money in people's faces, accompanying his flourish with the statement that the bills were going to Ohio to buy Democratic votes for James G. Blaine, the Republican presidential candidate.[37] In the drawing and engraving divisions, extra work was done for outside parties and the proceeds were distributed among the members of the divisions, although a number of laws forbade extra work for extra pay, unless explicitly provided for by appropriation acts.[38] Several times the assistant in charge of the Washington office put a stop to some of these informal arrangements, but they were never completely abolished while Hilgard was superintendent.

The ultimate defect in Hilgard was his habit of drinking too much. The superintendent could be counted upon to stay sober in the morning; by afternoon, however, his fatal habit possessed him—and the news became public enough by 1884 that clerks in a nearby dry goods store gossiped about him. Nausea and depression went with the drinking.[39] Inevitably, Hilgard's infirmity affected his control within the Coast Survey. He had always been a talkative person; now, in 1884, Charles O. Boutelle, the assistant in charge of the office, was reluctant to tell him about confidential aspects of congressional politics—in one instance, about a move to break up the Coast Survey. It became increasingly difficult to obtain action from the superintendent; important papers would lie on his desk, unread or unsigned, for weeks. And alas! his behavior proved contagious. Stories were told that bottles of liquor passed from room to room in the Survey building, and Schott wrote privately about the "drunken set" in the Survey.[40]

The Emergence of the Hydrographic Office

2

Like the Coast Survey, the Department of the Navy practiced scientific surveying in antebellum times. Twice it had been the sole surveyor of the American coastline, before the Coast Survey had fully organized its systematic mapping. Customarily, non-American shores and waters were the navy's exclusive domain. The climax of naval surveying came during the expedition to the South Pacific, commanded by Lieutenant Charles Wilkes. At home after 1842, Lieutenant Matthew F. Maury exercised leadership in naval science, occupying a dual position as superintendent of both the Naval Observatory and a "hydrographical" office. Maury, a Virginian who had been a midshipman in the navy, could no longer go to sea because of a serious knee injury. His chief rivalries in government science were with Joseph Henry of the Smithsonian over the control of land meteorology, and with Bache about deep-sea soundings in the Atlantic.

Maury made his name in world science when he transformed the hydrographic duties of his job, which, before his time, had merely required the administration of a depot for naval charts and instruments. He commenced with the painstaking collection of information from mariners' logs and, with the knowledge thus acquired, constructed wind and current charts for the Atlantic, Pacific, and Indian oceans. On several series of these charts he plotted

27

winds and currents, and collated statistics on their prevailing directions. He also drew the tracks and gave the names of vessels from whose logs the marine information was derived. Maury recorded water temperature, located breeding grounds of whales, and organized materials on the frequency of storms and rains. A second large accomplishment of this remarkable man was the compiling of sailing directions of coast pilots for coasts other than the American, where, of course, the Coast Survey presided. [1]

The Civil War ended forever Maury's association with governmental science, because he joined the Confederacy. For several years in the 1860s, no appropriation was forthcoming in support of his maritime projects. With the coming of peace, however, and given the friendly disposition toward governmental projects in science, which had inspired the expansion of the Coast Survey, a successful revival of Maury's pre-war hydrography came to pass. Shipmasters and insurance companies presented Congress with a lengthy memorial, Rear Admiral Charles H. Davis of the Bureau of Navigation and Bache of the Coast Survey collaborated, and a military-civilian board declared it a governmental responsibility to publish charts and books for American navigators. [2] Describing his project as a venture in "Foreign Hydrography," Admiral Davis proposed that naval vessels do coastal surveying abroad and that a hydrographic office engrave the results. [3] If charts of foreign shores were already available, let the new agency replenish them as they were disposed of. Also, Maury's wind and current charts would be republished.

In 1866, Congress passed "An Act to Establish a Hydrographic Office in the Navy Department"; this Act made the Office independent of the Naval Observatory and placed it in the Bureau of Navigation. The Treasury and the Bureau of Navigation arranged for the newly created Hydrographic Office to assume responsibility for publishing *The New American Practical Navigator,* which the concern of E. & G. W. Blunt of New York City had been bringing out all through the century. The Blunts were the foremost publishers of nautical textbooks in the United States, and these textbooks provided seamen with all the tables needed for determining latitude and longitude, if they also possessed the *Nautical Almanac,* which was already being published by the government. In 1867, the Navy Department, Gideon Welles being secretary, found $70,000 to pay the Blunts for the copyright and stereotype plates of the thirty-fifth edition of the *Practical Navigator*.

The Hydrographic Office flourished primarily as a maritime publishing company. During the early seventies, before an economy movement began to undermine government finances, it spent $100,000 annually (almost all of it in Washington) and operated at the well-known Octagon building with a staff of fifty persons, twenty of them naval officers. This place was a compiling, printing, and distributing center, based initially on the past projects of Lieutenant Maury. The new Hydrographic Office reprinted charts from Maury's copper plates, and then began its own engraving of revised charts, whose ancient originals by Maury were frequently overloaded with signs, figures, and lines. It also republished *The New American Practical Navigator*. In 1869 the Office began preparing notices to mariners about man-made and natural changes along all coasts save the American, for which the Lighthouse Board was responsible. Concurrently, the Bureau of Navigation organized an Admiralty chart room, and for many years the Hydrographic Office reproduced charts of the British government, then dominant in marine publishing. In 1870, Captain Robert Harris Wyman, author and translator of oceanographic materials, became the leader of the Hydrographic Office. He was the first to be called Hydrographer and served the longest in the agency's history—eight years.

The Office also originated other publishing ventures. Lieutenant Commander Henry H. Gorringe, who later won popular renown by delivering and putting up an obelisk in Central Park, commanded the USS *Gettysburg* in the Mediterranean from 1872 to 1876. Gorringe took soundings, measured winds and currents, described stretches of the coast, and learned about local laws and customs, all of which went into Office guidebooks. Gorringe insisted that he was not making a coast pilot for vessels of war, which, after all, could carry hundreds of charts. His purpose was to help the merchantmen who could not afford a nautical library. His *Coasts and Islands of the Mediterranean Sea*, published by the

Hydrographic Office in four volumes between 1875 and 1883, was called a "splendid sailing directory."[4] The reprinting of the pamphlet *Steam-Lanes across the Atlantic* represented a return to Maury, who had first placed the work before the public in the 1850s. The New York Board of Underwriters ordered a thousand copies. Ernst R. Knorr, the civilian head of the drafting department, translated a collective German work on the Gulf Stream, which improved on Maury's presentation of ocean temperature by drawing isothermal lines.

The officer corps of the Hydrographic Office projected their brightest hopes toward the Pacific Ocean, where they most wanted to do research. This ocean seemed the "natural and necessary highway"[5] of great trade to the Far East. The dream of an interoceanic canal also stirred the imagination of naval officers, and they looked expectantly to communication with Japan by cable. Scientific chartmaking on Mexico's Pacific Coast was the specific activity to which the corps gave their most earnest and continuous attention. Irregular, disconnected, or ancient surveys were characteristic of the long coastline south of the American border. It was easy to compile, from the best London charts, a page of errors on coastal positions, on offshore islands, and on depths and dangerous rocks. Officers hoped the results would compare favorably with the Coast Survey product and lead to the making by the Hydrographic Office of all the maritime charts for American territories around the Pacific basin.

In 1872 an appropriation of $50,000 allowed a start in Baja California and the Gulf of California.[6] For three years, until the lack of money closed down the operation, naval officer George Dewey, commanding the USS *Narragansett,* determined latitudes and longitudes, made soundings, and located positions by the measurement of horizontal angles with the sextant. On land and sea, he took the bearings of the principal peaks and their angular altitudes, and he sketched in the shore as he moved down the Mexican coast into the Gulf of California. To accompany this reconnaissance or running survey, Dewey provided information on winds, currents, and tides, on anchorage, channels, and drinking water. Recognizing Dewey's work as an improvement over the publication of its own Hydrographic Office,[7] the British Admiralty hastened to engrave the results, which was done before the American Office could secure publication funds from Congress.

The Caroline and Marshall Islands were another unknown and threatening region. These islands were the repository of thousands of dangers, many of which probably did not exist or were incorrectly located. Sometimes the same island had half a dozen positions assigned to it, with opinions differing by as much as fifty miles as to its proper location. The only thing that the Hydrographic Office could do at the time to keep ships from piling up on poorly located rocks, shoals, or islands was to update sounding sheets and reports and to publicize reported dangers to navigation in the North Pacific Ocean.

An impressive feat occurred in 1873, when Commander George E. Belknap sailed the USS *Tuscarora* on a deep-sea exploring expedition, his primary purpose being to determine the feasibility of laying a submarine cable between the United States and Japan. Maintaining the antebellum, innovative spirit of the American navy in marine technology, Belknap used steel wire instead of hemp line for the sounding machine, invented by William Thomson. Also, the commander was good at inventing cylinders or cups for bringing specimens up from the bottom. Northeast of Japan, he sounded five and one-quarter miles to pick up five ounces of mud; this was the greatest depth recorded until 1895, when two British ships secured bottom samples in the South Pacific at six miles.[8]

The next prominent hydrographer after Captain Wyman was Commander John Russell Bartlett, explorer, scientist, and naval officer, who made his regime of five years (1883–88) the nineteenth-century climax of the Hydrographic Office. Bartlett inspired his organization with a spirit of improvement that looked to the day when all aids to navigation would be "perfect."[9] He sought new ways of applying scientific knowledge to the navigation of the North Atlantic and hoped, through services performed, to raise the standing and influence of the navy with the commercial and seafaring classes. In his relations with Congress, he managed to reverse the downward trend of the annual budget and bring it back almost to the $100,000 level of Captain Wyman's early years at the Office.

Bartlett presided in the basement of what naval officers liked to call the New Navy Building, which actually was a section of the large and well-known State, War, and Navy edifice next to the Executive Mansion. Although in a basement, their quarters seemed palatial to the officers working there, some of whom remembered the small and crowded rooms in the Octagon building two blocks away, where the lighting had been bad and the corridors jammed with charts. The new rooms had Brussels carpets, oak cabinets, walnut screw stools, and glowing cherrywood desks with olive-green covering and brass handles. Very early in his tenure as Hydrographer, Bartlett felt compelled to assert authority within his own household. He thought that Knorr, the civilian chief draftsman and editor, had too much power and was making charts which lacked uniformity in lettering, abbreviations, and other graphic elements. Knorr's salary was soon reduced 50 percent, and the next year he was dismissed upon Bartlett's recommendation.[10]

Bartlett's happiest innovation, beginning in December 1883, was the publication of a monthly pilot chart for the North Atlantic. He saw how rapidly maritime knowledge was accumulating—from the increase of commerce on the North Atlantic, from the large number of fast steamers, and from the submarine cable—and he proposed that the Hydrographic Office disseminate this knowledge through pilot charts. The pilot chart was Maury's wind and current chart, revised more often now, and furnished with other information of contemporary maritime interest. A composite affair, it had as its base an ordinary chart of the North Atlantic on Mercator's projection, lithographed in black, with such permanent features as a compass card, magnetic variation curves, the line for the depth of 100 fathoms, and small black arrows for the drift of ocean currents. Overlaid in blue color were the weather conditions for the month of publication: blue arrows with crossbars for the frequency and force of winds and blue lines for the region of fogs and icebergs, the limits of trade winds, and the location of equatorial calms. These graphic materials were synopses rather than forecasts; they summarized the experience, since the middle of the century, of ships passing through different areas of the Atlantic Ocean. Steamship and sailing routes were also given. Printed in red on the pilot chart was information drawn from events of the month just before publication: derelict vessels, wrecks, icebergs, the belt of Newfoundland fog, and information about lights and buoys.

As if this was not enough, Bartlett put on the side or back of the pilot chart notices to mariners, weather reviews, listings of other published charts, the circulation of winds around low-barometer areas, and tables of barometric readings. The magazine *Science* thought it "almost impossible" to publish on one chart such a variety of information.[11]

Bartlett needed new institutional arrangements to make his program of pilot charts work. He felt he must get in touch with the captains of ocean steamers and the masters of merchant vessels to secure materials for the pilot charts, then distribute the finished product to the same people. He went to Congress, therefore, in 1884 and won permission to open branch hydrographic offices in the maritime exchanges of half a dozen leading American seaports: Boston, New York, Philadelphia, Baltimore, New Orleans, and San Francisco.[12] Manned by graduates of Annapolis, these branch offices became at once busy centers where "a continuous stream of people" sought "information of all kinds."[13] The naval officers in charge of these branches sent cards to masters, inviting them to call; they also urged the local press to publicize Navy Department activity; they mailed pilot charts, sorted notices to mariners sent from the central office, and above all talked to sea captains, vessel owners, insurance companies, and maritime associations about the latest nautical knowledge. In one year the New York branch office arranged visits to six thousand vessels, furnished information to eight thousand masters, distributed gratis ten thousand pilot charts, and forwarded to Washington thirty-five hundred reports for preparation of the monthly pilot charts.

The pilot charts and the branch offices were a spectacular success at home and abroad. Often called "aristocratic," the navy did well this time in reaching the man in the street and the man at sea. The Coast Survey had never distributed its own publications but used private agencies, which sold them at a profit. The *New York Herald* and the *Boston Post* were two newspapers which reproduced the monthly pilot chart. French and British sea captains were "extravagant" in their praise for the way the Hydrographic Office was collecting and disseminating valuable information.[14] They and American masters, in both steam and sail, showed keen interest in the routes marked on the pilot charts to avoid drifting ice, although the ever curious General Meigs of Civil War fame thought that this information was too general. The Liverpool Underwriters Association informed Bartlett in 1886 that it was impressed by the pilot charts, most of all because they showed that the Hydrographic Office was considerably ahead of the British Admiralty in broadcasting knowledge through charts and notices. And John Worthington, the American consul at Malta, was proud of the American charts because of their simplicity, completeness, and usefulness.[15]

One specialized topic which Bartlett exploited was the calming effect of oil on water. Not only were his efforts a service to maritime safety, but they revealed his conception of public science. The use of oil to quiet the seas had been, for the nineteenth century, more a proverb than a practical method of saving life and property from breaking seas, until Bartlett made it his responsibility to bring this matter to the notice of seamen in Europe and America. The Hydrographic Office published a pamphlet by Lieutenant George L. Dyer, *The Use of Oil to Lessen the Dangerous Effect of Heavy Seas,* and the pilot charts also spread the word. Laudatory statements followed quickly, one of the most impressive coming from Captain William J. L. Wharton, hydrographer to the British Admiralty, who said that "thanks to the efforts of the Americans, the facts are well known to all English-speaking mariners, and many are the instances of the successful use of oil."[16] Bartlett drew the greatest satisfaction from his success, which illustrated so nicely the kind of practical knowledge which he believed that governments should cultivate and distribute. The Hydrographic Office did not seek to explain the dynamics of thick, viscous oils; it was satisfied to tell everybody their protective effect in subduing large, damaging waves. "It is not the policy of this office," Bartlett once said, "to go at all into the region of theory; it is prepared only to state and to publish facts."[17] Bartlett's oversimplified approach is here in sharpest contrast with the method of the Coast Survey.

Bartlett watched closely the scientific surveying of his command on the west coast of Mexico and Central America, renewed in 1879 after abandonment for lack of money in 1875. He wanted a set of charts, ranging from San Francisco to Panama, which did not rely on old Spanish surveys of the eighteenth century, some of them fifteen miles off in longitude; and of course he hoped to show that the Hydrographic Office could do better than the Coast Survey.

The *Ranger* was the surveying vessel, the only one that the Hydrographic Office used almost exclusively for that purpose. Bartlett directed Charles E. Clark, the *Ranger* commander for three years, to follow Coast Survey methods closely, except for detail in topography. However, an inquiry from a European source caused the hydrographer to change his mind. An English mapping firm wanted to know if the contour lines on his charts of the west coast of Central America indicated actual heights, and Bartlett had to admit that the lines were there simply to strengthen the shading of the hills. Not long afterward, he ordered the *Ranger* to begin contour line drawing for Baja California and to measure more heights on the same peninsula.[18]

The range of activity of the Hydrographic Office is the final measure of an emerging government scientific organization in post-Appomattox America. Sailing directions for the west coast of Mexico and Central America were published and a copy was sent to the Pacific Mail Steamship Company, which happily acknowledged receipt.[19] In 1888 the Hydrographic Office published a fishery limits chart of Newfoundland, indicating where Americans could fish under treaties with Great Britain. The fishermen used this chart, and so did the Senate Foreign Relations Committee. A new U.S. Great-Circle Sailing Chart for the North Atlantic drew enthusiastic response from an officer on the Cunard liner *Etruria*, who thought the chart was "the nicest thing . . . ever given to Seamen."[20]

Before Bartlett, the Hydrographic Office had constructed a circumpolar chart of the Arctic, where European and American parties had been making their desperate exploration and rescue attempts. Bartlett compiled maps of the Arctic for the Greely Relief Board; and he republished the circumpolar chart, which Robert E. Peary, the explorer, wrote for immediately. The *Beacon,* a literary weekly in Boston, thought this new edition (in 1885) a marked improvement over current English and German products. It particularly liked the location of the North Pole in the center of the chart.[21] Work also continued toward determining secondary meridians by telegraph from the primary meridian at Greenwich. In Bartlett's time, a chain of these points girded the Caribbean and northern South America.

It was decisive for this story of science and scientific rivalry that not all the naval contingent in hydrography worked for the navy. One or two score officers and several hundred enlisted men did oceanographic research through assignment by the Navy Department to the Coast Survey, a practice begun in the antebellum period. That is to say, naval forces, with their ratings, pay, and rations, constituted the hydrographic parties of the Coast Survey. The Hydrographic Inspector, a naval officer in the Washington office of the Survey, supervised these hydrographic parties, which sometimes numbered a dozen yearly. These naval forces sailed the Survey ships and made the soundings for the charts, which developed the earth's solid surface beneath the waters in Maine on the East Coast, for Florida and Texas on the Gulf, and for the West Coast and Alaska. Lieutenants in command worried about the weather, the ships' boilers, and the supply of coal and fresh water, yet each was pleased to have an independent command in the Coast Survey, rather than standing watch in the navy proper. These officers believed they worked harder than their counterparts in the regular navy, and they were proud of the finished charts, which bore their names as a record of their contribution.

A typical day in hydrography began with a trip through the surf to build signals on trigonometrical positions provided by the Washington office, which in turn had received them from the triangulating forces of the Coast Survey. Reciprocal sighting between land and water was the method of recording positions. The ship, starting outward from a few meters offshore with a signal flying, took soundings with the lead while the ship's officers took angles on triangulation points ashore. Concurrently, personnel ashore sighted on the ship from the occupied points. At the end of the day, recorders transferred the results to the progress sheet. At times, lines of soundings were crossed to check for accuracy.[22]

The doings of these officers and men added one more distinguished chapter to the annals of science by the navy after the Civil War. In command of the *Blake,* a wooden schooner-rigged steamer belonging to the Coast Survey, Lieutenant Commander Charles Dwight Sigsbee made many offshore explorations from 1874 to 1878. Wanting to discover great depths of water (a passion of oceanographers in those days), Sigsbee, who later was to command the *Maine* at nearby Havana, ran thousands of miles of sounding lines in the Gulf of Mexico; and the superintendent, surprised by the depths of 2,000 fathoms discovered there, named two locations on the *Blake*'s tracks, Sigsbee Deep and Sigsbee Bank.[23]

John R. Bartlett followed Sigsbee on the *Blake,* and this second naval officer developed a submarine valley in the western part of the Caribbean, which the superintendent of the Coast Survey named the Bartlett Deep. Bartlett also constructed a model of the Gulf of Mexico bottom, which impressed many American scientists. All this was before Bartlett became head of the Hydrographic Office.

In 1883 the Coast Survey summed up the harvest of physiographic knowledge by constructing a relief model "of the depths of the sea" for the western Atlantic, the Gulf, and the Caribbean. This model was displayed at the London International Fisheries Exhibition and at the Philadelphia meeting of the AAAS, where it attracted "great attention and favorable comments."[24] After Bartlett came Commander Willard H. Brownson, who north and west of Puerto Rico found 4,500 fathoms of water—the greatest depth yet, he reported, to yield bottom specimens and temperature. The superintendent of the Coast Survey thought this discovery of Brownson's worthy of a special announcement, and the *American*

Journal of Science welcomed the "marvelous facts" about depth along the north shores of the West Indies.[25] One surprise was the revelation that, in the depths of the sea, the differences in height far surpassed those on land.

Naval officers were effective in their probing of ocean depth because they took pains with the technology of their operations. Commander Sigsbee seemed determined to modify and improve every mechanical device aboard the *Blake*. The pitching and rolling of a ship at sea put a heavy strain on the sounding wire, and surveying parties in England and America relieved this strain by using rubber bands called accumulators which, attached to the sounding wire, absorbed the constant jerking through their capacity to bear weight and to stretch. Sigsbee's accumulators were a series of round rubber objects that looked like doughnuts; fitted to the mast, they acted as a spring to absorb the sudden force imparted to the sounding wire by the heaving vessel.[26] He collaborated with Alexander Agassiz, when the Harvard zoologist came aboard early in 1878. Agassiz suggested that the wire rope used for sounding also be adopted for dredging and trawling, and Sigsbee made the successful change from hemp rope. Future oceanographic surveys would copy this change.

For five years after he left the *Blake* in 1878, Sigsbee heard praise of his work. In 1880 the Coast Survey brought out his authoritative publication, *Deep Sea Sounding and Dredging: A Description and Discussion of the Methods and Appliances Used on Board the Coast and Geodetic Steamer Blake*. Thomas A. Edison thought the Sigsbee publication an "original and splendid contribution." A professor at the University of London, who had been a naturalist on the *Challenger* exhibition, was convinced, after reading Sigsbee, that his methods in sounding and dredging were far superior to those of the British.[27] In 1883, Sigsbee, having built a deep-sea sounding machine modeled after William Thomson's ideas, won a gold medal at the International Fisheries Exhibition. Altogether, the commander constructed four machines for government use: one for the German navy, one for the American navy, one for the U.S. Fish Commission, and, of course, one for the Coast Survey.

Perhaps the most lasting contribution of the navy to Coast Survey and American science was the work by Lieutenant John E. Pillsbury on the Gulf Stream between 1885 and 1889, where Bache had introduced the Coast Survey before the Civil War. To locate the *Blake,* Pillsbury designed his equipment to distribute the force of the jerking vessel so that none of the parts—mast, boom, or deckhouse—would receive undue strain. He was able to use Sigsbee's accumulators or arrangement of rubber springs, which under a 15,000-pound strain would compress from 13 to 5 feet. He also designed a current meter, which he lowered by Sigsbee's sounding machine. Pillsbury's main objective was to anchor in the Gulf Stream and observe for current and temperature at various depths. For this purpose, he spent two years at stations established on a line across the Florida Straits from Fowey Rocks to Gun Cay. Afterward, stations on four other lines across the Florida Straits were occupied; one location off Cape Hatteras was made; and stations were established in the passages of the Windward Islands.

In his views on the Gulf Stream, Pillsbury accepted the tradition, now increasingly dominant, that the Stream was the result of water piling up in the Caribbean from wind-driven current, then overflowing north through the Gulf of Mexico and the Florida Straits, where it was joined by other wind-driven currents. Pillsbury fixed the fact, heretofore disputed, that there was a comparatively smooth bottom for the Gulf Stream in the Florida Straits and as far north as Cape Hatteras. Also, he located the axis or maximum flow of the Gulf Stream farther west than was previously supposed. He found no evidence of a polar countercurrent beneath the Gulf Stream, though such a current had been believed in since Bache's time. His laborious effort to show a correlation between changes in the Gulf Stream and changes in the position of the moon were not fruitful. Nevertheless, Pillsbury's scientific reputation endures because of his unique and valuable statistics on the temperature and velocity of the Gulf Stream, which grateful oceanographers have been using ever since.[28]

3 The Naval Challenge to Civilian Science and the Congressional Response

The rivalry between the Coast Survey and the Hydrographic Office in post-Reconstruction times did not, in the beginning, raise the question of the amount and kind of natural knowledge to cultivate, but whether a military or a civilian organization should direct the current operations. Before the Civil War, when both the army and the navy sponsored natural science, the merging of the two ranks with civilians in a common enterprise was popular, as in the Coast Survey and on the Lighthouse Board. After Appomattox, the army did not return to the Coast Survey, leaving to the Navy Department the chief initiative for science with a military cast. Continually, elements in and out of the Department strove to assume maritime responsibilities tangential to the central mission of defense. This ambition extended even to the consular service, but the major objective was always the science of the Coast Survey. The rhythm of the departmental desire revealed its incentive, which was to keep surplus manpower busy during peacetime. The motive had operated after the War of 1812, when the Coast Survey was twice transferred to the navy; after the Mexican War, when agitation was renewed by naval protagonists to move the civilian agency out of the Treasury; and after the Civil War, when the issue of the proper place of the Coast Survey in the government was

40

again raised in naval circles, amid the quickening of public activity in natural science.

The first move of the Navy Department after 1865 was toward regaining what had necessarily been lost during the civil conflict: the command and staffing of the hydrographical parties within the Coast Survey. In 1868, Admiral David D. Porter, of Civil War fame and ranking naval officer, who once wrote that the Coast Survey was one of the best schools the navy had, "broached the subject" of reunion to a Survey assistant, only to have Peirce refuse cooperation, although he was advised that naval officers had their legal position within the Coast Survey.[1]

Frustrated in this informal approach, several bureau officers applied public pressure through two newspaper articles early in 1872.[2] The *National Republican* of Washington took the high ground, arguing that a Department of Science was needed to regulate the "scientific undertakings" that had "grown wonderfully since the war," if the "great material interests of the country" were to be efficiently and usefully served. The *Boston Evening Journal* was more down to earth in labeling this idea of a Department of Science "A NAVAL PROPOSAL," whose first step was the merger of the Coast Survey with the Hydrographic Office, the latter being praised as "fast rising" and "under good management." Both newspapers saw the Coast Survey as tardy in the publication and revision of its charts, and too much "an adjunct of Harvard and the scientific ambitions of Cambridge Professors." Satisfaction of the navy's legitimate grievance at its exclusion from Coast Survey affairs came in 1874, when Carlile Pollock Patterson, under the aegis of Peirce, ascended to the superintendency. Once a midshipman in the navy, "Captain" Patterson, as he was called, moved immediately to restore naval prominence in his bureau. The scientific fruits and institutional arrangements of this reunion have already been recounted for this history.

Once the navy had been reestablished within the Coast Survey, the competition between naval and civilian forces shifted to the territory of Alaska, which Secretary Seward had summarily awarded to the Coast Survey. In 1869, the Department of the Navy issued a directory of the new possession—the same year that the

Coast Survey was bringing out its own publication on the Alaska coast. Because of protest by the civilians, the navy agreed to change the title of its publication and also to eliminate some materials by George Davidson, the Coast Survey's representative in Alaska.[3] The climax of the accommodation came in May 1881, when William H. Hunt, the new secretary of the navy, issued General Order No. 270, which acknowledged the surveying and publishing rights of the Coast Survey in the continental United States and Alaska.[4] This order told the navy not to maintain special surveying vessels along the American coast or in Alaska; any incidental surveys executed by the navy in American or Alaskan waters were to be forwarded to the superintendent of the Coast Survey for publication. Both the Hydrographic Office and the Coast Survey could conduct surveys of unknown coasts in Alaska. Neither the Bureau of Navigation nor its Hydrographic Office could publish charts of any harbor or portions of the United States or Alaska; but these two naval units were allowed to publish general route charts beyond the 100-fathom curve as part of their hydrographic work, to improve the navigation of world trade routes.

It was a mark of the delicate balance in feeling and purpose between the Coast Survey and Hydrographic Office that William E. Chandler, Hunt's successor as secretary of the navy in 1882, could so quickly and completely upset the statesmanship of his predecessor. A confidant of President Arthur's and a more partisan secretary than Hunt, Chandler seemed to fit better the presidential idea of what a cabinet member should be.

Chandler, a political personage from New Hampshire, had participated in local and national affairs for twenty years—in the legislature of his home state, under Lincoln in wartime Philadelphia and Washington, and through four presidential elections as either secretary of the Republican National Committee or its member from New Hampshire. Slight in stature yet bold and outspoken, Chandler possessed a ready store of classical references for oratorical display, and his sharp tongue gave him a reputation for liking and inspiring controversy. Politics and administration had made him a man of parts: alert, impatient, aggressive, confident, and energetic. The biographer of Chandler does well in relating these personal qualities to the secretary's three-year term in the naval office: he got "a good grip upon the Department," and mastered "thousands of details" within the eight bureaus.[5] In the building of the new navy he was a major participant.

The connection of Secretary Chandler with this story is not, however, because of his contribution to the new navy, but for what he wanted to do about the old one. With its 1,800 officers and 31 seagoing ships, it was suffering from severe underemployment, which Chandler proposed to alleviate in a hurry through bureaucratic expansion. "We claim everything belonging to the water," he said.[6] Chandler made his plan of expansion part of the navy's annual report in 1882, which he published to a startled Washington in December of that year. Chandler urged the establishment of a bureau of merchant marine within the Navy Department. To this bureau would be transferred six agencies of the Treasury Department: the Coast and Geodetic Survey, the Lighthouse Board, the Marine Hospital Service, the Lifesaving Service, the Steamboat Inspection Service, and the Revenue Marine Division. Chandler argued that these six agencies were maritime in nature and purpose, and belonged, therefore, in the Navy Department. With the exception of the Revenue Marine Division, they had little or no connection with the Treasury Department, he said.

Chandler also presented his plan as a consolidation, which he hoped would appeal to the depressed maritime interests of the nation. The shipping owners and interests, he claimed, needed a strong, centralized bureau to represent them; at present, they had to rely on a confederation of subordinate offices in the Treasury.[7] To show that he was serious about this report, Chandler had a bill introduced in the House of Representatives in January 1883 to organize a "bureau of mercantile marine" in the Navy Department.[8] Chandler was not the first to originate a congressional measure proposing the enlargement of the navy's scientific service; bills had appeared over the decades favoring the takeover of one or another of these agencies. The difference in Chandler's bill was that it virtually swept the board of the desirable agencies.

Chandler asked several officers of the navy to append to his annual report essays on desirable acquisitions from the Treasury.

Commander Sigsbee, of the *Blake,* spoke for the transfer of the Coast Survey. The Navy Department, said Sigsbee, was already contributing appropriations and men to the nautical work of this bureau. The navy had the facilities for fitting, docking, and repairing the ships which made the coastal surveys. Navy officers were making hydrographical surveys abroad and publishing every kind of foreign hydrographic survey. In England, Sigsbee concluded, all charts for sailors were made and published by sailors.

Lieutenant Seaton Schroeder, who had worked for the Hydrographic Office in the Mediterranean, along with Gorringe, wanted to relieve the Treasury of the Lighthouse Board, because this board required technical skills "widely differing" from those used in Treasury business.[9] Also, naval officers were the best judges of the efficiency of lights, and the best caretakers for all aids to navigation.

A third officer would transfer the Marine Hospital Service, which cared for merchant seamen, from the Treasury to the hospital establishment in the Navy Department. Charged with the health interest of officers and enlisted men, this Service was competent to take care of merchant seamen as well; there was no need for two organizations.

Chandler showed more impudence than anything else when he put the Revenue Marine Division on his list of proscribed Treasury agencies, because its very name designated an obvious Treasury function, the collection of revenue. Nevertheless, he found a junior grade officer, Master G. H. Peters, to justify the transfer. The Revenue Marine Division was essentially a naval service, Peters argued. Its ships carried guns and its crews performed naval drills; in war, the government would have to make use of these same revenue vessels. Meanwhile, younger officers from Annapolis would receive valuable experience in commanding them.

Certainly, Chandler merits praise in seeking opportunities of usefulness and prominence for his underemployed naval officers, but his proposals ran into such a storm of criticism and abuse from the Treasury agencies that their political future was immediately hopeless. In this instance, the Department of the Navy was no match for the Department of the Treasury. Hilgard made the mildest reply. He argued the legitimacy of the present coastal surveying, which had worked well for forty years and used military officers when they were available, but did not try to transform them into professional scientists.

Several of the other chiefs asserted that Chandler's measure violated the spirit and traditions of American government.[10] "The people," said E. W. Clark, chief of the Revenue Marine Division, "have always jealously guarded the civil functions from the encroachments of the military power . . . [and] any attempt to induct the Army and Navy into the civil offices had been met and properly restrained by adverse public sentiment." "The navy," said S. I. Kimball, superintendent of the Lifesaving Service, was "naturally unrepublican" and a "dangerous enemy to the public liberty if elevated from its useful subordination as a military arm of the nation to practical control of the civil service of the country." J. A. Dumont, the supervising inspector general in the Steamboat Inspection Service, broadened the attack by portraying the navy as a menace to the whole social fabric. He said that he had heard the claim made in Washington that the navy was *the only aristocracy* in the United States." From personal observation, Dumont knew that officers of the navy were "frequently aristocratic and tyrannical when dealing with people they deem unequal to themselves in the social standing their position gives them." To these ruminations on the threat to liberty and equality of military power and authority, Clark, of the Revenue Marine Division, added words of sarcasm and abuse. He charged naval officers with introducing dutiable goods in their baggage and inquired whether smugglers would make good customs officers. The navy at large was in a state of "degeneracy and ruin," he went on; the ratio of officers to enlisted men was more than double that of any other nation, a situation which rendered these officials a "horde of idlers" and the navy itself one "floating mass of incompetency."

By itself, Secretary Chandler's plan was futile and unwise. What gave it a future, nevertheless, was its preemption by an alert House member, Samuel J. Randall of Pennsylvania, who proposed allying the expansionist aims of the navy with a strong economy movement, of which he was the leader in Congress. In this way the rivalry of the Coast Survey and the Hydrographic Office spread to Capitol Hill, where it was to remain a burning issue for the rest of the century. Indeed Randall, by his initiative, pressed upon congressional attention a third broad issue of the size and scope of governmental science.

Randall was a Democrat and an urban congressman from Philadelphia, where businessmen, mechanics, and factory and dock workers were his steadfast constituency from 1863 to 1890, when he died. These groups gave him a long tenure in the House, and he in turn pleased them by advocating protectionism, although he was a member of the low-tariff Democratic party. As chairman of the Appropriations Committee in the Forty-fourth Congress (1875–77), Randall had insisted that the Coast Survey contribute to his economy drive in agreeing to a slash in its budget of $150,000, and now, for the Forty-eighth Congress (1883–85), he perceived in a modification of the Chandler proposal a means of advancing both economy and military science. Move the Coast Survey out of the Treasury, he said, by sending its hydrography to the navy and its geodesy to the Interior Department—a division which he knew would appeal to the House Naval Affairs Committee. At the same time, he said, $150,000 more could be saved in the Coast Survey, thus associating economy and military science in a common enterprise. In June 1884, Randall and two other members of the subcommittee of the Appropriations Committee approved the division and transfer proposal and placed it in the Sundry Civil Appropriations bill.

The narrative pauses at this point to allow the author the opportunity to expound on congressional opinion about science and spending. The materials are drawn mainly from public documents and individual biographies when they record the speaking, voting, and other behavior of senators and representatives toward natural knowledge. Relevant information has been found for some 142 members. The lines of congressional opinion about science and government originate in opposing ideologies, and the conflicting views coalesce around the two parties, with the Republicans favoring science and generosity in expenditure for it and the Democrats expressing hostility toward natural knowledge and its expense. That is to say, the partisan confrontation is dialectic between the forces of liberality and economy.

Liberality appeared after Appomattox in the flush and relaxation of victory, when a rejuvenated government conceived of new projects and movements for the saved political system. And there was extra money within the departments, as they sold off their war-accumulated surpluses. Regularly, through the rest of the century, upswings of the business cycle renewed the bursts of spending; prosperous times in the early seventies inspired the generosity of the Forty-first Congress (1869–71) and in the late eighties sparked a similar reaction in the Fifty-first Congress (1889–91). Leading Republicans identified larger appropriations with progress and as part of the inevitable scheme of things. The times were moving ahead, they said, the country was growing rapidly, and the government was expected to do more business, for there were more groups and interests in need of public attention.

Representative Charles O'Neill told the House that "The republicans . . . sent me here from the city of Philadelphia . . . to vote for appropriations which will give progress to every interest of the country . . . to vote for river and harbor improvements . . . to represent the . . . citizens of a commercial city, a manufacturing city, a city that has grown faster and greater then any other city on this continent." And Charles A. Boutelle, Republican from Maine and longtime naval expert in the House, informed listening members that "the people of this country have . . . long been accustomed to look to the Republican organization to assume responsibility, to make requisite provision for great public enterprises and to foster great public interests."[11]

The economy movement, under the aegis of the Democratic party or "the Democracy," as it liked to call itself, started in the summer of 1868 and, after initial disappointment in the presidential campaign of 1872, moved ahead rapidly in the following year, driven by public indignation over the Credit Mobilier, by the anger at the vote in House and Senate the year before on a salary increase or "grab" (retroactive for two years), and in response to the depression that began in the autumn of that year (1873). Under the banner of retrenchment and reform, this movement called for frugality, purity, and simplicity in government. These ideas and their practice had been present since the early Republic, but only in the 1870s did they rise to the stature of a major, independent force or issue in American politics. In the long run, economy fared better on the downside of the business cycle in the Forty-fourth Congress (1875–77), during the depression of 1873–77, and in the Fifty-third Congress (1893–95), when there was a deficit in the Treasury, resulting from a slide in the nation's economic affairs in 1893 and 1894. The climax of the movement came early in its life, in 1876, when the House of Representatives of the Forty-fourth Congress, Democratic for the first time since before the Civil War, and led by Chairman Randall, reduced government salaries 10 to 20 percent, and shrank the number of employees some 20 percent. The budget total also turned downward.

The ideal that Democrats saw themselves defending through economy was the laboring man, his hard-earned wages, and the daily bread he bought. The gravest threat to this threefold reality was the government and its power to levy taxes. If it forgot that this revenue from taxation, even in the Treasury, belonged to the people, then any scoundrel could reach his arm in and live off the labor of others. For Democrats, the favorite example of such activity was government spending, which they termed "steals" of the taxpayer's painfully acquired wages.[12] In a litany they never tired of chanting, Democrats charged the government with using the people's money for extravagant, profligate, and even monstrous purposes. To illustrate their case they pointed to the new look of American cities and towns, arising out of their growth and prosperity.

Adoniram J. Warner, Democrat of Ohio, saw a "mania" for the construction of palatial postoffices and customhouses; Milton J. Durham, Democrat of Kentucky, sneered at the "tinsel and foolish ornament" in these structures, agreeing with other Democrats, who said that plain, humble buildings would have been better. William Jennings Bryan mourned that the House seemed to prefer a splendid land to a happy one. Benjamin A. Willis, Democrat of New York, expanded the critique of spending to complain that the modest demeanor and cheap government of the democratic system was losing out to inordinate salaries, high living, and costly appointments.[13]

Other Democrats made the explicit contrast of present and past; they praised "the good old days of the Republic" and "old General Jackson's" time, when government was limited, expenditures were small, and the economy was severe. Thus, Democrats were traditionalists.[14] Richard Townshend, Democrat from Illinois, urged the enactment of a specific feature of the past. In 1878 he rose in the House to propose that the principal examiners in the Patent Office (scientists or lawyers) should have their salaries reduced to $2,500. Why? Because that was the payment for these examiners in 1848. Those were "the halcyon days of our country," Townshend proclaimed, and the policy of the Democratic party at that time was "the chief glory of the Republic."[15]

Townshend's motion showed that the parties were assimilating government science into the liberal-conservative division concerning public spending. When talking about research, Republicans informed their statements with a cosmic perspective. Nature and man, commerce and things, land and sea, adventure and the unknown were the broad dualities likely to enter their political discourse. A tone of celebration prevailed about natural knowledge. "God speed to the achievements of science," cried James B. Belford, Colorado Republican, "and to the victories of the General Government whose beneficent influence contemplates the advancement of all its individual citizens (Applause)."[16] When the Coast Survey's geodesy came under attack, Representative James A. Garfield spoke with eloquence and enthusiasm about the continental chain of triangles, which would bring to surveying in the interior the same high standard of accuracy which underlay the coastal work. Republicans drew confidence and example from the current successes of science policy. The weather forecasting and accompanying maps of the Signal Service of the army, begun in 1870, were "considered important by people in gathering their crops, in taking their journeys, and killing and packing their pork," said Henry L. Dawes, Republican of Massachusetts, first in the House and then in the Senate.[17] Farmers, sailors, and shopkeepers formed a broad constituency which did not seem too distressed at the frequent failures of this first weather bureau. The Fish Commission, founded in 1871, propagated species in new localities, or replenished them in traditional fishing grounds, thereby endearing itself to large numbers who worked for a living. Republicans saw many other uses in the national life for the shoreline mapping and sounding of the Coast Survey on the East and West Coasts and along the Gulf. James G. Blaine of Maine came from a state with a long and much-indented coastline. When the Coast Survey, in a deliberate bid for his support and to help American yachtsmen, operated continuously on the Maine coast after 1865, Blaine, first in the House and then in the Senate, responded effectively in getting money for the bureau.

Not understanding science, and perhaps not even interested in it, Democrats on the Hill were content mainly to dismiss research proposals. A common reaction was to attack certain social types as surrogates for the knowledge they were unwilling to spend money on. Thus aristocrats, capitalists, intellectuals, and esthetes became the symbolic representation of the science that these politicians did not know or would not accept.

Antagonizing specific knowledge, James R. Beck of Kentucky, later a senator, sought to strike transcontinental geodesy from the budget of the Coast Survey. So far, he said, the only result had been to discover that Columbus, Ohio, was two or three miles away from where it was supposed to be. This discovery was of "no possible good to anybody." James H. Blount of Georgia, afterward commissioner and minister to Hawaii, disparaged the place of geodesy in the workaday world, although he did admit that this science would realize itself in the next century. Geodesy, he said, was "pleasure and entertainment" for scientific gentlemen, but it had no connection with the land surveys and would not be completed for a hundred years.[18]

Democrats compared science unfavorably with other realms of human experience. They could not or would not distinguish traditional religion from modern science. Benton McMillin of Tennessee, afterward of ministerial rank in the diplomatic service, placed fossils in the setting of the biblical flood, and Martin Maginnis, territorial representative from Montana and also a newspaper owner and publisher, said that settlers did not want to know whether the rotundity of the earth put them farther away from the "central fire" than their neighbors.[19] In saying that scientific knowledge lacked a moral message, Joseph A. Bailey, a representative from Texas, and later a senator, demonstrated that he did not understand the difference between moral education and research. Speaking of zoological collections, Bailey asked "what man will be wiser" because of them? "What woman will derive refinement or grace" from them? "What child will be taught to tread the path of virtue?" In the same vein, Hiester Clymer of Pennsylvania, manufacturer and banker, insisted that material progress could not "compensate for the loss of virtue."[20]

The public lives of four political leaders confirm the partisan division about science on Capitol Hill. Two of them were Republicans, Representative Joseph G. Cannon of Illinois and Senator William B. Allison of Iowa; two of them were House Democrats, William S. Holman of Indiana and Hilary A. Herbert of Alabama.

As a member of the House Appropriations Committee, Representative Cannon consistently and effectively stood with government science during the period of this history. Cannon's philosophy made this valuable contribution possible. One of his biographers informs us that he was "an evolutionist," by which Cannon meant that things were always changing—slowly, to be sure—but the direction of this change was forward looking. Cannon had faith in "the ascent of men" and in material and spiritual progress through civilization. The world was a better place to live in than it had been when he was a boy.[21] In the debate over the founding of the U.S. Geological Survey in 1879, he cheered Congressman Hewitt's eloquent speech in behalf of the new bureau, and seven years later he testified for Powell's leadership when the permanence of the bureau was at stake. In 1891, he delayed for one year the setback of the Geological Survey because of its Western land policies. Concerning the Coast Survey, Cannon established a relationship of trust and respect with Superintendent Mendenhall (in office 1889–94), whom he considered the best administrator of science in Washington. In a later Congress, he approved an amendment from the floor to raise the Coast Survey budget a little. And in 1900 he climaxed his service to orderly and progressive science by taking the side of the civilian Coast Survey in its deadly rivalry with the navy's Hydrographic Office over the mapping of America's new territorial possessions.

The counterpart of Cannon in the House was Allison in the Senate. For two years in the mid-eighties, Allison presided with moderation and good sense over a joint commission to study and resolve the postbellum rivalries in government science. The influential report of the majority—three Republicans and one Democrat—stabilized the positions of both the Geological Survey and the Coast Survey against the dissenting minority of two Democrats. In Cleveland's first administration, Allison refused spoilsmen the opportunity to entrench themselves within the Coast Survey by congressional permission. Another time in the nineties, he set a floor on the reduction of the budget, upon the appeal of the ruling assistant in the bureau's Washington office.

Holman ranked so high with congressional Democrats because he articulated their representative ideas and led their parliamentary maneuvering. Of course, he disparaged science all the time, a fact that T. C. Smith, the biographer of Garfield, commented on. Although Holman owned a farm in Indiana, he had little use for the scientists of the Department of Agriculture, who, he claimed quite unfairly, learned their agrarian knowledge from "the bucolics of Virgil and the old romances of the Greeks and Romans." He was eloquent, in a perverse way, about "certain gentlemen of elegant leisure" who wanted to view, at government expense, the transit of Venus across the face of the sun. "The movement of that goddess among the heavenly bodies is well enough," he said, "for curious and speculative inquiry, but you have no right to tax the people for any such purpose." He viewed the Botanical Garden as too "fancy" in a country demanding retrenchment and reform. And he expressed continued irritation at the government's publishing books to further scientific medicine, especially the index catalogue of the library of the Surgeon General's office, which was a job for private enterprise, he maintained. Most of all, he disliked the free distribution of this serial, which violated proper business relations between citizens and their government.[22]

Like other Democrats, Holman distrusted the present and admired the purer and better days of the past. The splendor of public buildings and the high life in contemporary America were contrary to the "genius and character of our government." He charged that American society was now ruled by an alliance of bankers and capitalists, who had centralized the wealth of the nation and whose agents were in Congress. He also raised the specter of land monopoly, whose "Dead Sea" fruits were opulence and luxury for the few and poverty and wretchedness for the many. He admitted that public policy could increase the aggregate wealth, but "the sigh of labor" would resound throughout the land, and the only true wealth and glory of the Republic would disappear—that is, a virtuous and contented people. The survival of the Republic, he said on another occasion, depended on the restoration of "the economy and severe simplicity" so gloried in by the fathers of this generation.[23]

Holman's performance on the floor of the House was little short of sensational. Early in 1876, during the Forty-fourth Congress, he managed a change in the rules of procedure to allow amendments to appropriation bills when the subject was germane and the result would be to reduce expenses. This amendment, Rule 120 or XXI, which made it regular and in order to graft new legislation on money bills in the direction of economy, Randall characterized as "one of the chief jewels in the crown of the democratic House." Holman dominated the offering of money-saving amendments under his own rule, and Randall used the same rule to fortify his leadership.[24]

Herbert, the second Democrat, was the kind of man who could achieve prominence in anything he put his mind to. He came out of the Confederate army with a useless left arm after the Battle of the Wilderness; he succeeded in law practice in Montgomery, Alabama, and as representative in Congress for sixteen years, where he was a leader in three fields. He wrote and compiled a book with the title *Why the Solid South? or, Reconstruction and Its Results* (1890), which was accepted as reality and history by several generations of Americans, including historians. And today he is, among historians, the symbol of American thinking about race and Reconstruction in the late nineteenth and early twentieth centuries. Herbert was also a big navy man, later serving for four years as department secretary.

Along with Holman and Randall, Herbert led the fight against science. His sweeping objective was the destruction of the government's two leading science agencies of the nineteenth century, the Coast Survey and the Geological Survey. Laissez-faire was the point of departure of Herbert's thinking, and he cited as authorities three Englishmen, Adam Smith, Mill, and Buckle, and three Americans, Jefferson, Benton, and Calhoun. Like Cannon, he subscribed to the doctrine of evolution—in his case, to justify open competition and the survival of the fittest. Like Holman, he believed in the doctrines of the old Democratic party. He opposed making the Department of Agriculture of cabinet rank, because the research it did belonged to the universities. Also, he antagonized the founding of the naval war college and the establishment of a popular zoological park in the District.

Whenever he attacked the Coast Survey and the Geological Survey, Herbert was the clever and unscrupulous lawyer. His method in each case was to ridicule a branch of knowledge: geodesy in the Coast Survey and paleontology in the Geological Survey. It seemed absurdly funny to him that the Coast Survey would put Barnum's menagerie with its prominent tower on a coastal map, and that the Geological Survey would publish drawings and descriptions of birds with teeth. When confronted with a statement by Director Powell of the Geological Survey on the glacier theory of the earth's history, Herbert asked if this theory was not disputed, thereby suggesting scientific parity for Ignatius Donnelly's idea that the glacial mantle was the tail of a comet which had come near the earth.[25] He was one of the two dissenting Democrats on the Allison Commission, and once during its proceedings he had the gall to ignore the advice of an expert who had informed him privately of the scientific value for Alabama's coal and iron industry in the research which the Geological Survey was doing.

The twofold dialectic of liberality in science versus economy in science and of Republican versus Democratic will be illustrated as this story proceeds. Nevertheless, an approach through the positioning of opposites can never describe historical reality completely or neatly, for this reality always escapes to some degree any pattern that the historian would impose. In this combined history of the Coast Survey and the Hydrographic Office, individual behavior sometimes did not correspond to theory. Chairman Randall was cleverer than his fellow Democrats, Beck and Blount, when he criticized geodesy. The man from Philadelphia said that another science, geology, was more deserving of governmental support. In favoring mineral science over geodetic science, Randall cited the growing force and importance of industry in the national economy and the need for a geological survey to find natural resources, which would energize this sector of the economy. Randall's thinking implied that Coast Survey science, traditionally connected with trade and commerce, was less relevant in an industrial era.[26] The institutional result in the 1880s was the rapid rise of the Geological Survey and the decline of the Coast Survey.

In general, Republicans praised scientific knowledge; but the most sweeping attack on high science came from Republican Stephen B. Elkins, a territorial representative of New Mexico—and later a senator from West Virginia and a legislator on railroads. In 1877, during the debate on the appropriation for the General Land Office, Elkins declared that "the people on the frontier care nothing about geodetic points, isothermal lines, and the Silurian system; they want homes, farms, and mines, and therefore they desire the public domain surveyed."[27] Herbert, though professing laissez-faire, was an enthusiast for the navy, whose growing expense slowly undermined economy. Holman placed patronage above principle by never attacking the Geological Survey, because Director Powell made Paul Holman, the worthless son of the representative, an assistant topographer in the bureau.

In that other part of science policy, the organization of the governmental work, whether by civilians or the military, there was no chance of a second dialectic emerging from the ranks of Republicans or Democrats to complement the syndrome of liberal and economy-minded people. The politicians were too divided or changeable. Three Republicans in the Senate stood for the Hydrographic Office doing coastal science, but four House Republicans fought naval science as a portent of militarism; and a prominent Democrat joined the latter four. In the Naval Affairs Committee of the House, a Republican and a Democrat urged the cause of the Hydrographic Office. However, a third Democratic member of the committee switched from military to civilian advocacy. For all his support for coastal mapping by the navy while in the Executive branch, Chandler, upon becoming a senator, advocated civilian control in the Naval Observatory.

The best statement on the effectiveness of military science came from Representative Nathaniel P. Banks, a Massachusetts Republican, who had been an active (if unsuccessful) general during the Civil War. General Banks hailed the union of "science and force . . . to direct, execute and protect" the weather effort of the Signal Service; he looked for "the vigor, skill [and] discipline . . . of a military establishment" to advance the science of meteorology.[28] Nevertheless, Banks had words of praise for the civilian Coast Survey. The switch of Amos J. Cummings, Democrat of New Jersey—who, when younger, held editorial positions on three New York newspapers—from military to civilian advocacy on the key question of territorial coastal mapping will be decisive in this story of the rivalry of Coast Survey and Hydrographic Office.

Although divided in principle on the related issues of science and economy, Republicans and Democrats often worked together. They united in demanding Coast Survey science when Baltimore interests needed revised sheets of Chesapeake Bay and when Westerners of both parties insisted upon scientific mapping in Puget Sound and near San Francisco and Los Angeles. For their part, Republicans gave many pledges of economy, and because they feared the force of public opinion, as expressed pungently in Democratic journals, voted repeatedly for the idea in Congress. There were Democrats in this period who advocated government science with skill and distinction. Representatives Abram S. Hewitt of New York City and John D. C. Atkins of Tennessee were two of the founders of the Geological Survey; Senator Wilkinson Call of Florida spoke warmly and frequently about the same bureau; and

Representative Robert Lowry, judge and congressman from Indiana, would help government science at one critical moment later in this account.

Often, Democrats did not practice what they preached, a failing pointed out by several of their own members. In 1878, Representative Ebenezer B. Finley, Democrat from Ohio, agreed that in the memorable Forty-fourth Congress the Democratic party carried out its pledge to economy, but the Forty-fifth Congress was not making good in the same way. Finley blamed "a clique or a combination . . . in behalf of . . . appropriations for customhouses and postoffices." As late as 1900, William J. Talbert of South Carolina, farmer and member of the Farmers' Alliance, speaking in the House, mourned that "my brother Democrats believe in denouncing extravagance upon the floor, but when it comes to opposing and voting against extravagant pension claims, they fail to come up to . . . scratch."[29]

Despite all these reservations about the partisan division between Republicans and Democrats concerning science and economy, and science and its organization within the government, the reality and influence of the split remained substantial. An analysis of the lives of the involved Republicans and Democrats provides some explanation for the gulf between the parties. Though neither party could claim a research scientist within its ranks, Republicans had more acquaintance with scientific knowledge and method. Senator Nathaniel P. Hill was a former professor of chemistry at Brown, before he went west to apply his knowledge in Colorado toward separating gold and copper; Representative Horace Maynard taught mathematics and natural history for six years at East Tennessee College; Representative Clifton B. Bush, a Cleveland manufacturer, took out patents for his inventions with the general government; and Omar B. Conger, who served in both the House and Senate, helped Michigan's first geological survey in the exploration of the Lake Superior region. As a reporter, Representative Robert Adams of Philadelphia had traveled with geologist Ferdinand V. Hayden in the Yellowstone country, and James W. Patterson had taught mathematics, astronomy, and meteorology at Dartmouth College in New Hampshire. On the Democratic side, only Hewitt, an iron and steel manufacturer, had any significant connection with science and technology.

Because more Republicans than Democrats were college graduates (46–25), it is not surprising that they received more honorary degrees (23–4) and sat on more governing boards in academe (13–1), where, inevitably, they gained a better idea of modern science. In the national capital, more Republicans were regents of the Smithsonian (23–17) and members of the Cosmos Club (7–2). Democrats were more naive than Republicans in their mixing of religion and scientific language or symbols. Denominational differences did not affect attitudes toward science; however, the four Unitarians and two Quakers were Republicans. Differences in age and congressional tenure seemed too slight to affect ideological patterns. Although there were many more wealthy Republicans than Democrats, the connection of this disparity with the issue of knowledge is elusive.

Randall was no more successful than Chandler with a program to break up the Coast Survey, and this second attack also provoked controversy. One Coast Survey assistant wrote to thirty congressmen. Robert Lowry, of the House, asked thirty-seven people in science, government, and academe their opinion, and he did not receive one reply that was favorable to Randall.[30] Philadelphia, Randall's home town, was the center of public protest. The major insurance companies there spoke up, as well as the Board of Trade, the Engineers Club, the Franklin Institute, and the American Philosophical Society. In New England, the Yale faculty, the "leading men" of New Haven, thirty-one citizens from New Hampshire, and the American Academy of Arts and Sciences in Boston opposed the transfer. Another organization that complained was the St. Louis Academy of Science. Prominent officials who supported the Coast Survey included the governor of Maryland, the state geologist of New Jersey, and the president of Columbia College. Several members of Congress pledged themselves to fight the transfer bill, when it reached the House and Senate floors.

The response to the Lowry inquiry demonstrated that among scientists and civilian engineers the Coast Survey was a very popular government bureau. Charles A. Young, an astronomer at Princeton, was sure that he spoke for nine-tenths of the scientific men of the nation when he said that "the abolition of the Coast and Geodetic Survey and the transfer of its duties to other organizations would be considered nothing less than [a] calamity." "High scientific ability" and "a remarkable standard of accuracy" were two other comments by respondents, and several of them praised the Survey as one of the world's greatest.[31] Fairman Rogers, civil engineer of Philadelphia and a founding member of the National Academy of Sciences, expressed pleasure at the excellent rapport he had with the bureau. The college professors who did summer geodetic work were also favorably disposed.

The idea of scientists in subordination to military authority moved several civilian engineers to protest Randall's move in the House committee. These engineers were thinking of their own unhappy position in public works managed by the Corps of Engineers. The military engineers were an aristocracy, charged the civilian engineers, who monopolized the top jobs and received all the credit for federal projects, when four or five times as many civilian engineers worked for the Corps on the same projects.[32]

Several letters to Lowry scoffed at naval officers in government science. Lewis M. Haupt, prominent civil engineer in large waterway projects, would not put them in charge of coastal surveying, because they "may have forgotten" all their astronomy, spherical trigonometry, and physics. And James T. Gardiner, civil engineer and geodesist in New York state, insisted that surveying was a profession which only professional surveyors could practice; no one could aspire to master three or four different professions, he added. Admiral Porter considered the Coast Survey "a most important national institution," and he could not believe that naval officers "would be brash enough" to recommend its dismemberment. Nor did the admiral suppose that the Hydrographic Office, "with its limited arrangements[,] would aspire to attach the Coast Survey to its train."[33]

A strong and unusual composition came from the pen of Assistant Bache of New Haven fame, who wrote anonymously in *The United Service Magazine*. Accusing Randall of being "daft with his economy," he combined and directed satire, reason, and rhetoric against the House chairman. "O Uncle Sam, dear Uncle Sam," Bache apostrophized, "your coat may be shortwaisted, your trousers skimpy, your face weazen, and your nose a trifle sharp, but not a mean bone have you in your body." Bache conceded the virtue of economy within the household: to save the cheese parings and the candle ends and to count the potatoes was not degenerate there. About the public economy, however, Bache articulated the Whig view of the function of government. He insisted that the lawmakers saved by spending, if they wished to maintain the natural balance of production and distribution. The wider the territory of a nation and the more diversified its industries, the more the legislators needed intelligence and skill to understand the relations of production, distribution, and protection and "to further their harmonious . . . development." Bache ended with a peroration that compared the Coast Survey to the Greek warrior Achilles. "Like Achilles, the Survey has lived in the light of open day, fearing no man, invulnerable to attack in front." Like Achilles, the Survey was "capable of speaking winged words," because they were the words of truth. Like Achilles, it was also capable "in its wrath of dragging its foe behind its chariot around the plain of Troy. And like him, it can, after having spoken, be silent and as calmly die."[34]

In the face of the general and articulate uproar, the House Appropriations Committee was soon ready to back down from Randall's division and transfer plan. The constructive move was a resolution, introduced within the committee, proposing that a joint congressional commission be established through the Sundry Civil bill to investigate the relation of the Coast Survey to the Hydrographic Office and the Geological Survey. Immediately, within the committee, the scope of the commission's work was broadened to include the Signal Service (weather bureau), whose controversial position within the War Department had long perplexed conscientious members of both House and Senate.

Thus originated the six-member joint commission, with Senator William B. Allison of Iowa as chairman, founded by the Forty-eighth Congress in its Sundry Civil Appropriations Act of July 8, 1884, and charged to investigate disputes in the Executive branch involving old and new government science, to further economy and efficiency in government science, and to consider and decide upon civilian-military relations.

Emerging from a decade of naval challenge to established science and House friendliness to economy, the Allison Commission became a historical force in its own right, whose course has been well marked for years by historians.[35] The idea of a Department of Science, the principles of government which four science agencies should build upon, the testimony of their chiefs, and the report two years later and its significance—these have been the major topics developed by present-day scholars. This account will focus on how the Commission related to the scientific rivalry between the military and the civilians and to the confrontation between the secretary of the navy and the head of the Hydrographic Office, on the one hand, and the Coast Survey superintendent on the other.

The preliminaries to the hearings of the Commission took the form of a discussion and report by a nine-member committee of the National Academy of Sciences, chaired by Montgomery C. Meigs, quartermaster general during the Civil War, architect of the Pension Building, and now retired from the Corps of Engineers. The secretary of the committee was Colonel Cyrus Comstock, also of the Corps. Just as six years ago, in 1878—when President Othniel C. Marsh appointed an Academy committee on the Western scientific surveys—his choices in the summer of 1884 provoked a complaint by the military about its representation.

The great objector was Secretary Chandler, who, upon seeing Marsh's list of members, must have resented the weak presence of the navy and the Hydrographic Office and the strong representation for the Coast Survey. The sole naval person was Simon Newcomb, a civilian astronomer and mathematician at the Naval Observatory. Two-thirds of the committee were civilians from college campuses or observatories, including three astronomers, and a majority of the committee were on record as praising the Coast Survey. Chandler proposed to undermine the Academy committee by joining with

Secretary of War Robert T. Lincoln in ousting Chairman Meigs and the two other military representatives, Newcomb and Comstock. The two Cabinet members held common ground. Although Chandler would increase naval science, nevertheless, like Secretary Lincoln, he was a civilian and stood for the supremacy of that status in American government. Concerning the action by the Academy committee, Chandler and Lincoln shared the common principle that officers of the navy and army should not "sit in judgment" on the government science of their departments, "except at the desire and under the direction" of these departments. Both feared lest a military officer assume supervisory functions over the head of his own (or another) department of the government.

When Lincoln, prodded by Chandler, sought to force the three resignations, Newcomb and Comstock complied, although the secretary of war had acted so slowly that the two had had time to influence the proceedings of the Academy committee. If Meigs had also resigned, Chandler's riposte would have finished the committee, but the distinguished Civil War veteran refused to budge. The quartermaster general was strong for army officers engaging in scientific surveys, believing that their participation in the Coast Survey before the Civil War had made them persons of larger knowledge, grasp, and power. As to speaking up in public discussion or in committee, he asserted that "opinion is free in our republic, even in the Army and Navy," although he admitted that expression of an opinion by an officer might become a grave offense against military discipline.

Meigs also went on the offensive against civilians. He interpreted the rivalry of the Hydrographic Office and the Coast Survey as a struggle for place and power, and he charged that in this struggle the civilians were jealous of the military. This feeling of jealousy, Meigs said, was felt "in all free states" against "the natural tendency of the military spirit and training, to grasp at power, and to acquire more than their fair share of public employment and service."[36]

In the fall of 1884, Meigs and the six remaining members of the Academy committee reported back to the Allison Commission. They blamed Congress for duplicating geodetic surveying among the War, Treasury, and Interior Departments, the legislators having ignored the recommendation of the Academy in 1878 that the Coast Survey have charge of all scientific mapping. The committee cleverly handled the sentiment for giving the coastal surveying to the navy. Instead of rejecting naval ambitions outright, it proposed that the Coast Survey complete its charting and mapping of the American coasts. Then, perhaps, the reexamining and resounding might go to the navy. This statement could hardly have satisfied naval protagonists, and they must have been irritated when they read in the report that the committee was not prepared to recommend that the work of the Hydrographic Office be detached "in any way" from the Navy Department.[37] Was anyone seriously proposing this?

A statement of geologist Dana and Meigs' commentary on it gives other relevant thinking within the committee, which did not appear in its report. Having praised the charting and mapping by the Coast Survey around New Haven as a model for the engineering and academic world to follow,[38] Dana insisted to Meigs that the bureau should make the same kind of map for the nation. Meigs agreed that the most accurate map was the best, but he thought that it was better to have a fair national map from Powell and the Geological Survey than none at all. The Coast Survey worked too slowly, said Meigs, to receive legislative support for a national mapping project. A map for the nation of the kind that New Haven enjoyed would not come for another century, he believed.[39]

When the Allison Commission convened for hearings in December 1884, Secretary Chandler did his best to demonstrate that the Coast Survey was a misfit as a scientific bureau. Its location in the Department of the Treasury, a bureau of fiscal affairs, was wrong; and the emphasis of its science was erroneous, because the legitimate work, the hydrography, was overshadowed by geodesy and topography. Since the government's hydrography was now executed by naval officers in either the Coast Survey or the Hydrographic Office, let the two groups unite within the Navy Department and let the other science of the Coast Survey go to the Geological Survey.

Chandler appealed to the prejudice against permanent bureaus by saying that the Coast Survey would have completed its main job of coastal surveying by now, had it not taken up geodesy. Representative Theodore Lyman of greater Boston, an independent in politics, who served with Lowry on the subcommittee of the Commission for the Coast Survey and was the only research scientist in Congress in this period, contradicted Chandler the most. Lyman doubted that the hydrography of the Coast Survey could be separated from the geodetic work, "any more than you can separate a man's skin from his muscle." He also questioned whether the artistic work of Coast Survey topographers could be done by naval men on a three-year assignment.

When Chandler, seeking to gain the initiative, said he was not in favor of letting well enough alone, Lyman replied that with the Coast Survey perhaps it was a question of letting "*very* well alone." This answer prompted Chandler to remark that he did not suppose that the Coast Survey was immaculate, or that it personified Achilles, as some of its admirers seemed to think. Thereupon, Eugene Hale of Maine, longtime manager in the Senate for naval legislation, member of the Allison Commission, and associated with Herbert as a subcommittee member of the Commission for the Hydrographic Office, said that the feeling was general that the work of the Coast Survey had been good, and that it had been headed by able and devoted men.[40]

Bartlett, once in command of the *Blake* and now Chandler's appointee to the Hydrographic Office, followed the secretary before the Commission. Bartlett expanded on the naval criticism of the Coast Survey, first presented in the *National Republican* years before. The ultimate science of the Coast Survey, geodesy, assured high quality for its maps, Bartlett admitted, but what use did they serve for the actual navigator or hydrographer, he asked. The triangulation across the continent had no more to do with the coast than the "Desert of Sahara." Bartlett then managed a dialogue with Chandler which gave the impression that the civilians in the Coast Survey were for the most part doing geodesy in the interior, while the naval officers engaged themselves in the proper hydrographic work on the coast. Seeking to erase the memory of the unsatisfactory work earlier in the century, when the navy controlled domestic coastal surveying, he said that naval officers were now trained at Annapolis, one of the best scientific schools in the nation. On the Pacific coast of Mexico, the USS *Ranger,* a Hydrographic Office vessel, was conducting a survey which answered all the needs of sailors. Latitude, longitude, variation in the compass, and the range of tides were determined; also, the positions of soundings were fixed through triangulation.

Bartlett admitted that geodetic refinement and details of topography were not attempted by the *Ranger* because such science was "foreign to the objects of a nautical survey." Bartlett also cited the party of naval officers sent in 1882 to survey the Gulf of Samana in Santo Domingo. "A base line was measured, positions were established astronomically, and the whole Gulf [was] enclosed in a complete system of triangulation," he said.[41]

Bartlett made much in his testimony of the elaborate and expensive topographical detail in Coast Survey maps. Nowadays, he said, when artificial aids to navigation were so numerous, seamen could get along with very little topography. In his correspondence (interpolated here as addenda to the testimony), Bartlett also accused the Coast Survey of procrastination. He disliked being told by the Coast Survey office that a locality reported to have shoaling water would be "examined when the opportunity offers." When a famous engineering project in the East River was consummated and Flood Rock blown up, Bartlett waited eight months, then complained that the Coast Survey had not publicized the new soundings. In a letter he composed for the secretary of the navy to send to the secretary of the treasury, he gave the number of months (one to four) that the Hydrographic Office, downtown in Washington, had to wait for charts requested from the Coast Survey on Capitol Hill.[42]

Before the Commission, Superintendent Hilgard successfully defended the geodesy, which Chandler, Bartlett, and the Democratic leadership in Congress were attacking so openly. Hilgard hinged the difference between the Coast Survey and the Hydrographic Office on this science. "The hydrographic survey along our shore," he said, "is . . . not a nautical survey, but, properly speaking, a *trigonometrical* survey." Positions of depths, rocks, and shoals were determined by the observation of angles on shore; and these objects on shore were located through geodetic triangulation and topographical work. Bartlett had accused the Coast Survey of "running off into the interior," and Hilgard admitted it. More than one chain of geodetic triangles was necessary, he said, to secure the framework of accurate distances, points, and directions necessary for the support of charting in shallow waters. If a survey, starting from a single point or measured line, proceeded down the coast, errors of observation accumulated within the chain of small triangles that was constructed. These errors might not cause trouble at the time of the survey, but later, when the attempt was made to join adjacent surveys, instead of the two fitting together, there would be gaps, offsets, and overlays.

Maps constructed without a geodetic base were an obvious failure, and Hilgard cited the American experience. When the results of various land surveys were collated, errors of one or two miles in latitude and longitude were common. Between the land surveys of Illinois and Missouri, the Mississippi River was in some places a wide lake; in other places it entirely disappeared. In the best maps of Ohio, Indiana, and Kentucky, the Ohio River disappeared. The way the Coast Survey avoided such glaring errors was to develop, away from the coast, a second chain of long triangles to form the backbone of the smaller chain. At frequent intervals, this second chain was extended seaward to check the coastal chain. Hilgard placed the work of the *Ranger* off the Pacific coast of Mexico in the category of unsatisfactory mapping, because it was not based on geodetic triangulation. Nor was there, he testified, any "accurate trace" made of the shoreline. It was similar to the exploratory work that the Coast Survey was doing in Alaska.

The topographical refinement which Bartlett disowned, Hilgard stressed. Coast Survey topographers had to have the ability to draw from nature, to see and represent land forms quickly and well, he said. If they tried to measure every line, the detail would never be finished; therefore, they learned to sketch the coastline between the points ashore and fill in the contours of the hills. They became as gifted as artists, the superintendent claimed.[43]

By the end of January, the Allison Commission knew that it

could not complete its task during the Forty-eighth Congress. Consequently, it secured a new legislative lease of life on March 3, 1885, and planned to resume hearings when the Forty-ninth Congress was first to meet, in December 1885.

4

The Ordeal of the Coast Survey under Cleveland in the Eighties

Two events introduced a new tension and urgency into the relations between the Hydrographic Office and the Coast Survey: the return of the Democrats to the Executive branch after an absence of twenty-four years, and the personal attention given to the business of the Coast Survey by President Grover Cleveland, the leader of the Democratic party.

Several months after the inauguration of Cleveland in March 1885, the Executive branch moved against the Coast Survey. The action came in July out of a Cabinet meeting and represented a major decision about the spirit and purpose of the new administration. Cleveland and his Cabinet complained that, in Republican administrations, accounting officials honored too easily the requisitions for money by heads of departments and agencies, without ascertaining whether Congress had authorized the spending. Disavowing this "Republican habit," the president and his advisers agreed to ask auditors and comptrollers of their administration to see that expenditures were legal and that proper protocol was followed. This emphasis on accountability and bookkeeping defined one very important meaning of economy and reform in government for the Democracy and for Cleveland's administration, which picked the Coast Survey to become the "practical exemplification" of the new procedures and preciseness.[1]

The events and drama of this planned crisis centered in the office of the Coast Survey, located at 205 New Jersey Avenue on the south side of Capitol Hill, a hundred yards from the House of Representatives wing of the Capitol itself. The office, including workrooms and shops, was a large, five-story brick building, perhaps originally intended as a hotel but immediately on construction leased to the Coast Survey. It had a hip roof, ornate front, and iron-spiked fence topped with fleurs-de-lis. The entrance was framed in fluted chocolate-color sandstone pilasters with a Corinthian motif and the steps were flanked with low balustrades, also made of chocolate-color sandstone. A back wing of the building, which looked like a barrack, extended toward South Capitol Street.

Action was harsh and sudden. On Friday, July 24, 1885, two assistant secretaries of the treasury, C. S. Fairchild and C. E. Coon, called at 205 New Jersey Avenue and, entering the office of the assistant in charge rather than Hilgard's, presented letters from Secretary of the Treasury Daniel Manning that suspended Hilgard and dismissed four other persons: Charles O. Boutelle, the assistant in charge of the office; Morgan, the disbursing agent; Saegmuller, the foreman of the instrument division; and Anton Zumbrock, electro-typist and photographer in the engraving division. Frank Manly Thorn—lawyer, journalist, and longtime friend and supporter of the president in Buffalo—who had accompanied the two assistant secretaries to the Survey building, became acting superintendent. Assistant Benjamin A. Colonna was called into Boutelle's crowded office and introduced to Thorn, who asked:

"Can you conduct this office for a short time?"

"Not as well as Captain Boutelle," replied Colonna.

"You are assistant in charge," said Thorn.[2]

Colonna had joined the bureau in 1870; he was a Virginian, a graduate of Virginia Military Institute in 1864, and a soldier for the Confederacy in the Battle of Newmarket. In the Survey, he passed through the usual experience of the field force in all branches, and in 1879 contributed a "valuable paper" on the transit of Mercury.[3]

On the recommendation of J. Q. Chenoweth, Cleveland's First

Auditor of the Treasury, Thorn also headed a three-man commission of the Treasury to investigate the Coast Survey, and twelve days later, on Wednesday, August 5, the Thorn commission brought in a report. A headline on the first page of the *Washington Post* on Friday, August 7, dramatized the report with words and punctuation, "INTOXICATED *** DEMORALIZED." In a sweeping generalization, the Coast Survey was described as "inefficient," "unjust," and "disreputable." The commission announced Hilgard's confession of intemperance and recommended his removal, and the superintendent resigned the same day.[4]

The Thorn commission report was the initial step in carrying out the wishes and philosophy of the Cleveland administration concerning the Coast Survey. The commission thought that the scientific force of assistants could be "considerably reduced" and that none of them need be paid over three thousand dollars. On the lookout for employees who did no work, the commission pointed to Samuel Hein, seventy-six years of age, who had been with the Coast Survey forty-eight years and now was blind. Hein, once the disbursing agent, was carried on the payroll as a librarian at $150 per month. Three other examples were given of persons receiving pay but doing no work.

Bent upon a scrupulous accounting for government property and its use, the commission reported that several of the scientists, including Hilgard, used chronometer watches of the Coast Survey as their personal timepieces. It noted, correctly, that two hundred books of the Coast Survey library were in the possession of Assistant Peirce. The records of the instrument division showed that valuable instruments of the Survey had been charged to persons no longer employed by the Survey or had been loaned, without authority, to institutions of learning. The commission heartily disliked the position of Saegmuller as foreman of the instrument division and partner in the firm of Fauth & Company, which sold thousands of dollars of instruments every year to the bureau. Against Hilgard, it chalked up another score when it reported that he had sold a black mare, belonging to the Coast Survey, for $50 and pocketed the money.[5]

Because the Thorn commission was in a hurry and because it

listened uncritically to scandalmongers in the Survey office, it made a number of incomplete, unfair, or exaggerated statements. Had Thorn delayed his report for a few weeks, he could have included the subsequent discovery of Hilgard's manipulation of vouchers, when the *Patterson* was launched and Kübel was confronted in a Survey washroom. Also, the commission would not have charged Morgan with being "entirely passive" about unusual vouchers submitted by the superintendent, for the disbursing agent had twice refused Hilgard's vouchers on the occasion of the launching. Alexander McCue, the solicitor of the Treasury, later gave his opinion that there was a lack of evidence in two of the cases described by the commission as pay without work.

The castigation of the superintendent in the Bradford incident seems harsh and less than frank. Bradford was the skillful compiler and editor of the *Atlantic Coast Pilot,* who, falling into debt in 1883 because of his gambling, was caught taking Coast Survey funds through false vouchers. Hilgard had threatened charges against him as a "thief, drunkard and forger," thus forcing Bradford's wife to borrow a thousand dollars, at 15 percent, to refund the money taken from the government. The next year (1884), Bradford's salary was raised $60 a month, a generous action on Hilgard's part, which the commission characterized as a "deliberate condonation of embezzlement, forgery, and drunkenness"—without telling that Hilgard, by his positive reaction to Bradford's bad conduct, had retrieved the government's money.

The commission probably exaggerated the importance of one irregular voucher submitted by Boutelle, the dismissed assistant in charge of the office. Boutelle had persuaded a liveryman, who had not serviced him, to sign a voucher for $18, the amount that Boutelle spent on cab fares to the Survey office while he was sick. Boutelle, fighting back, convinced Cleveland's secretary of war, William C. Endicott, that the charge against him was petty, and Secretary Endicott appealed to Secretary Manning of the Treasury, who restored Boutelle to the list of assistants on August 7, the very day that the Thorn commission made the headlines.[6]

Disciplinary and investigatory actions dominated Survey affairs for several months. Thorn dismissed the blind librarian, Samuel

Hein, and two others with forty years or more of service, who were doing no work. Bradford resigned to avoid a public investigation of his past as a gambler, and so did W. T. Bright, chief clerk of the drawing division, who, like Hilgard, had succumbed to the drinking habit. A daughter of Patterson, the deceased superintendent, also lost her job. Before the year was out, fourteen persons had perforce left the Coast Survey office.[7]

The high point of his activity came in late September, when Thorn reported to the secretary of the treasury the discovery of eight transactions by Hilgard that justified, Thorn said, a government claim for money against the former superintendent. In the middle of October, Hilgard accepted his financial liability in six of these transactions and deposited a check with the solicitor of the Treasury for $1,100, payable to the order of Daniel Manning, secretary of the treasury. By this payment, Hilgard admitted putting misleading or untrue information on five Coast Survey vouchers: in two cases where no bona fide work had been done, in one when an imaginary name had been used, and in the *Patterson* and Kübel affairs. The feature of the sixth transaction which had induced financial redress by Hilgard was his failure to keep a record of cash received when he traded off Survey instruments.[8]

Sensitive about his responsibility for government property, Thorn ordered an inventory of Survey belongings. He collected chronometers from Hilgard and other scientists, and he called for instruments from scores of colleges. Two theodolites were missing, which had been paid for but, apparently, never delivered by Fauth & Company, Washington instrument makers. A four hundred dollar overcharge on another instrument was also uncovered. After six months, Superintendent Thorn informed President Cleveland of "the restitution of instruments worth $2,395 of spurious vouchers."[9] In a determined effort to change the mood of the Survey office, Thorn issued orders against smoking, newspaper reading, and gossiping. Daily luncheon spreads, served by messengers, ceased, and after-hour work was discontinued in all departments. "No more idling, fooling & trickery," reported Schott to Davidson.[10]

Under Thorn, the Coast Survey lost power to Treasury officials. This development was not surprising in an administration where secretaries of departments found their orders for expenditures frequently countermanded by comptrollers and auditors. Nor would Cleveland intervene to support the "injured dignity" of the Cabinet members.

The Treasury officials who wielded the most power in the Coast Survey were J. Q. Chenoweth, the First Auditor, and M. J. Durham, the First Comptroller, who used their high rank to issue legalistic and rigid rulings. For example, they combined to throw into doubt for eighteen months the power of the Coast Survey to make a topographic survey of the District of Columbia. To complaints reaching Durham about the injustice of his opinions, the comptroller replied, more than once, that he must construe the law as he found it. Congress should provide, he said, for the hardship cases. According to Assistant Secretary Fairchild, the valuable work being performed by the Coast Survey in establishing state lines, often in collaboration with a state boundary commission, was unauthorized, and he urged Thorn to obtain a law from Congress to justify this activity.

Another outsider who exercised great power in Survey business was G. A. Bartlett, disbursing agent of the Treasury, who took charge of the Survey's accounting division upon Morgan's dismissal. Bartlett organized a force of twenty clerks to read, construe, and sometimes reject Survey accounts. This analysis was so intensive, Bartlett admitted, that what was formerly a matter of minutes now became the "labor of hours."[11]

It was rare that Thorn could prevail over this battery of Treasury personnel, but he did once—when the Treasury challenged the longstanding and necessary practice of the Coast Survey of making cash advances to field parties that operated in remote areas where there were no banks, or where field parties needed to spend such small sums that checks or drafts were not practical. There never had been high authority for these advances; indeed, they were contrary to law. Nevertheless, Thorn was emphatic when he told Secretary Manning that the practice, despite its illegality, must continue; and within a week after his imperative letter an order from the Executive Mansion approved the advance of money if bond was given by the entrusted employees.[12] Thereafter, appropriations for the Coast Survey carried a provision for cash advances if bond was given.

A central figure in the storm of controversy which swirled about the Coast Survey was Charles S. Peirce, son of Benjamin and representative on the Coast Survey of one of the enduring influences of the Peirce regime; for the father had introduced, through his offspring, another phase of geodetic work which would lead to knowledge of the shape of the earth beyond what triangulation provided. This phase or advance was to measure the acceleration of a body under the force of universal gravitation at various places on the surface of the earth. Since geodesists knew then that the earth was not a perfect sphere, but flattened at the poles and, according to them, bulging at the equator, the force of acceleration, because it was related inversely to the square of the distance from the earth's center, diminished as one moved from the poles to the equator; that is, it varied with the latitude. In this change of gravity lay a change of shape (the ellipticity), which the measuring of the force could lead to. Local forces of attraction and the earth's gravitation were two other factors which affected the field of gravity on the earth's surface. In the 1860s, there had been a new upsurge of pendulum swinging in Europe to collect more data on gravity on the earth's surface; also, an International Geodetic Association had been established. Peirce lined up the Coast Survey in 1872 to do its share, by putting his son in charge of American research.

The instrument for measuring gravity was the pendulum, which Peirce the younger defined as "a body so suspended from a fixed point so as to move to and from by the alternate action of gravity and its acquired energy of motion."[13]

Since Galileo's time and the rise of classical mechanics, several varieties of pendulums had come into use among scientists.[14] Initially, they swung a bob or weight, suspended by wire or string to a fixed support. In the nineteenth century they turned to bar, rod, or tubular pendulums. The Kater pendulum of that period was perhaps the most famous of stable, rigid bodies used to measure gravity. Henry Kater, an Englishman, had constructed a bar pendulum which swung on two fixed knife edges, located on opposite sides of the center of gravity of the bar. He swung the bar pendulum on each knife edge in turn, and so adjusted the weight of the pendulum that the periods of swing on both knife edges were identical. Kater's was called an invariable, convertible, unsymmetrical pendulum. After 1860, another popular type of instrument was the Bessel-Repsold pendulum, named after a German scientist and a German instrumentmaker. This pendulum was symmetrical and also had two knife edges, but they were interchangeable. The Bessel-Repsold was called a reversible pendulum.

By the nineteenth century, geodesists had clarified their idea or model of the pendulum. They used the identifying term, simple pendulum, which meant in theory that the mass lay all in one point, and the string or wire connecting the body to the fixed point was without mass and inextensible. This simple pendulum was also conceived as vibrating seconds; that is, one second was the period of the swing, defined as half the distance between the top of the swing on one side to the top of the swing on the other side. In short, the simple pendulum was also a seconds pendulum.

Realistically, geodesists knew that they could only approximate their ideal pendulum. An actual bar pendulum of the nineteenth century had two knife edges, which lay at different distances from the center of gravity and were so located that the period of swing, the half phase, was near one second for each. The geodesist then designated the distance between two such knife edges with the common period as the length of the ideal, simple-pendulum vibrating seconds. Then the geodesist could go on to calculate g, the acceleration of a freely falling body from the formula that T (the period) equaled $\pi\sqrt{L/g}$. In other words, the period of the simple pendulum, oscillating seconds, varied as the square root of the length.[15]

Another method for finding the intensity of gravity dispensed with measuring the length of the pendulum, thereby saving much labor and expense. This was to carry the pendulum from a place where gravity itself had been determined—called absolute gravity—to a second place where the period alone was measured, common to both knife edges there. Then, with the ratio of the squares of the periods at the two stations in hand, the geodesist could introduce another ratio: the change in the intensity of gravity at the second station (called relative gravity) as related to the intensity of gravity per se at the first station, and then proceed with geodetic calculations to find the ellipticity of the earth's surface, as expressed in the fractional relationship of the equatorial radius of the earth to its polar radius.

The thirty-three-year-old son was the beneficiary of an act of manifest nepotism, but science advanced nonetheless. In a decade, "Charlie"—as he was called by his fond father—fashioned a brilliant career for himself in gravity studies. He educated himself rapidly and thoroughly on the assigned topic by reading "all the epoch-making works" on the pendulum. He supervised the construction at the Coast Survey of invariable pendulums with conical bobs, and swung them at Northampton, Cambridge, and in the Hoosac Tunnel. In 1875 he sailed for Europe for a year's tour of duty, to observe the best practice in pendulum swinging and to pick up a Repsold pendulum that he had ordered made at Hamburg in a shop with that name. He buttonholed Clerk Maxwell, G. G. Stokes, and Airy in England; talked to Theodor von Oppolzer in Vienna; and saw others in Germany and Geneva. Collecting the Repsold pendulum at Hamburg, he swung the instrument at Kew, Berlin, Geneva, and Paris, where the earlier great men in gravity studies of the nineteenth century had done likewise. Of course, he attended meetings of the International Geodetic Association as representative of the Coast Survey.

Soon he was making his own contribution as a relentless investigator of error-making in current pendulum swinging. He discovered a defect in the Repsold pendulum, believed by himself and many other scientists to be the successor to the Kater as the best apparatus for obtaining gravity data. Overhearing in Europe the casual remark that the stand for the Repsold pendulum might be unstable, he checked this type of pendulum and found that it put its stand in vibration and that the vibration of the stand affected the time of oscillation. After an initial division among European scientists about Peirce's findings, with the Germans and the French supporting him and the Swiss and the Austrians expressing skepticism, all the European experts came to praise him for the correctness of his critical analysis.

Peirce's international reputation was made. (Later, he considered the possibility of swinging two similar pendulums from the same support to overcome the swaying of the stand.) He took the statements of the president of the Bureau of Longitude in France in support of his idea and made analytical and mechanical investigation of their practicality. In 1880 he appeared before the Paris Academy of Sciences to demonstrate that his measurements of the acceleration of gravity at Paris were superior to those of the two celebrated physicists, J. C. Borda and J. B. Biot, whose work, Peirce said, needed only the corrections he proposed to put them in harmony with his own.[16]

With the Repsold, Peirce initiated a second round of pendulum swinging in the United States, at Hoboken. Then he moved on to Allegheny, Ebensburgh, and York in Pennsylvania. In the early eighties he had four reversible pendulums of cylindrical form made at the Coast Survey, and with them he began a new round of swinging at the Smithsonian, Hoboken, Montreal, Albany, Madison, and Ithaca. In 1882, at a conference organized in Washington by Hilgard for considering the usefulness and scientific accuracy of pendulum swinging, he engaged in debate with Colonel John Herschel of England on whether the invariable or the reversible pendulum was better for determinations of gravity. Another trip to Europe, in 1883, resulted in an order to the workshop of P. F. Gautier in Paris for new, reversible pendulums. Gautier was the mechanician for the French Bureau of Longitude and the observatory at Paris.

Early in August 1885, Peirce was swinging his domestic-made, reversible pendulums at Ann Arbor, Michigan, when the news came of harsh criticism by the Thorn commission of him and his work. The commission asserted the "meagre value" of pendulum experiments, which had cost $31,000 since 1879, and it connected this putative poverty of return with Peirce's "utter disregard" of recordkeeping. This scientist, said the commission's report, had been independent "at all times" of control or discipline; he was also identified as the assistant who had in his possession two hundred books belonging to the Coast Survey library. Interviewed in the *Washington Post* the day before the Thorn report appeared, Chenoweth sneered at the "so-called" scientists in the Coast Survey; in September, he was reported as making "cheap jibes" at pendulum swinging.[17]

Peirce met the attack boldly and publicly. Within a two-week period he sent twenty-one letters or telegrams from Ann Arbor to the Coast Survey office, the strongest communication being his letter of resignation addressed to Secretary Manning. He had a broadside printed, defending himself and his work, which was published in the *New York Evening Post* and the magazine *Science*. A fortunate circumstance for him was the meeting that same August in Ann Arbor of the American Association for the Advancement of Science, and that group, urged on by Peirce, responded with a set of resolutions for President Cleveland, Secretary Manning, and the newspapers. These resolutions twice urged the government to judge the merits of its scientific work by consulting with scientists. A superintendent was called for who had the "highest possible standing among scientific men" and commanded "their entire confidence." There was also lavish praise for Peirce's gravity studies and "earnest sympathy" for the government in its effort to make the public service efficient.[18]

For the next six years, between 1885 and 1891, Peirce and the government would be at swords' points over his gravity research. The scientific principles that Peirce stood for, the policies springing from these principles which he would follow about pendulum swinging, and the nature and effect of his distinctive personality all merged in tension and conflict with collectivities and individuals within the government—with the Executive, with Congress, and with dominating persons and their philosophy within Cleveland Democracy.

Because Cleveland and his Democrats had called for efficiency and earnestness in government procedures and for businesslike methods in all public activity, the Thorn commission had directed much of its fire against Peirce's habits in official matters. Peirce was poor at logistics, although the necessities of his science required planning for the frequent transportation of meter-long pendulums, which made for heavy and cumbersome equipment. He left boxes and packages in customhouses or postoffices for months at a time; and he performed no better with books. The two hundred books that belonged to the Coast Survey library suffered severe damage in two fires, and while he was lecturing at Johns Hopkins University (from 1879 to 1884) he borrowed "valuable and rare" volumes from its library, which several years later President D. C. Gilman was still trying to retrieve. Gilman learned of two of these books, borrowed by Peirce, when they were sold as unclaimed packages in Washington, D.C.[19]

Usually, Peirce had not filed the results of his pendulum experiments in duplicate to satisfy regulations. "What would have happened differently," he asked Thorn, "if I had filed the records?" And he rationalized his lifetime behavior by telling the Allison Commission that "the highest kind of scientific work" could not result from "mere" organization. Original work, he insisted, came from "individual genius."[20]

Peirce's eccentricities cannot be dismissed simply as the amusing, personal side of a very talented scientist and philosopher. His outspokenness made him a public figure in political circles and the stories about him, along with Hilgard's disgrace, fed the prejudiced opinion in Washington that men of science had little aptitude for administrative work or practical affairs.

Although early in September Peirce humbly expressed the "wish and intention" to conform to Survey regulations in the filing of records and computations, he soon backslid on his resolution. Bills continued to slip his mind and vouchers were lost track of. "Charles Peirce about crazes me," wrote Colonna, the new assistant in charge of the Washington office; "he has no system, and no idea of order or business."[21] Thorn, too, complained that Peirce ignored official correspondence and refused courteous requests to acknowledge the receipt of such communications.

Peirce increased the tension with the superintendent, early in 1887, after a locked room in the national office, which he had used as storage space, was appropriated for Survey purposes and

Peirce's materials were put in a general storeroom. He charged that powerful persons were making war on him, or planning to get rid of him. In a letter, which Thorn doubtless saw, Peirce charged that "Thorn is mad, I can see, as people generally are with those who save them from acts of folly." Thorn got many direct complaints from Peirce in his mail. In one such letter, Peirce offered himself for martyrdom; he was, he wrote the superintendent, "pretty well habituated to unfair treatment."[22]

One of the brighter features of Thorn's administration was his handling of the eccentric scientist. He withheld Peirce's impulsive letter of resignation from Secretary Manning, taking the advice of Schott, who argued the loss to the higher scientific work of the Survey if Peirce should resign. Peirce had built, at home and abroad, a reputation which the Coast Survey was proud of. With the period of experimentation in gravity measurement by the Survey drawing to a close, Schott thought that Peirce would soon begin the systematic areal work, leading to better knowledge of the earth's figure. Thorn replied with patience to Peirce's blunt letters. No one in the national office, he said truthfully, was trying to get rid of Peirce, and he characterized some of the letters as "ridiculous hysterics." At the same time, he acknowledged Peirce's "great ability" and expressed "genuine admiration of some traits of your character." In a lighter vein, Thorn said that Peirce was good at turning the "humdrum routine of official intercourse into a series of lively episodes."[23]

Personal tensions and byplay should not obscure the issue about which Peirce would differ with three superintendents: Hilgard, Thorn, and Mendenhall. He insisted that for first-class work he needed the Gautier pendulums ordered in 1883, and that he should be allowed to go forthwith to Europe and supervise their construction. Unhappy with this proposal, Hilgard threatened to assume personal direction of the pendulum swinging, whereupon Peirce talked of resigning. Thorn's reaction was to consult Schott, but this time the Washington assistant would not support Peirce, saying that his arrangements with Gautier were a "defective bargain" and that Thorn, like Hilgard, should refuse to buy the Parisian instruments. Let them be made at home instead.[24]

Nor could Peirce stay away from the most theoretical and abstract parts of geodesy to concentrate on measuring relative gravity, which all agreed was the practical objective. He informed Thorn in 1887 that he was improving on the mathematical theory of Britain's Stokes as to the effect of small jars on the period of the pendulum; and the following year he reported that he had made a "new calculation of the compression of the earth," which Schott called irrelevant to the pendulum observations.[25]

In his philosophy of science, Peirce would not consider any system of priorities, to allow focusing on immediate goals and putting off ultimate problems. At the conference with Colonel Herschel in 1882, called to consider the practical return as well as the scientific quality of pendulum swinging, Schott and Hilgard were present, and Peirce showed that he was not restricting the range of his thinking in the light of any political situation. He defined his task in a way that collapsed any distinction between the theoretical and the practical. "Too great stress ought not to be put upon the demands of the practically useful," he said; and "the knowledge of the force of gravity is not a matter of utility alone, but it is also one of the fundamental units of quantity which is the business of geodetic surveys to measure."[26]

In the end, Peirce suffered a serious loss of independence. Thorn shut down on his field work and ordered him to concentrate on putting in finished and available form all the records of his observations at American gravity stations. Peirce's reaction was far from manly. He soldiered on the job, became morose, showed his wounds in the newspapers ("they were unbounded lies"), talked of maintaining himself independently of his Survey salary, and turned to other work, such as writing articles on logic and philosophy for the *Century Dictionary* or book reviews for *The Nation*. He who had spoken up so boldly from Ann Arbor in 1885, in 1889 expressed supersensitive feelings about "the rude and insulting communications" from the Coast Survey office. They have, he wrote eloquently, "depressed my spirits, taken away my heart, poisoned every motive and exertion, slacked my energy, and dulled my intellectual keenness." Even the eventual retraction of most of the charges did not still his grumbling at the statement of the Thorn commission that he had not been under proper control and discipline. "Of course I have had my way," he wrote; "I know the questions and facts, [and] my ideas are clearer and reasonable."[27] His ultimate protest was to leave the coastal and urban areas, where he had lived and worked most of his life, to reside near Port Jervis, where New York, New Jersey, and Pennsylvania come together. To this isolated spot his annual salary of $3,000 continued to come from the Coast Survey.

Those who next experienced the shock and turmoil of the Thorn regime were the field geodesists and topographers, already generalized about somewhat and presented individually through Davidson, Bache, Rodgers, Mitchell, and Pratt. Proud of themselves as manly scientists, they held expectations about rewards which had become part of the practice or custom of the Coast Survey. They considered their salaries low, and realistically looked to no great or sudden change for the better. Promotions were few, coming only when vacancies occurred; longevity increases or retirement pay did not exist. They came to rely, therefore, on other Survey advantages, which either supplemented their incomes or compensated them in other ways for their low salaries. A large per diem allowance or subsistence was one of these advantages, and furlough with no diminution of income was another, as well as uninterrupted pay during periods of sickness, disability, and old age. If challenged to justify these supplementary benefits, the assistants would cite the eminence and laboriousness of their service. Only an inhuman person, they asserted, would begrudge them their privileges. It was the retention of the aged into their seventies and eighties which particularly angered Cleveland Democrats; it amounted, they said, to a system of pensions. And pensions were, for them, the symbol and evidence of a decadent aristocracy.[28]

For all their qualities and common experience, the assistants could not find the will and the unity to oppose Thorn or the Treasury effectively. They had relied too long on sympathetic superintendents for their perquisites and their independence. The senior assistants, who had successfully led a fight against Patterson's move in 1881 to curb their privileges in the name of economy, were demoralized by the charges of drunkenness and corruption against the Coast Survey; they were likened to a Grecian chorus which interpreted "what the play was about" by making "dumb motions of despair."[29] Mitchell, the distinguished hydrographer and member of the National Academy of Sciences, seemed the most likely leader in opposition, but his knowledge and prestige were of no avail when he faced Thorn, who met the assistant's dissatisfaction with mockery of his technical learning and his personality.[30] Ultimately, Mitchell resigned.

In the middle of September, Thorn announced the policies which were to hurt the assistants most. Implementing the promise of economy in his August report, the superintendent forced substantial reductions in the income of all the civilian scientists. His method was to eliminate or reduce the per diem allowance or subsistence, which both the office and the field force among the assistants enjoyed and which meant yearly increments to formal salaries of up to one thousand dollars a year. Subsistence, Thorn ruled, belonged only to those engaged in actual field work; therefore, the assistants who were permanently in the national office could have no regular income from this source. Then he narrowed the definition of field work for those located outside the national office, so that they also were deprived of large amounts of subsistence allowance.[31] The annual sums that were lost to members and saved on the Coast Survey budget ranged from two hundred to nine hundred dollars. To show that he meant business, Thorn let it be known that resignations in twenty-four hours would be asked from any complaining assistants. As late as 1920, one of Thorn's successors was lamenting the financial burden placed upon field workers, who lost subsistence when they came to the national office.

A second severe shock to the corps of assistants came in February 1886, when First Comptroller Durham challenged $29,000 in salaries and expenses paid them by former disbursing agent Morgan during 1884 and through July 23, 1885.[32] The proposed disallowances on salaries affected 30 persons and concerned 119 payments; the challenged expenses involved 106 persons and 900 items. The cost of finding geodetic points for the states and working up the transcontinental geodesy were two of the disallowed expenses. If the challenged accounts were ultimately disallowed, then the assistants would be responsible for the amounts improperly paid them. Meanwhile, in anticipation of final disallowance, deductions from salaries, amounting to hundreds of dollars, were levelled against many assistants. In justification of this retroactive step, Durham cited the 1881 edition of Coast Survey regulations, which Patterson had promulgated as an economy measure.

In this revision, Patterson had denied subsistence for office work at home, where much of the field force stayed for many weeks between seasons. He had eliminated compensation while on furlough, and had inserted a 25 percent reduction in salary for assistants awaiting orders to proceed into the field.[33] The assistants had fought these new regulations so effectively, hiring a lawyer and rallying college professors to their side, that Patterson had to back down. And Hilgard, his successor, took a relaxed attitude toward them. They remained, however, part of the formal law of the Coast Survey, and Durham used them as the basis of his $29,000 challenge. For his part, Thorn required the assistants to follow the ignored regulations closely in the future and, as we have seen, he expanded the antisubsistence provision to include the office force in Washington.

The field assistants now entered a period of rule by financial officers. It almost seemed that the rendering of accounts took priority over scientific affairs. The correspondence with Washington on fiscal matters increased enormously, and so did the paper work to verify field expenses. For a time, "almost continual disallowance" plagued the assistants when they provided verification of their expenditures from local legal officers. Insisting that vouchers for money spent be validated by documentation, the Treasury often returned the vouchers and the notarized affidavits, which accompanied them, on the grounds that the fees of the notaries were excessive. Worst of all, deductions from salaries became a familiar part of Coast Survey life, not simply because of the accounts through July 23, 1885, but also because of new interpretations of the rules. In the third quarter of 1886, for example, fifty-one persons of the Coast Survey had $2,300 in increased salaries disallowed for failing to take an oath of office at the time of the promotion which brought the increased salaries.[34]

The experience of the talented and energetic Pratt communicates vividly what the new controls meant. At the time of Hilgard's resignation, he was directing topographical and hydrographical work in Puget Sound and the Straits of San Juan de Fuca. The arbitrary manner of the accountants kept Pratt in a constant state of irritation or anger. It seemed to him that they made no effort to lighten or simplify his task; they showed no sense for the human situation. They slashed items "right and left," regardless of who was at fault, and more than once returned a whole month of accounts because of one offensive voucher. Pratt begged Treasury officials to send back the offensive voucher with the month's account, so that when the recipient of public money was asked for a second voucher, he would not think that the government was being charged a second time.[35]

When Pratt claimed freight costs on a shipment of goods bought with subsistence money, Bartlett of the Treasury ruled that the subsistence payment itself should cover the freight expenses. Going aboard the Coast Survey schooner *Yukon* at Seattle to prepare it for the field season, a task which took several weeks, Pratt claimed subsistence for field work, only to be told that he was doing office work and could not claim subsistence. He asked Treasury officials how he could obtain affidavits about money payments from the officers of corporations in the Puget Sound country when, for the most part, these officers were large capitalists residing in either New York or Philadelphia. One challenged expenditure under Durham's sweeping revocation of Morgan's accounts went back to the summer of 1884, when, under an order to join a Coast Survey party in Vancouver, whose leader had been stricken with paralysis, Pratt rowed eighteen miles at four in the morning to intercept the steamer bound for the Canadian city.[36]

In 1886 Pratt suffered a suspension of $64 in salary payments, while Comptroller Durham reviewed a subsistence payment to the assistant in 1884. Durham wanted to apply Patterson's unenforced regulation that an assistant awaiting instructions to proceed into the field was temporarily unemployed and therefore should accept a 25 percent reduction of salary. In a strong rebuttal, Pratt admitted to awaiting instructions one time in 1884, but he vehemently denied that he was unemployed. In the interim period cited by Durham, he had designed and built a twenty-two-foot topographical boat, made of white oak frame and cedar planks with copper fastenings. The cost in materials came to $65, and the boat could not be replaced for $225. To take away some of his salary, when he had been so busy, was simply wrong: "if the decision is made against me," Pratt wrote, "it is both morally and legally unjust and the government is in *wrongful* possession of the results of my labor during the time it affirms that I was doing nothing."[37] On this occasion Pratt carried the day, and for a man who was reputed to be hot-tempered, he remained marvelously calm. Nevertheless, his annual salary was drifting downward during this vexatious period, until by 1890 he was receiving $360 less than in 1885.

Richard M. Bache, Randall's tormentor and the Survey's literary figure, was another assistant who skillfully fought the forces of Cleveland's bureaucracy. He received notice from Thorn in May 1886 to go on furlough, which under the new dispensation meant that he drew a diminished salary while in that status. Bache admitted that the regulations gave the superintendent the power to "grant" furlough; but he argued that use of the word "grant" implied a request from the assistant that he receive furlough, and Bache had not asked for it. After correspondence with Bache, Thorn, and the secretary of the treasury, McCue supported Bache. Thorn, in pique, ordered Bache to await instructions, whereupon Bache replied that he had already been posted to Rehoboth Bay and Staten Island. This time Durham supported Thorn, and Bache perforce received only three-fourths of his salary for a fortnight in May.[38]

In the fall of 1885, the purge of the Coast Survey having passed its climax, activity by the president and Congress gave further impetus to the course of events. President Cleveland intervened in the most personal and direct way in the affairs of the Coast Survey, and on Capitol Hill the Allison Commission, after many months of inactivity, resumed its hearings. Representative John T. Wait of Connecticut replaced Theodore Lyman, and Senator John T. Morgan of Alabama filled in for Pendleton of Ohio.

Cleveland ascended to the presidency with as strong a prejudice as anyone in the Democratic party against the science of the Coast Survey. In 1884 as governor of New York, he wiped out with a veto the geodetic survey of the state of New York, because it was elaborate, slow, and expensive. Cleveland had expressed the opinion then that a "correct and exact location of boundary lines and monuments to answer every useful purpose could be conducted . . . at a comparatively small expense."[39] After his summer participation in the initial movement against the Coast Survey, Cleveland in September sought Alexander Agassiz as superintendent, and failing in this, he sent Thorn his commission in October, the Treasury having refused to pay the full salary of $6,000 because Thorn was only acting head. Thus Cleveland made the first presidential appointment of the superintendent, assuming a power previously exercised by the secretary of the treasury.

In December came his first State of the Union message, which castigated the Coast Survey for its "abuses" and "reckless disregard of duty" and called for the enforcement of "economies" and "business methods." Cleveland charged the Coast Survey with taking to itself "powers and objects not contemplated in its creation," and appealing to the Allison Commission, he urged legislation to transfer the coastal surveying to the Navy Department. If the other science of the Coast Survey was to continue, it should be executed with an awareness of state authority and individual enterprise in scientific inquiry. After the message, Thorn sent the president a letter informing him of a plan to insert in the testimony before the Allison Commission an anonymous memorandum favoring civilian control in the Coast Survey. Thorn, however, volunteered to "suppress" this material, since it conflicted with the thrust of the presidential message. The president had only to let him know. A second letter to the president carried the denial by Thorn of a newspaper story that he had recommended continuance of the Survey as presently organized.[40]

Before the Allison Commission in mid-December, with Hilgard gone and Thorn not appearing, the assistants for once held the initiative. They submitted good papers, and one of them—by Schott, Mitchell, and Colonna on hydrography—was read into the final report of the Commission. These three men explained the triangulation, astronomy, leveling, and topography which must be done by the land forces of the Coast Survey so that the naval parties could have the maps they needed for their hydrographical work. Only upon such maps could these parties properly locate the soundings which they made. Imagining the hydrography transferred to the navy, the assistants viewed with skepticism the prospect of cooperation between two independent organizations, one military and the other civilian, in putting together the land and sea parts of an engraved map. If the entire Coast Survey were transferred to the navy—what Secretary Chandler wanted—then naval officers would be entering a new profession.

Mitchell, who led off the assistants before the Commission, dispersed wishful thinking about the end of coastal surveying on the Atlantic side. He impressed the members with the need for resurveys, as the sea bottoms shifted and alluvial shores accumulated. He pointed to Nantucket Shoals as one place where hydrographical knowledge needed continual renewal for the protection of the thousands of persons and millions of dollars worth of property passing daily there at certain seasons.

In the presentations by the assistants there was only one tactical mistake. Carrying the burden of the congressional cross-examination, Assistant Colonna praised naval officers as good fighters; "but they are not," he went on, "surveyors . . . in a practical sense." Elsewhere, he called the navy the "enemy to our time-honored institution."[41] At a time of crisis and peril, Colonna was perceived by several scientists as unnecessarily provoking their naval opponents with his remarks.

At the beginning of the new year, 1886, as the Allison Commission hearings ended, anxiety within the Coast Survey mounted. There was a long wait for the report of the Commission, and although there was no reason to feel pessimistic from the tendency of the hearings, Schott thought that the Coast Survey should be ready for anything. Behind that awaited event loomed Congress and another trial about appropriations, with Randall and other

Democrats certain to try again for large economies. Pressure from the Hydrographic Office increased, as Bartlett cultivated an expectant attitude toward the transfer of hydrography. The commander predicted new duties for the Hydrographic Office, and he campaigned for support from merchants' exchanges and marine magazines. He asked G. H. Eldridge, the chartmaker, to explain the reasoning behind the decision to buy Coast Survey charts and eliminate land detail before resale to mariners. Moreover, his criticism of Coast Survey maps became sharper. Money, one circular of the Hydrographic Office said, was "thrown away" on topography.[42] The chart of New York Harbor, which depicted roads, farms, and fences on Staten Island, was more appropriate in a library or gallery than aboard ship.

Another demoralizing situation developed in the national office, where behavior descended to a new low. Political appointees were the primary cause of this descent into semianarchy. Many of these appointees were mean and quarrelsome persons, who terrorized the Survey headquarters and sought to make public scandal of their stories and complaints. According to Simon Newcomb, of the Naval Observatory, when two persons at the Coast Survey office became dissatisfied with each other, they did not appeal to the superintendent but proceeded either to "fight it out with their fists" or prefer charges to some Treasury official. Schott, who in January saw nothing in Survey affairs to sustain hope, reported in the spring that "we have not yet reached bottom in our misery," with informers "defaming us in the newspapers" and with "spies all around us."[43]

The chief troublemaker was an accountant with the Dickensian name of V. J. Fagin, who had come to the Survey in Hilgard's time and was a protégé of Republican Congressman Benjamin Butterworth of Ohio, later commissioner of patents. Fagin's "despotic rule" in the disbursing division dismayed the field assistants. He once knocked down a waiter in a Washington restaurant; and he told a House committee in the spring of 1886 that the Coast Survey was paying a number of consulting astronomers $5,000 each in salary, when the last person to hold such a consulting position was Benjamin Peirce, who died in 1880.

Thorn, who could have been expected to stop the decline in

manners, lacked the personal confidence or the political power. On the defensive because he was not a scientist, he more than once said publicly that he would gladly relinquish his post, if only Cleveland would give the word. Regarded as only temporary, he continually heard rumors that some naval critic or military engineer would replace him. Nor could he keep the Treasury or Congress from forcing disreputable or worthless people on him as patronage. The most flagrant instance of forced hiring came after Fairchild had failed for three months in Wall Street to find the kind of an accountant, which he thought the Coast Survey needed in place of the dismissed Morgan. Thorn was summoned to Manning's office and, in the presence of Readjuster Senator Harrison H. Riddleberger of Virginia, was "requested" by the secretary to accept "an ex-clerk of a little country store" in Virginia, who was "absolutely without experience as a bookkeeper." When Thorn objected, the secretary urged him to do the best he could with the candidate. His name was Roger C. Glascock; and besides being quite useless, he was to be very troublesome to Thorn's successor.[44]

Next to Thorn, the person who might have pacified the Coast Survey was Assistant Colonna, whom chance, more than anything else, had brought into the Washington office. In 1884, while head of a working party in the San Juan de Fuca Straits, he had fallen and suffered partial paralysis. Needing a cane or crutches for some time, he never returned to field work. His appointment to take charge of the Washington office probably came from his political connections in Virginia and the Treasury. Certainly his rank in the lower third of the assistants did not justify a promotion, which brought with it a doubling of salary. Thorn relied on Colonna so much that, in effect, the assistant was often the superintendent. Colonna was willing to work long hours; he knew the Survey well enough to keep it going in the customary way; and he lobbied better than anyone else in the Capitol, where he had the confidence and friendship of a number of senators and representatives. Confronted with political appointees, however, Colonna only aggravated a tense situation. He was by nature truculent, unscrupulous, and not above using threats with the assistants and blows with the skilled workmen. He feuded with Fagin, called him a Radical Republican, and spread noisome stories about him.[45]

Two newspaper stories, one in March and another in April 1886, dramatized the plight of the Coast Survey as it waited for the report of the Allison Commission on its future. On March 8, the *New York Evening Post* carried an editorial on the condition of the Coast Survey. Unavoidably, this editorial was inaccurate on the subject of corruption, since no responsible person had tried to correct or supplement the statements in the Thorn report. The issues between field and office were fairly stated, and the conclusion was given that Thorn had been "severe" with his clerical and scientific staff. It declared that Thorn's position was not respected either in the Survey or in the Treasury; and Chenoweth considered him to be a subordinate.

The surprise was not that Thorn replied to the editorial, but that he wrote so vehemently about it. His charge against Hilgard of "shameless misconduct" and "grave malfeasance," while harsh, was not too wide of the mark. He completely lost control of himself, however, when he made a sweeping statement about "slobbering sycophants" in the Coast Survey. These "pseudo-scientists," he wrote, who "chafe at my profanation of the place [the Coast Survey office] were calmly content while one of their ilk [Hilgard] was befouling and converting it into the 'mother of dead dogs.'" The second story, in the *Washington Post* on April 16, was even more troublesome, because it threatened an alliance between Fagin and Randall. Bearing the headline "Overhauling the Coast Survey," it reported the close examination of Fagin by Randall and other members of the House Appropriations Committee. Fagin charged the Coast Survey with slackness in neglecting to keep its assistants busy, when they were not in the field; and he also told his story of the expensive consulting scientists who rendered no service. The article predicted that Randall's committee would "cut down" the number of assistants from sixty to sixteen.[46]

In late spring, after a year of bad news, the findings of the Allison Commission brought welcome relief to the Coast Survey and brightened its chances for survival. A majority of four stood with the scientists, whose authority they used in deciding the issues. That one of this majority, Lowry, was a Democrat made the findings of the Commission even more persuasive for contemporaries. The Coast Survey work, said the Commission, should continue as before with a person of the "highest scientific attainment" at the head, whose office should control the triple duties of triangulation, topography, and hydrography. The justification for Coast Survey refinements in chartmaking was their universal approval by scientists at home and abroad. Adopting the tactic of the Meigs committee of the National Academy, the Commission said there would be time enough to consider transfer when the original survey of the coast was completed. As for the geodetic survey of the interior, every civilized country had one; in Europe, such surveys were a common venture at public expense. Praising Bartlett and the Hydrographic Office, the Commission did not doubt that naval officers could perform the entire spectrum of Coast Survey science; but this responsibility would compel them to abandon their own profession, which was not practical.[47] In its determination to understand government science and clarify its position, the Commission was admirable; in defending the Coast Survey and the Geological Survey, the Commission stood with American civilian scientists at large, who wanted little or no association with the military in their scientific enterprises. Its only real failure was neglect to expose the Coast Survey in December 1884, thus leaving Hilgard in power for many more months.

The opinion of the Commission minority, expressed by Herbert and Morgan, Democrats of Alabama, was informed with a hostile spirit toward science and scientists. Civilian scientists were not the people to consult about what should be put on a chart; sailors best knew what was needed, and naval officers were the educated sailormen who executed surveys on every coast except the American. Those who applauded the extensive and elaborate topography of Coast Survey charts were college professors, mathematicians, astronomers, and geodesists. The minority report made the charge, as Cleveland had in his first annual message, that the pristine task of coastal surveying to warn sailors of the perils of the sea through extensive soundings was forgotten in the introduction of large, national programs in geodesy and topography. The Coast Survey had a tendency to involve itself in "the boundless field of physical science." The arc of triangulation along the Appalachian Mountains particularly irked the minority members.[48]

The Allison Commission disposed of the transfer issue for the Forty-ninth Congress, and indeed for the rest of the decade. Formal debate, however, about spending for the science of the Coast Survey rose between the parties. Late in June 1886 the House Appropriations Committee of the Forty-ninth Congress, with Randall as chairman, reported a reduction of $150,000 for the Coast Survey in the Sundry Civil bill. Herbert gave a long, derogatory speech: the geodetic work was done by professors in colleges "who never had a theodolite in their hands"; local pilots had little use for the Survey's nautical charts. He spoke of the expensive engraving for the island of Mount Desert in the Gulf of Maine.

The Coast Survey had its defenders—who did not move, however, to restore any of the items which the Appropriations Committee had slashed. Congressman James B. Everhart, Republican of Pennsylvania, was the most exciting, for he brought applause with his praise for the Coast Survey because it disclosed "to government and people the border perils and safeguards of commerce and the country." Congressman Boutelle told the House that, relying on Coast Survey charts, he had taken vessels in and out of "nearly every indentation upon the coast," from New York to Galveston.[49]

One outsider intervened during the June debate in the House: Director J. W. Powell of the Geological Survey, which, like the Coast Survey, did scientific surveying and mapping. Indeed, while the Coast Survey stood on the defensive during the eighties, the Geological Survey, under Powell's leadership, launched the large project of making a national topographical map. The advantage of the Geological Survey was its willingness to do topographical mapping more cheaply and faster than the Coast Survey. To the debate in the House Powell contributed a letter, not to challenge the work of the Coast Survey but to praise it. He apologized handsomely for his failure before the Allison Commission to take into account the military purpose of coastal defense for Coast Survey charts. Powell was sure that this military purpose, by no means disavowed in the 1880s, had been prominent in the decision to develop topographical and cultural detail.

Two army engineers, probably exasperated at the harping of

Herbert and Bartlett on the subject of detail, also spoke in praise of Coast Survey mapping. Henry G. Wright was former chief of the Corps; William F. Smith had seen long service in the field during the Civil War, and had been engineer-secretary of the Lighthouse Board. If anything, Wright wrote, the war showed that the Coast Survey charts did not have enough detail to satisfy the leaders of coastal expeditions against the South. Smith insisted that the failure of any field commander to demand and use detailed maps showed "utter want of knowledge of fundamental rules in warfare." No general was fitted for command who did not take into account all the topographical and cultural detail of positions to be defended or assailed. At Fredericksburg, want of knowledge of a canal ditch had proven disastrous.[50]

The Republican Senate would not go along with the Democratic House. The thinking of the upper house, expressed through Senator Allison of Iowa, was that in reducing the Coast Survey so drastically the House had abolished old offices, created new ones, and changed salaries. Reorganization was always a proper consideration of legislative bodies, but the Senate, explained Allison, wanted to wait until a scientist was in command of the Coast Survey, who then could submit his recommendations on these changes of the House.

In early August, the two legislatures were negotiating through conferees. Eventually, the Senate agreed to a House proposal that there should be no new appointment in the field ranks of assistant, subassistant, or aide until the total number of this field force was reduced from 63 to 52. In this way the House backed off from its radical attack on the number of the assistants. After the compromise, the appropriation amounted to $503,000, down $65,000 from the previous year. The Coast Survey money provided through the naval appropriations bill remained at $200,000.

The trouble for the rest of the year came from the political appointees, above all from Fagin. With evident satisfaction, Colonna handed him his dismissal in August, and before he left the Survey office—indeed on the day of dismissal—he hit one of the scientists of the tidal division. More was heard from Fagin, for in October he inspired a fellow accountant, H. E. Coleman, who had also clashed with Colonna, to lodge charges with the public prosecutor of the District of Columbia against Thorn, Colonna, and half a dozen others of the national office, implicating them in the issue of false vouchers. The charges involved the signing of salary vouchers for three oldsters of the Survey, "absent from the office for periods of four months to two years," whom Thorn paid for the month of July 1885 (before he dismissed them), although they had done no work during that month. The charges did not go beyond the grand jury, but the *Washington Post* wondered if "a year or two more such as the last" would leave anything "worth preserving" in the Coast Survey.[51]

Also in October, the Coast Survey made it into the Democratic campaign book for the congressional elections. Bureau personnel were called "the silk-stocking gentry"; the Survey itself was the "acme of perfection in robbery and jobbery," $100,000 yearly having been diverted. The chief of the bureau, Hilgard, was said to be the prime mover in the frauds, and he had grown rich at public expense.[52] Meanwhile, Fagin departed the city to help ex-Congressman Butterworth regain the congressional seat which he had lost in 1884. Upon Butterworth's victory, and perhaps feeling that a Republican landslide was in the offing, Fagin sent Thorn a telegram on election night, 1886, asking "Has Grover fired you yet?" This telegram prompted Thorn to write Cleveland a long letter denouncing "Faginism" and admitting that, for some weeks in the summer of 1885, "I was misled" by the ruffian.[53]

In 1887, the economizers of the Forty-ninth Congress tried again, with the House Appropriations Committee reducing estimates for field expenses in the Sundry Civil bill from $244,000 to $125,000. "Sheer butchery," Thorn called it. It was Colonna, however, who did the fighting on Capitol Hill. He visited Senator Allison of the Senate Appropriations Committee, who said that "he did not like the democratic way of doing things" and promised, if he had a letter from Secretary Manning in favor of the Coast Survey, that he would work to restore the money. The letter from Thorn to Manning, read on the floor of the Senate, said that Coast Survey salaries were already on the average $700 less than those of the Geological Survey. If the House reductions were accepted, then the average salary difference between the two science agencies would rise to $1,200. In the end, the House and Senate conferees agreed on a sum for the Coast Survey below $500,000, but close to the appropriation of the previous year.[54]

During the debate on the Sundry Civil bill, the chief vehicle of appropriations for government science, Randall contrasted the Democratic House and the Republican Senate. In 1884 the Senate had added $4 million to the sum which the House authorized in that bill. And when for three years in a row—1886, 1887, and 1888—the House and the Senate, controlled by Democrats and Republicans respectively, divided over the amount in the bill, with the House reducing the estimates from the bureaus and the Senate restoring all or a considerable part of the excised sums, the awareness of an issue between the two bodies sharpened. Randall and other leading Democrats defined the issue as the economical House versus the profligate Senate. One representative charged that in Cleveland's years during interlegislative negotiations on the Sundry Civil bill the Republican Senate forced twenty-three million unwanted dollars on the Democratic House.

The Democrats now had one more glorious past to look upon: the Forty-fourth Congress and its curbing of expenditures. Congressman Thomas B. Reed of Maine, very much the Republican spokesman, chided Randall for taking "gentle refuge in the past"—"that home of the Democracy," said Reed, "the place where they live and from which they never go."[55] On the defensive, Senator Allison had to admit that the Senate had twice in the Forty-ninth Congress moved back toward the original estimates for the Coast Survey, after the House had done some cutting. He denied, however, that in light of all the appropriation acts the House was more economical than the Senate, and he complained that he and the Senate at large were "held up and gibbeted on the cross roads of public opinion" for their profligacy. Republican Senator Joseph R. Hawley of Connecticut came to Allison's side in the exchange about Coast Survey expenditures: "Democracy . . . is . . . stinginess," he declaimed.[56]

Despite these legislative scares, the Coast Survey exercised more control of events after the Allison Commission had reported. The internecine warfare seemed to die down; or if the fisticuffs continued, they no longer created public scandal. Representative Herbert could not move a transfer bill out of his Committee on Naval Affairs. In the spring of 1888 Commander Bartlett, who had brought the Hydrographic Office so high, asked to be relieved of his duty there. The magazine *Science* reported his disappointment that the Office had not been given bureau status. And slowly, the Treasury and the Coast Survey moved toward the settlement of Morgan's accounts.

Colonna took the initiative here, and by persistence gradually got the disallowances reduced from their high of $29,000. And when the election of 1888 went against the Cleveland administration, the Treasury and the Coast Survey agreed that the whole business should be settled before the Democratic administration left office. The result was the payment to the Survey scientists of the money withheld from their salaries since February 1886. Small sums of money were lost to eight assistants because of rulings on subsistence, but this loss amounted to no more than $150. Hilgard contributed $455 to cover further overcharges on instruments, and Morgan had to submit a check for $433 to meet the final disallowance figure on his accounts. In the end, the Treasury made good only $1,000 on its claim of $29,000 upon Morgan's accounts. After Morgan paid his debt in February 1889, he was reinstated as disbursing agent, granted thirty days leave with pay by C. S. Fairchild, now secretary of the treasury, and his resignation was accepted. According to the annual report of the Coast Survey for 1889, probably written by Colonna, what happened to Morgan was "a triumph" for him and "a vindication of the Survey as a body, after it had been most sorely tried and cruelly persecuted for three and a half years."[57]

The story of the Thorn regime closes properly with an appraisal of the superintendent's place in the completed history of the Coast Survey from 1885 to 1889. Thorn did his duty and eliminated drunken behavior and financial corruption in the national office. He also forced payments to the government of $4,600 in cash and property. His second and related objective was economy, and here he secured annual savings of $50,000 a year, most of which represented reductions in pay of the office and field forces. The savings were accomplished in the face of rising production and distribution of the Coast Survey product. New charts increased in number from 28 in 1885 to 92 in 1889; 37,000 copies of charts, new and old, came off the Coast Survey presses in 1885, and 78,000 in 1889. Thorn got more results for less money out of Coast Survey personnel. It is a fair criticism, however, to wonder if he really saved any money, for the reason that numerous clerks in the Treasury to oversee the Coast Survey accounts probably cost as much as the superintendent was saving. And the reduction in income for the honest, able, and hard-working men in the field force is not easy to justify.

As a lawyer and journalist, Thorn made a reluctant superintendent. Hoping for many months that Cleveland would relieve him, he insisted, to the detriment of his authority, that he was only temporary at the Coast Survey office. Ignorant of science, he could not avoid having an alter ego to advise him. The trouble was that he allowed the Treasury to select Colonna as his adviser, and Colonna's faults inspired a new source of disorder.

Thorn could make friends with the assistants. Indeed, ten of them collectively praised his tenure of office when he departed, and his patience with Peirce was extraordinary. Other times, however, he found the tension between layman and expert unbearable, and then he would exercise his talent for abuse. A *New York Times* article of April 14, 1889, which summed up his accomplishments as he viewed them, ended with a paragraph on "pseudo-scientific monkies" in the government service.[58]

In the politics of legislation Thorn's record was not good. Privately, he defended the Coast Survey in Cleveland's presence, reminding the surprised president that putting the Coast Survey under the navy had been tried earlier in the century with no great success.[59] But in public, he would not uphold the integrity of the Coast Survey against its naval and congressional critics. Nor would he play the political game in Congress for the sake of appropriations, which numbers of scientists had learned about since the Civil War and which was absolutely necessary for the survival of the Coast Survey. His failure to establish some measure of independence from the Treasury brought him and the Coast Survey to the brink of another disaster, in the further breakdown of discipline. Quarrelsome, useless placemen were the worst heritage bequeathed by Thorn to his successor.

One of Thorn's last official acts was to participate in the transition to the new administration. In February 1889 the Fiftieth Congress passed legislation which envisaged the departure of Thorn from the Coast Survey and laid down a new condition for the appointment of his successor. Seeing that Cleveland had taken into his own hands the selection of the superintendent, the Senate asserted its classic role in presidential appointments and placed in the Sundry Civil bill an amendment requiring that the superintendent be chosen by the president, with the advice and consent of the Senate.[60] Effective July 1, 1889, this amendment precluded Thorn's serving as superintendent after June 30, for he had never received senatorial confirmation, and one of his last official acts (on June 22) was to inform President Harrison and Secretary of the Treasury William Windom that appointment of a superintendent would be necessary at the end of the fiscal year. Early in July 1889, the president temporarily commissioned Thomas C. Mendenhall as superintendent, and in December the Senate confirmed the appointment.

5 The Ordeal Renewed in the Nineties

Thomas Corwin Mendenhall, the seventh superintendent of the Coast Survey in the nineteenth century, had been a teacher and researcher in physics, mostly at Ohio State University but also in the Signal Service and at the Imperial University in Tokyo. His best science came in Tokyo, where he employed pendulum swinging to find relative and absolute gravity and to arrive at a respectable figure for the mean density of the earth. Immediately before coming to the Coast Survey, he was president of Rose Polytechnic Institute of Indiana.

The new superintendent wanted first to restore the position of the Survey scientists. In the national office, he promised to deal with them directly rather than through Colonna, as Thorn had done, declaring that they were not clerks but his confidential advisers. He organized two unprecedented and exciting conferences in Washington, one for the topographers lasting six weeks in the winter of 1892 and another of equal length for the geodesists in 1894. He relaxed regulations so that members of the field force could take time off without going on furlough (when salaries were stopped) or being classified as temporarily unemployed (when regular pay was reduced 25 percent). His ultimate action toward improvement was finding $4,000 to compensate some thirty persons from the three grades of assistant, subassistant, and aide for their loss of subsistence in 1885. Twenty assistants, for example, received raises of $100 to $400.

In managing these salary hikes, Mendenhall had no more money from Congress. Instead, he framed the budget passed by the Fifty-first Congress in 1890 to draw on the wage fund of his skilled workmen. He forced two of them out in the instrument division and reduced the pay of eight others in that division and in the engraving division. The plate printers of the engraving division suffered the most reduction in pay. To justify subordinating his workers to his scientists, the superintendent argued that wages in the engraving and instrument divisions were higher than what was paid to comparable workers in private shops throughout the country. This statement by the superintendent on comparative wages within the Survey and outside in the major cities of the country was never challenged. One item of information in line with his assertion appeared in a volume of the Eleventh Census (1890) on statistics in the cities for manufacturing industries. A table, giving the wages of employees in "Printing and Publishing, Book and Job," cited the "high average earnings" of workers under this heading for Washington, D.C. In the Eleventh Census, plate printers fell within the category of "Printing and Publishing, Book and Job," and no doubt those in this class from the engraving division shared in the high local earnings, before the superintendent moved against them.[1]

Another major objective of Mendenhall's was to keep his administration free of partisan aims or conduct. His appointment, he knew, did not result from party activity or pressure; Powell of the Geological Survey and Secretary Langley of the Smithsonian were his chief sponsors in Washington, and he made it a condition with President Harrison that there be "no political or other interference with my selection of subordinates or employees." As a consequence of this negotiated understanding, the superintendent had everything his own way with Windom, Harrison's first secretary of the treasury, who had learned something about the Coast Survey during his brief tenure with Garfield in the same capacity. Upon Windom's sudden death early in 1891, Charles Foster became secretary of the treasury, and he, unlike Windom, held the view that good Republicans should have the government jobs. But Mendenhall successfully opposed him, for after "one or two good-natured 'rows'" Foster told his friends that he controlled every bureau of the Treasury except the Coast Survey.[2]

The most serious struggle between the two men came over the office of disbursing agent, held by John W. Parsons, Morgan's successor. This job did not demand very difficult qualifications, and the salary was good. One pressing candidate, who was from Ohio (Secretary Foster's home state) and had been a customs officer in New York City, brought his wife along when he came to see the superintendent. The couple complained about party ingratitude and threatened to see James G. Blaine and other Republican leaders. Foster's private secretary told Mendenhall that "numberless Republicans" wanted the job held by Marshal W. Wines, chief of the Miscellaneous Division of the Coast Survey, and the superintendent was urged to write the secretary explaining why Wines should not be removed.[3] Within the Coast Survey, Mendenhall dismissed Glascock, the most useless of the holdovers from Democratic times.

Mendenhall ascended to his office in 1889, the year the Fifty-first Congress began. It was the most liberal body about expenditures since the Forty-first Congress, twenty years before, and has always been known as the "billion-dollar Congress" because it appropriated that amount during the two years of its duration. In control after the election of Harrison in 1888, Republican leaders set the tone and pace of this Fifty-first Congress and elaborated on their ongoing dialogue with economy-minded Democrats. Representative Cannon, chairman of the Appropriations Committee, said in 1890 that the country was growing, was going ahead and not looking back, and an increase of government expenditures was to be expected. He might have added that there was a surplus in the Treasury. Republican Senator Nelson Dingley of Maine asserted in 1896 that government expenses grew regardless of the party in power, because the population increased, and so did the material interests to be served. From the same point of view, Boutelle, after lauding the Republican party for its statesmanship (see Chapter 3), asserted that the popular expectation of the Democratic party was that it would "act as a clog upon progress and as a brake upon all national advancement."[4]

For science, this billion-dollar Congress established a zoological park, gave the Naval Observatory a new building, and built an astrophysics observatory. It also provided for the movement of weather forecasting out of the army and into the Department of Agriculture. General A. W. Greely, who presided over this transfer from military to civilian status, did not foresee any lessening of expense. In the Signal Service, his noncommissioned subordinates worked thirteen hours a day, and the officers did their military duties, performed as executives, and predicted the weather. In the Department of Agriculture, said Greely, each civilian would have his own specialty, and that alone.

For the Coast Survey, the Fifty-first Congress raised the annual appropriation to $580,000, the level in Hilgard's favorable years. This sum included grants for new steamers and schooners, and there was more money for chart printing to meet the growing demand. The Fifty-first Congress also showed respect for science and scientists. In 1891 a committee of Cannon's and one from the Treasury examined the expenditures and policies of the Coast Survey. Cannon was impressed; the Coast Survey was conducted, he reported, in an "economical, praiseworthy and profitable way."[5] Later he asserted that Mendenhall was the most competent person ever to preside as superintendent.

Mendenhall was as eloquent as Peirce about the Survey's mission. Addressing the conference of geodesists, he defined his agency as a "great governmental bureau which is notably engaged in the investigation and application of the most refined methods of science." The objectives were noble and manifold: "the betterment and amelioration of the conditions surrounding mankind, the diffusion of general knowledge, and the protection and development, by means of its perfect surveys of navigable waters, of the commerce of a great and growing country."[6]

Satisfaction showed through the announcement in 1891 of the completion of "the most extensive mapping project on so large a scale as 1-4800 ever performed in the United States."[7] This was the topographical survey with five-foot contours of sixty square miles in the District of Columbia. The following year, sheets from this survey were dispatched to the World's Fair at Chicago. Boston Harbor had not been surveyed since 1860; so in 1893 seven topographers were put to work on its shoreline and adjacent territory, including nearby cities and towns. In the South, phosphate workings inspired activity—in the resurvey of the Ashley, Cooper, and Wando rivers in South Carolina and in the original survey of the Caloosahatchee River in Florida. In Texas, there were examinations and surveys at the entrance to the Brazos River, where land and river improvements had substantial support. On the West Coast, the Survey returned to San Diego, after forty years, to record the new railroads, wagon roads, and wharves. Far to the north at Coos Bay, Oregon, another Coast Survey assistant found new towns, wharves, and streets to survey. Of course, a resurvey was required in the harbor of Seattle and adjacent waters. A population which had numbered ten thousand in the early eighties numbered fifty thousand in 1891, and the assistants saw many new shipyards and lumber mills. Other projects, demonstrating the range of the Coast Survey at this time, were a trial course south of Block Island and Long Island for the new armored cruiser *Philadelphia,* a survey of Virginia's oyster bed, demarcation of the boundary between Ohio and Indiana, a town boundary survey in Massachusetts, and special surveys for the city and county of San Francisco.

The new frontier of the Coast Survey under Mendenhall was Alaska. Because the territory was so huge, little had been done there for many years, given the priorities elsewhere. After the first rush in the summer of 1867, when Davidson used historical documents more than scientific instruments, only now and then were geodesy and topography applied—at key locations like Sitka, where longitude was determined, or through triangulation in small amounts in the channels of the Alexander Archipelago of southeastern Alaska. Clearly, it was going to take more than naval vessels, whalers, and codfish fleets to bring the Coast Survey more actively into the territory.

One new impulse proved to be political: the decision of the United States and Britain in 1892 to establish the boundary between Canada and Alaska. "Boundary lines," observed Rodgers in 1895, "seem to be of special interest to the San Francisco newspapers."[8] Pursuant to the Anglo-American agreement, President Harrison appointed Mendenhall as U.S. Commissioner, and he met with W. F. King, the Canadian commissioner and chief astronomer of his country. The two agreed to send their respective national parties into the field in the spring of 1893 with the purpose of finishing the job in two years.

In the division of labor, the Americans mapped the continental coastline, jagged with bays, rivers, and channels, from the bottom of Alaska north to Mount St. Elias, while the Canadians did the topography in the interior and between the watercourses. There was no question of refined surveying as practiced in the States, based on elaborate triangulation and detailed delineation of topography. The Americans determined latitude and longitude at the mouths of important rivers, ran traverses up these rivers, and landed here and there on the long coast. The fifty-sixth parallel, near the southern boundary of American Alaska, was one area where astronomical positions were determined and new triangulation was executed. Americans for the first time were learning to use the camera at great heights to facilitate the taking of topography. Both sides were on the lookout for one long mountain range, a few miles from the sea, whose well-defined heights could furnish a convenient boundary line between the two countries; but none was found. Each commissioner had the right, which was exercised often, of sending his scientists along as observers with the parties of the other nationality.

Determining the boundary line for Alaska proper, where it lay straight against Canada north and south along the one hundred and forty-first meridian, was easier because Canadians and Americans had only to apply their science. By treaty, this part of the boundary had been clearly declared, but it had not been marked anywhere on the ground. It began at Mount St. Elias, which stands at the head of the Alaskan panhandle, and extended along the one hundred and forty-first meridian to the Arctic Ocean. Two assistants were sent out late in Thorn's regime to determine three positions on this north and south line, at its junction with the

Yukon and Porcupine rivers and on the Arctic Ocean. Later in the 1890s, after correspondence between the State Department and Her Majesty's government and a joint resolution from Congress appropriating money for American expenses, Coast Survey assistants and Canadian surveyors began putting down a line of monuments between Mount St. Elias and the Arctic Ocean, which gave latitude, altitude, and longitude.

The climax of this scientific effort was not in the field, but in Washington and London. The Washington office made atlases of the twelve American and the twenty-four Canadian maps, which were submitted to the Alaska Boundary Tribunal when that body was established in 1903. Two officers of the Coast Survey accompanied the U.S. agent when he went to London to appear before this tribunal. Afterward, Coast Survey assistants returned to the field with Canadian scientists to trace and mark the boundary as awarded.

The other event propelling the Coast Survey into the Far North carried assistants out of southeastern Alaska through the fog-shrouded passes of the Aleutian Islands into the Bering Sea. This event was the discovery, late in the decade, of gold in the Klondike, along the border between Alaska and the British Northwest Territory, and the movement of thirty thousand miners through Alaskan and Canadian passes into the Yukon River basin. Congress, for its part, appropriated $100,000 to survey the Yukon River, which became one of the passageways into the new gold fields.

The leader of the Survey force was Pratt, who worked with some forty-five persons out of Dutch Harbor. He took pains with shipmasters, who waited in line to talk with him, seeking their confidence and friendship, for he knew their feelings would be hurt if he did not see them, even though he had to listen to many erroneous opinions. Pratt directed surveys for one hundred and fifty miles in the delta of the Yukon. In the vicinity of one river mouth, the shore was about twenty-five miles farther west into the Bering Sea than the published charts indicated. Twenty-five hundred square miles, said Pratt, were added to American territory. Pratt looked for the depth of water on the bars in front of the delta, and through a running reconnaissance examined the principal passes for the river into the sea. Of course, he laid down triangulation to control the topographical and hydrographical work. He logged the streams and swung the plotted work into place by astronomic positions.

Survey scientists soon discovered that outdoor life in Alaska was even more grueling than in the States. One kind of exhaustive and dangerous work was the running of traverses in the southeast panhandle on the short rivers, which came down from permanent snowfields. One assistant found the current in the Unuk River so strong that a canoe could not be paddled against it, and so hemmed in by cliffs and gorges that Indian guides said a canoe could not be taken through. Nonetheless, he hauled the canoes with lines, while up to his knees in water, grabbing brush, clumps of grass, and jutting rocks to establish a hold.[9] The Americans saw that the Canadians were better equipped for mountain work, with snowshoes, alpenstocks, and waterproof moccasins.

In the Yukon, Pratt added to the saga of his hardships and feats. The floating ice, strong currents, and tide rips made surfboat work dangerous. Pratt said he was living more in a minute than ordinarily in a year. While surveying in the delta, the men were soaked, and usually there was little chance of drying their clothes. According to another assistant, "we generally wrung out the clothes and then lay down in them, our body warmth getting them dry before morning." As a field worker, this assistant found the mud exasperating; it was sticky and wretched to walk through. He had to keep moving, for if he stayed in one spot, he sank. Therefore, the readings over mud had to be done quickly; in some spots, "it took us many minutes to release one another from the quick-sand-like mud."[10]

Above all, Pratt remembered the squalls of hurricane force and violence in the Bering Sea.[11] The cross-seas were mountainous, he reported. All the lead flushing in the *Patterson* was broken in the companionways, hatch coverings, waterways, and skyloft. The spar deck leaked so badly that the wardroom and cabin floors were awash; "the groaning of the joiner work between the decks was 'pandemonium let loose'"; and the rudder was almost lost. Pratt believed that another week would have finished the *Patterson*, that he had gone through a nightmare; yet he could do no less than pay his respects to the captain who had designed the craft named after him. The *Patterson* had been built inexpensively for work in the inland passages of southeast Alaska, rather than for continuous ocean cruising. Put to an unexpected test in the Bering Sea, the vessel demonstrated that the captain had designed a buoyant and seaworthy model with comprehensive rig. No other superintendent, concluded Pratt, was so thoroughly experienced in the construction and maintenance of Survey vessels.

A usual feature of Survey science at any given time was the personal research of the superintendent, who naturally wanted to make an original contribution in his chosen field. Mendenhall collaborated with several assistants and with Ernest G. Fischer, the chief mechanician, to build a new pendulum, which was only a quarter of a meter long, beat half seconds, and swung within an airtight case. Using a new European practice, he substituted a chronometer for the pendulum clock, whose coincidence in swing with the long pendulum had traditionally given the period of that pendulum. To find the period of the short pendulum beating half seconds, Mendenhall and his colleagues used the coincidence of two flashes of light, thrown on two mirrors within the receiver or case which enclosed the suspended pendulum. One mirror was mounted on a fixed plate near the head of the pendulum and received a flash of light each second, when an electromagnet in the circuit of the chronometer moved a shutter. The other mirror was placed in the head of the pendulum, right next to the fixed mirror, so that when the pendulum hung freely the flashes of light from the two mirrors almost coincided. When the pendulum with the mirror in its head was moving, the flashes of light would not, most of the time, come near coincidence, and at times there were no flashes from the second mirror because it had moved out of the field of sight of the observer, who looked at the mirrors through a small telescope. When the pendulum was swinging and the fixed and movable flashes coincided, the period of the pendulum could be decided.[12]

In pressing his new pendulum on the Coast Survey, the superintendent had very much in mind measuring gravity more cheaply and quickly. To reach this goal, the superintendent cut back on the objectives of the pendulum swinging. His pendulum measured only relative gravity, the change in the intensity of the force at one place as compared with the intensity at another. He sought the ratio of the value of g at two places, whereas Peirce had measured the value per se, called absolute gravity, at every station. This change spared the superintendent a time-consuming and expensive task: measurement of the length of the pendulum at each place selected for swinging; for in solving the equation for relative gravity he needed only the period of the pendulum swing. Also, the superintendent reduced the "magnitude and complexity of the instrumental outfit," and speeded up the preparation of a station for swinging. In the new dispensation, the Coast Survey could determine gravity at six to twelve stations a month, whereas Peirce, in his quest for absolute gravity, required more than one month for a single measurement. The cost per station fell 90 percent.[13]

Mendenhall's other decision about pendulum swinging was to ask for Peirce's resignation. This assistant had continued on his independent way, exercising that critical candor in science which he was so good at. A further objective now was Mendenhall's half-second instrument. The trouble with the goal of economy, Peirce said, was that it endangered accuracy, and if accuracy was lacking, then the time and money were thrown away. The grave source of error in Mendenhall's creation lay in the length of the pendulum, which should be invariable, if scientific accuracy was to be realized. But Peirce could not see that proper precautions had been taken to secure this invariability.[14]

During Mendenhall's first year Peirce submitted the report, which the Thorn administration had asked him to prepare, on his gravity determinations at the Smithsonian, Ann Arbor, Madison, and Ithaca. This report carried the results of observations of oscillations at the four places and the reduction of observed gravity to sea level and the equator. Because this was a report by Peirce, there were proposals on corrections for air resistance and for differences of temperature along the pendulum staff. There was also a new calculation of the compression of the earth and a statement on an-

other effect of the atmosphere, through its viscosity, on the swinging period of the pendulum.[15] The report submitted, it immediately became an issue between the two men. Mendenhall was
inclined to refuse it in its offered form, while Peirce asserted a
prior agreement with Thorn that it would appear as the author
wanted it.

The technical disagreement was about the numerical expression
for the length of the pendulum, length being a prime objective of
those who measured the force of gravity. Peirce used a logarithmic
expression to represent this length, rather than metric measurement. After asking advice about Peirce's manuscript from four scientists, who were divided in their reaction, with William Ferrel
approving Peirce's idea about a second atmospheric effect, the superintendent refused publication and asked for Peirce's resignation. The assistant did not put up much of a fight. He denied that
he had been idle. He thought his services could be useful, but if
they were not, then he had no desire to stay. The resignation took
effect at the end of the year 1891.[16]

The departure of Peirce meant the end of world renown for the
Coast Survey in gravity studies. The Royal Prussian Geodetic Institute, at Potsdam, soon assumed leadership, and in the twentieth
century, as long as pendulum swinging was customary, the figure of
the Institute for absolute gravity prevailed. To compete with Euro-
peans, Peirce would have needed a lot of money and the willingness
to agree with other Survey geodesists on a common program. Although he admitted more than once that the Coast Survey should
do relative gravity measurements, he was not much interested in
taking that course. It can be argued that Peirce's continuing presence
on the Survey would have made little difference anyway, because the
forces of economy were so strong that further gravity studies were
politically impossible. Mendenhall soon had difficulty defending
geodetic surveying, let alone gravity studies. Certainly, he owed
Peirce publication of the gravity measurements and the man's mathematical calculations. Pendulum swinging has passed into disuse as
a laboratory device; today, scientists measure free fall directly. At
the Washington conference with Peirce in 1882, Colonel Herschel
complained of the "inexplicable contradictions and anomalies in-

dicative of unknown causes of error" which surrounded the measurement of gravity by pendulums.[17] Before the recent demise of
the knife-edge pendulum, geodesists found another source of error,
which seemed impossible to remedy. No matter how carefully knife
and plane were brought into contact, a series of spots on the knife
edge became possible points of support. Moreover, the effective
point of support changed from time to time, with a consequent
change of the period of the pendulum.[18]

The American government has never had a more famous
thinker than Charles S. Peirce, although any number of public
men probably have surpassed him in the importance and contribution of their day-to-day duties. On the larger stage of philosophy,
logic, and mathematics, Peirce remains supreme. In the 1920s he
was acknowledged as one of the founders of pragmatism, the only
truly American philosophy. After World War II, his reputation
soared at home and abroad. Books about him, a new edition of his
writings, a journal of research devoted to him, his recognition as a
forerunner in the new discipline of semiotics—all these elements
now enter into the appraisal of this man of genius.

Good feeling and success characterized Mendenhall's first three
years; mean politics and too much failure marked his last two
years. The explanation of the sharp contrast begins with the
changed composition and spirit of the Fifty-second and Fifty-third
Congresses from 1891 to 1895. The former was Democratic in the
House, reflecting the revulsion of the American people against the
billion-dollar Congress; the latter was a depression Congress,
Democratic in both House and Senate.

As in previous debates, the two major parties split in their thinking and voting about science and spending. Randall had died in
1890, but Holman of Indiana made a fitting successor as chairman
of the Appropriations Committee. He called the Fifty-first Congress profligate and cried down the "idea of the Government publishing books for the benefit of a particular profession whether law,
medicine, or any other."[19] Another Democrat, Henry C. Snodgrass
of Tennessee, denied that the American people should shelter "the
creeping and slimy things of the earth."[20] After the exuberant years

under Harrison, Republicans could only complain about the turn in political fortune. Replying to Holman's charge that the Republican Senate always revised upward the House's schedules in the Sundry Civil bill, and no doubt thinking of other appropriations, Representative Reed scoffed at this tenth annual charade of the economic House and the profligate Senate. Henry H. Bingham, Republican of Philadelphia, accused the national Democratic party of "striking down scientific work necessary to the people and the Government." Fellow party members cheered.[21]

In the spring of 1892, Democrats went to work with determination on their favorite vehicle for saving money, the Sundry Civil bill, and soon half a dozen major science agencies of the government were in trouble with their budgets. In mid-March, Mendenhall received two letters from the clerk of the House Appropriations Committee: one asked him to resubmit his estimates for the coming year with a revision downward of $60,000; the second inquired for the amount of money spent on geodetic work. Sending his replies to Joseph D. Sayers of Texas, Democratic chairman of the subcommittee of the House Appropriations Committee, Mendenhall stood his ground. The request to reduce estimates $60,000, if carried out, would mean the lowest budget in a quarter of a century. Every operation of the Coast Survey was geodetic in character, he said, or was directly dependent on geodetic work, whether the operation was to take soundings, to locate lighthouses and tidal stations, to do topographical surveying, or to find altitudes by leveling.[22]

Holman guided the Sundry Civil bill, with its reductions amounting to $13 million, through the debate in the House. He called the Coast Survey "a purely scientific service" whose activity could just as well be postponed. Herbert of Alabama made the astonishing statement that the Coast Survey had not begun geodetic work until 1874. Benjamin A. Enloe, Democrat of Tennessee, introduced a new argument against the Coast Survey and Mendenhall. He took the side of the bureau's workers, whose wages had been reduced by the superintendent, so that many members of the scientific force could receive raises. This course of action, said Enloe, was salary-grabbing at the expense of those who earned their bread by the sweat of their brow. Enloe represented a labor organization, the Plate Printers' Protective Union, whose members came mostly from three hundred workers in the Bureau of Engraving, who were now striking back at Mendenhall for his tough policy on wages toward their fellow craftsmen in the Coast Survey. There was no doubt about sentiment in the House after the overwhelming defeat of an amendment by William Cogswell, Republican from Salem, Massachusetts, who tried to restore the $60,000 for field expenses eliminated in committee. The Senate, for its part, insisted on many amendments, thereby increasing expenditures, and a number of the science agencies found their positions improved. Although most of the House reduction for the Coast Survey was negated, the final appropriation sank below $500,000, as it had once before in Thorn's time.[23]

In the second or short session of the Fifty-second Congress (early in 1893), the House reduced the Survey estimate and the Senate restored the excised amount. Once again the Coast Survey figures had been returned with the request for a $60,000 reduction. The superintendent replied with a letter to Holman claiming violation of an understanding that if the estimates were on the level of last year's appropriation—that is, just below $500,000—they would be acceptable to the committee. Contrary to what Holman had said on the floor of the House, Mendenhall insisted that the Coast Survey was a bureau of applied science, and he found it difficult to believe that Holman's committee or Congress would intentionally "sacrifice" so valuable a service as the Coast Survey. Soon the superintendent heard, through another congressman, that both Holman and Sayers had been offended by the letter.[24]

In the all-Democratic Fifty-third Congress (1893–95), Enloe, making the crisis worse, revived the objective of abolishing the Coast Survey by dividing it between the Navy and the Interior Departments. His vehicle was the Sundry Civil Appropriations bill, and the time was March 15 and 16, 1894. The strength of his position lay in the concern for the workers of the Coast Survey, who, no more than the assistants, had been able to protect themselves from the arbitrary power of the superintendent. The weakness of Enloe's position was that he did not take up the topic of comparative wages in the Survey and in major cities of the nation, or dispute in any way the thesis of the superintendent that some skilled operatives in the Survey were paid substantially above the going rates in these major cities. Instead, the congressman, both on the floor and in committee, waged a campaign of misinformation and abuse.

Enloe found his materials where he could: from the Thorn report; from persons like Glascock, whom Mendenhall had dismissed; and from a naval officer like Sigsbee, now head of the Hydrographic Office. Leading off the debate on his amendments, Enloe asserted that all practical work of the Coast Survey for the past twenty years had been done by naval officers. He charged that Peirce was drawing pay and doing no work. He castigated the topographical detail on the chart of New York Harbor, and he called the Coast Survey "shamefully corrupt." He also read letters from Secretary of the Treasury Carlisle and Secretary of the Navy Herbert, supporting the transfer idea.

Enloe was no expert in legislative procedure, and objections of a parliamentary nature soon stalled his amendments. The House was working in Committee of the Whole under a rule permitting only those changes to the Sundry Civil bill which reduced expenditures, and Enloe could not prove that money would be saved if his transfer proposals were carried out. After a while, the presiding officer ruled them out of order. Enloe then switched to an amendment which was ruled *in* order: that the Dockery-Cockrell Commission, an existing congressional body, which was looking into the organization of the Executive departments and their efficiency, be asked to investigate the feasibility of transferring the Coast Survey to other departments. Discussion of this motion was the nearest the House came to considering the abolition of the Coast Survey.

In this situation, partisans of the Coast Survey were inspired to seize the initiative and draw applause. Thaddeus M. Mahon, Republican representative from Pennsylvania, said that the bureau was worthy and efficient. Mahon did not believe that the government could put on "the movements of the crab" and "go backward"; as long as there were "Yankee brains and ingenuity," appliances "giving safety to navigation and commerce" would be invented and used. Daniel E. Sickles of New York, a Democrat, reminisced about an international geographical congress which he once attended, where every book exhibited by the U.S. government had won a prize for contributing to the advance of science and its application to "the practical uses of civilization." Listeners applauded this praise of books. As a result, the investigatory amendment was lost, 81 to 105, with most of the negative votes coming from the Republican side.[25]

Another amendment was also lost, which would have reduced the superintendent's salary by $1,000. Protagonists of the Survey may have shamed the House into opposing this last change. Mendenhall was described as traveling to Passamaquoddy Bay to check the line between Maine and Canada, journeying to Alaska as commissioner on locating the northwest boundary between Canada and the United States, and sailing the Bering Sea as a commissioner on the dispute about the seals. Was the House to sit in Washington and discuss whether to reduce the salary of this hard-working scientist? somebody asked.

The exchange in committee, which came after the debate on the floor, was even more one-sided. Enloe's separate bill to execute the transfer was referred to the Committee on Naval Affairs, which held eleven days of hearings in May and June 1894. The best that Enloe and Glascock could do was to taunt the Coast Survey with its unhappy past. Enloe made the Thorn report part of the records of the hearings; Glascock offered the materials from the Democratic campaign book for 1886, which accused the Coast Survey of "robbery and jobbery." The way was left clear, then, for Mendenhall and other scientists to monopolize the respectable parts of the hearings with their knowledgeable discourse. Mendenhall hammered away at the question of relations with the Navy Department so effectively that one wonders why any of the military allowed themselves to become involved with Enloe. The superintendent knew that Sigsbee, Schley, and "one or two other naval officers"[26] had been in conference with Enloe, and he paid his respects to them with a passing reference to a few grasping naval officers. In a fine sentence, which suggested that the naval advocates were consulting their own interest and not the public interest, he insisted that "The Coast Survey is for the benefit of the commerce of the United States and not especially for the benefit of the Navy." He pointed to one important field of Coast Survey science, "the influence of currents, winds, tides on the coast line as a matter of prediction," which naval officers did not cultivate very much. The superintendent counted 119 learned papers by civilians on this major topic of physical hydrography, and 11 by naval officers. He was glad to have the charting by naval officers off Alaska and the west coast of Mexico, but their surveys were preliminary; they did not "hitch together," he explained; "the parts are disjointed."[27]

Mendenhall expressed the overwhelming sentiment of American scientists, founded on their perception of military behavior, when he said that army or navy discipline was incompatible with the freedom which scientists needed in their work. And he seized upon a trend which foreshadowed the demise of the navy in Coast Survey affairs; naval officers, he informed the committee, were not as available as they used to be. Their average complement in the Coast Survey was thirty-five a year, in contrast to the seventy or eighty of years ago. In other words, the demands of the new navy for personnel were beginning to shut off the participation of its officers in the Coast Survey.

A formidable advocate of the Coast Survey was Robert S. Woodward, a professor at Columbia College, New York, who was asked by Mendenhall to testify. Woodward refused to be put on the defensive because he came from a college campus. "I am not a doctrinaire," he told the committee, "who has been locked up in a closet in some college."[28] He had served successively with the U.S. Lake Survey, the U.S. Geological Survey, and from 1890 to 1893 with the Coast Survey as an appointee of Mendenhall's, before he departed for academic life. In the twentieth century, he would be president of the Carnegie Institution of Washington.

Woodward's scientific specialty was baseline measuring apparatus, which must be an instrument of precision because the accuracy of all the *computed* lines of the system or chain of triangles depend in the first instance on the accuracy of the *measured* line of the first triangle. An error in the measurement of this baseline was carried along and magnified in the completed scheme of triangulation and computation. While he was with the army engineers in the U.S. Lake Survey, Woodward had demonstrated that steel tape for baseline measuring, used at night when the expansion of the metal tape through heat was avoided, permitted rapid and accurate work. For the Coast Survey, Woodward designed an ice-bar measuring apparatus which gave ultimate satisfaction as to accuracy. This apparatus involved a metal trough, filled with melting ice, in which the base bar was kept, thereby eliminating the temperature error. The disadvantage of this instrument was the great expense per kilometer of baseline measured, when compared with the cost of using steel tape.

Woodward condemned the part-time naval scientist. He readily conceded the ability of the navy to do science; he denied, however, that it was properly organized or motivated for the task. The custom of the navy, requiring tours of duty of limited duration from its officer corps, meant that the inventive or scientifically inclined officer could usually devote only a few years to his interest, and then he must move on. This rapid turnover encouraged dilettantism and obscured, said Woodward, the fundamental reality that science was serious business and a lifelong work. He cited a report from the Hydrographic Office on the work of the USS *Ranger* on the west coast of Mexico, where the navy had introduced a measured baseline into its surveying. The account of the laying down of the baseline honestly admitted a discrepancy in measurement of three yards. Woodward termed this discrepancy a "gross error," and "a disgrace to any sort of scientific work."[29]

Also, he confirmed Mendenhall's testimony on civilian scientists' perception of the military by saying that "a scientific man who has knowledge does not like to be lorded over by an Army or Navy officer." If the transfer to the navy occurred, it was his opinion that most of the Coast Survey assistants would resign.

Woodward offered some commentary on Herbert's ideas. Herbert, he said, was "totally unaware of the progress of modern science" and "he seems to have a curious notion that these bureaus like the Geological Survey and the Coast and Geodetic Survey are due not to the phenomena of nature, but to the machinations of scientific men." To the demand of some Democratic leaders that science bureaus finish their work and go out of business, Woodward replied that science was "part of civilization," and its research would continue "so long as the earth turns, so long as you can see stars, so long as we have navigation and tides, and phenomena of nature."[30]

As in the eighties, academic persons organized a demonstration. A resolution from the faculty at the University of Wisconsin said that "the Coast Survey was the first scientific bureau of this government to win the respect and admiration of scientific men throughout the world." Other petitions or letters indicated that the Coast Survey had maintained its position as the preeminent American bureau in the eyes of world science.[31] Civil engineers expressed skepticism of any broad naval program to do mapping; they were also critical of what the Geological Survey was doing, but for the Coast Survey there was "absolute unanimity among scientists of the world" as to the usefulness of its work. Estevan A. Fuertes, dean of civil engineering at Cornell, thought the scientific training at Annapolis was "inferior" to what was done at "a hundred private schools," not because of any inherent fault in naval institutions but because Congress would not appropriate money for expensive training. He also said that the times demanded "specialization in everything."[32]

The important consequence of the hearings was the conversion of one man, Democrat Cummings of New Jersey, the chairman of the Naval Affairs Committee. He came over to the Coast Survey point of view, and Enloe's bill died in committee.

Congress had frustrated Superintendent Mendenhall since 1892, and had even menaced him, but still he did not find the situation intolerable. However, events became impossible in the Executive branch, after the Cleveland Democrats returned to power in 1893. The superintendent faced a father-and-son combination from Kentucky: James G. Carlisle, former representative and now secretary of the treasury, and Logan Carlisle, chief of the appointments division of the Treasury. These two men were resolute spoilsmen who demanded more than the usual patronage in watchmen and messengers. They wanted Democratic placemen in the high administrative positions within the Survey: as disbursing agent, in the library, and to head the Miscellaneous Division. They also expected a partisan Democrat to be in charge of the Coast Survey office and another to be secretary to the superintendent. Father and son were not squeamish about pressuring the superintendent. One devious maneuver was for Secretary Carlisle to talk with "the greatest fairness" in interviews with Mendenhall, assuring him that he could run his bureau to suit himself and that this was what President Cleveland wanted. Whereupon Logan Carlisle, the son, would make demands for patronage in disagreeable interviews with Mendenhall or Colonna.[33] Then, rumors appeared in the newspapers that the bureau was going to be reorganized, and in January 1894 Secretary Carlisle gave an interview to fifteen businessmen from Philadelphia who asked for the removal of Mendenhall.[34]

The raw politics of the Carlisles came as a shock to the superintendent, and for months he wondered what to do. If he let the spoilsmen in, his fine reputation for conducting the Survey on business principles would soon vanish. He drew some solace from the belief that Cleveland was not listening to those who would dismiss him. Gardiner G. Hubbard, father-in-law of Alexander Graham Bell, one of the owners of *Science,* and president of the Joint Commission of Scientific Societies in Washington, obtained an interview with Cleveland, who disavowed any intention of removing Mendenhall. The superintendent did not believe, however, that the president would stand by him in a public confrontation with the secretary of the treasury.

Then, in the early months of 1894, Mendenhall felt his health slipping away. In March, Parsons, his choice as a disbursing agent when the Coast Survey regained its own financial officer, had to resign, and R. J. Griffin, a Carlisle appointee from Georgia, took the position. At the end of April, the superintendent quietly accepted the presidency of Worcester Polytechnic Institute. He still had a job to do with the House Naval Affairs Committee in June, and then he intended to resign.

Out of the circumstances of this resignation issued the final event of the Mendenhall regime. On the morning of June 20, 1894, the superintendent went to the Executive Mansion with Democratic Congressman Joseph H. Outhwaite of Ohio. They met with the president at 10 A.M., and the superintendent handed him a letter of resignation. The letter gave as the grounds for resignation the fact that the secretary of the treasury had interfered with the working of the bureau "by the retirement of experts and the substitution of inefficient men," to such an extent that it was no longer possible "to conduct the bureau on a scientific basis."[35] Cleveland expressed regret at the prospect of Mendenhall's departure, asking the superintendent to pocket his letter of resignation and say nothing about what had happened. Mendenhall took ten days before returning to the president and agreeing to this condition of his departure. In this period, he became embarrassed about the secrecy of his resignation, because reporters got wind of his presidential visits and came around to see him. He gave them the disclaimer that "I was still Superintendent of the Coast and Geodetic Survey and as far as I knew I would continue to be for some time to come."[36] Early in July he left for Europe on a three-month vacation, still on the Survey payroll. Mendenhall's public affirmation of his status was not untrue, but it deceived his colleagues in the Coast Survey who, taking it literally, concluded that the newspaper stories about his resignation were canards. The result was that they took no steps to prepare against the troubles which soon overwhelmed them, looking instead for the return from Europe of the superintendent to set things right. For all intents and purposes, Mendenhall had ceased to be superintendent on June 30, when he left the Executive Mansion after his second visit.

The first bad news came in early July, when Mendenhall's plan was overturned to have Colonna of the Washington office and assistant Henry L. Whiting, a longtime and skillful topographer, share the superintendent's authority while he was away. When Whiting came to Washington on July 8 to take up his new duties, he found a written communication from Secretary Carlisle saying that the action of Mendenhall "was illegal and of no effect." In his uncertainty, Whiting sought out Attorney General Richard Olney, a fellow New Englander, who gave him a card of introduction to the president. Calling on Cleveland, Whiting was informed that the acting superintendent should be some person in the government who, like the superintendent, had had his appointment confirmed by the Senate. Cleveland told Whiting that such a person would soon be appointed.[37] On July 13, Whiting and others in the Coast Survey learned that Cleveland had appointed a Treasury tax official, William H. Pugh, as superintendent in the absence of Mendenhall. Late in August, Pugh fired several persons whom Mendenhall had been defending: Francis H. Parsons, the librarian; Wines, the head of the Miscellaneous Division; and Martin Hensel, the superintendent's private secretary. For the first time, members of the field force (two in number) were dismissed; also, seventeen salaries of the field force were raised and sixteen were reduced.[38] On September 20, Secretary Carlisle accepted the resignation of Mendenhall, who had returned from Europe.

For several years Mendenhall was probably the most successful superintendent since Bache, who ruled before the Civil War. Pleasant, composed, mild-mannered, conscientious, and efficient, he made a good administrator, having none of that wildness which had hurt both Hilgard and Thorn. Except for Peirce, he had empathy for the scientists of the Coast Survey and a sense of their importance and worth. He restored their dignity, relieved their oppression, and represented them well before the Fifty-first Congress. His major handicap was his physical health, which tended to deteriorate after long sieges of work and pressure; and the superintendent dated this weakness from the early eighties, when he worked for the Weather Bureau in an uncomfortable basement room west of the Executive Mansion.

The crisis of his last year subtracts from his performance. To maintain the Survey position before Congress, he relied too heavily on knowledge and efficiency, when strategic friendships in the Democratic party were needed. He refused to play the role of spoilsman, which Powell among the geologists excelled at. Whereas Powell had kept Holman's worthless son in the Geological Survey, Mendenhall spent an hour explaining geodesy to the father. The superintendent seemed weakest in failing to secure for the Coast Survey a reputable successor. Colonna thought he had acted cowardly during the summer of 1894 by going on a long vacation to Europe and leaving his scientific corps helpless in the hands of scheming Democratic politicians.[39]

The years after Mendenhall's departure were the nadir of Survey affairs in the nineteenth century. In 1892, the superintendent had faced the dismal prospect of a Survey budget near $400,000; after 1894, this low level was the usual experience. The mood among the assistants was blacker than ever, as powerful officials reiterated the divide and transfer principle. The number of assistants tended downward, as purges were proposed or executed every year, in an agency where dismissals among the scientists had been rare. The reduction in the eighties had affected those in the office; in the nineties it cut into the technical force. The number of field assistants declined, from fifty-seven to forty-three, while the number and expense of clerks, messengers, and laborers in the Washington office changed but little.[40]

A decisive event was the appointment of a new superintendent in September 1894. Cleveland was getting nowhere in his search, when Don M. Dickinson of Michigan, who had been postmaster general briefly under the president and served him as an adviser on many matters, recommended William Ward Duffield of Detroit. Cleveland consulted his chief adviser, Secretary of War Daniel S. Lamont, about Duffield, and Lamont spoke highly of him. Duffield had been a railroad engineer, land surveyor, state senator, and a wounded and defeated general at Murfreesboro. He was seventy years old.

Duffield soon became disenchanted with his job. Three months after calling him to Washington to become head of the Coast Survey, President Cleveland, saying nothing good about the bureau in his annual message of December 3, 1894, urged its abolition. The same month, the Dockery-Cockrell Commission made a similar proposal, saying seventy-nine clerks and $100,000 could be saved.[41] Next, in January 1895, during the all-Democratic Fifty-third Congress, Chairman Sayers of the House Appropriations Committee and committee member Alexander M. Dockery took advantage of Duffield's inexperience. Instead of discussing the budget with the superintendent, the committee presented him with a letter to sign, in which he agreed to a reduction of eight in the number of assistants. The threat of no appropriation was made if he did not sign, and Duffield, falling for the bluff and not consulting anyone in the Washington office, signed. Many times in the past twenty years, the Appropriations Committee had reduced the Coast Survey budget, but this was the first occasion when it had the written consent of the superintendent. Made public on the floor of the House later in January, the letter helped secure approval of the revised Survey budget by the legislators, who were worried about the depression deficit of the Treasury. A reduction of the superintendent's salary to $5,000 was secured in Committee of the Whole. In the general dismay and gloom at the Cosmos Club, someone said that Duffield had not been hired as the head of a scientific bureau but as an undertaker. In the usual pattern, Colonna buttonholed important senators and three of the assistant positions were restored to the budget, but a floor amendment in the Senate to restore Duffield's salary to $6,000 was overwhelmingly defeated.[42] The superintendent came under the harshest attack ever made on Capitol Hill against a Coast Survey official. Senators were suspicious of his failure to make a committee appearance in the House and skeptical of his excuse that he was not yet familiar enough with Survey affairs to make decisions about them. They wanted to know the reason for the reduction of salary by the House, and wondered if there was a hidden history to the story of the Coast Survey appropriation. Duffield was also charged with slurring older members of the Survey.[43]

In the end, eight assistants lost their jobs in the spring and summer of 1895, because Superintendent Duffield had to make room for his son, Will Ward, Jr., as well as enforce the reductions required by Congress.

The first to go was Colonna, who as assistant in charge of the office had been a major figure in the political battles and dismissals of the Thorn regime. He blamed the South, the Democratic party, and the Carlisles for what was happening to the Survey. Not even the fear of Negro supremacy would whip him into allegiance to the Democratic party, Colonna wrote privately.[44] The conviction of Treasury officials that he was not a loyal Democrat probably contributed to his downfall. The removal of William H. Dennis, in charge of the drawing division, opened a position for the superintendent's son in the national office. Richard M. Bache (age 65) and George Davidson (age 70) also received dismissals. Some of the discharges were probably a result of the political suspicion that the Coast Survey was maintaining an informal pension system, yet the assistant nearest eighty, who needed an aide to do his field work, escaped. As if to demonstrate the arbitrary nature of the shakeup, John E. McGrath, one of the youngest and most active assistants, who had worked along the Alaskan boundary, received notice of termination. Herbert G. Ogden, head of the engraving division, was marked for dismissal, but he found out about it and, although a Republican, used his Democratic friends to foil the deed. However, he lost the headship of the engraving division, which was consolidated with the drawing division, to provide a headship for W. W. Duffield, Jr. Five hundred dollars of the $3,000 paid to the superintendent's son were taken from the salary of Eimbeck, the skilled geodesist who had been prominent in the triangulation between the Atlantic and the Pacific.[45]

The character and style of the Duffield administration was now set. The superintendent took counsel of the Democratic partisans around him: of R. J. Griffin, the disbursing agent; of H. S. King, the librarian; and of John F. Renfro, his private secretary. Although Duffield wanted Glascock in the Coast Survey office as an assistant, the Civil Service Commission protested the appointment of this "illiterate and discharged clerk," and it had to be withdrawn. Thought was given to bringing Glascock in as Duffield's private secretary after Renfro had resigned, having been caught purloining money from a registered letter. Fortunately, Glascock never got on the payroll, although at one point Logan Carlisle told Duffield to be sure that he was not a free-silver man, before hiring him as a confidential clerk.[46]

In 1896, a purge threatened three assistants, Dallas B. Wainwright, John W. Donn, and Ogden—each of whom had spent thirty years with the Survey. The superintendent justified his proposed triple dismissal with the charge of intrigue. However, Duffield could not make the dismissal stick with Wainwright, who brought naval influence to bear, or with Ogden, who appealed successfully to John R. Proctor, head of the Civil Service Commission. Donn, the only victim, had good and recent credentials because during the year of his dismissal he had made a survey of the Naval Academy grounds at Annapolis, which had brought commendatory letters from the superintendent of the Academy and from Secretary Herbert of the navy. Hubbard, again speaking for seven scientific societies and their two thousand members in Washington, queried Duffield on the procedural aspects of Donn's dismissal. It was not enough, Hubbard said, for the superintendent to make charges to the secretary of the treasury and for the accused to reply; there should be a fair and open hearing. Other knowledgeable observers were less patient than Hubbard, and the statement circulated that there was no place in Washington "nearer Hell than the Coast Survey office."[47]

Even in the abysmal year 1896 there were signs that the economy movement was losing its grip. Baltimore interests agitated for a resurvey of the Chesapeake Bay, last mapped fifty years before. In the Treasury, Superintendent Duffield sought to respond by asking for an increase of money for field work from $110,000 to $169,000, only to have Secretary Carlisle slash the sum to $45,800. In the Republican House of the Fifty-fourth Congress, Joshua W. Miles, Democrat of Maryland, moved to add $7,000 to Carlisle's depleted figure for beginning on the resurvey of Chesapeake Bay. Chairman Cannon of the Appropriations Committee expressed satisfaction with the Miles amendment, which squeaked by (amid applause) on a vote of 55 to 54. Grove L. Johnson, Republican of California and father of Senator Hiram W. Johnson, wanted no one to wear "the old clothes of the gentleman from Indiana," for "the day of the watchdog of the Treasury is passed," he said, "and we ought now to meet matters upon their own merits."[48] Johnson was prophetic. Two years later, in February 1898, Cannon formally closed the nineteenth-century economy movement, which had lasted thirty years. Without consulting any House member, he moved an emergency appropriation of $50 million to prepare for war with Spain.

An incident in 1897 was the most bizarre of all, because it happened after the return of the Republicans under McKinley and after a new Treasury investigating committee had recommended that Duffield be replaced. The Treasury was ready to make the removal, but Secretary of War Russell A. Alger chose to defend the old general, and no one in the Cabinet seemed ready, at least right away, to start an argument. Instead of going the dismissal route, Duffield lowered his objective and sought to relieve three divisional heads of their executive positions: Tittmann, Pratt, and Schott. Tittmann, whom Duffield himself had appointed assistant in charge of the office, was "insubordinate and disloyal" when testifying before the Treasury's new investigating committee. Duffield also claimed that Tittmann had originated nothing of value in thirty years with the Coast Survey. A disagreement about personnel contributed to the tension between the two men, and demonstrated that an older evil was still plaguing the Coast Survey. As assistant in charge, Tittmann had asked Duffield to relieve Assistant Stehman Forney, who was acting chief of the drawing and engraving division in the absence of the superintendent's son in Alaska. Forney, charged Tittmann, had been under the influence of liquor for two days straight in the Coast Survey office. Despite a hearing where several witnesses testified to the smell of liquor on Forney, Duffield refused to relieve him.[49]

Concerning Pratt, who had come from the West Coast at Duffield's request to be head of the instrument division, the superintendent said that he showed favoritism in the distribution of instruments, was tardy in finishing his Pacific topographical sheets, and wrote impertinent letters to the hydrographic officer. Schott, the third assistant to feel the wrath of Duffield on this occasion, was head of the computing division. The work of this division was several years in arrears, the superintendent asserted.[50]

The superintendent could not have chosen three more useful and respectable members of the scientific corps to denigrate. Otto Hilgard Tittmann, Hilgard's nephew, had been an excellent draftsman since the day in 1867 when he came to the Survey from St. Louis high school, and he turned out to be one of the all-around scientists of the Survey as well. Reproached for lack of originality, he admitted that few persons "originate things which are of great moment," but he thought that he had introduced into the Office of Weights and Measure "modern methods" in thermometry and in the comparison of length standards.[51] At the beginning of the twentieth century, he was to be superintendent of the Coast Survey for fifteen years, the longest term since Bache.

Answering Duffield, Pratt listed the many new fields of his work in the Pacific Northwest, which had delayed the completion of earlier sheets: Alaska's boundary, the Port Townsend resurvey, gravity work in Seattle, and longitude determination at Sitka. Pratt also began submitting drafts of letters to the hydrographic officer for Duffield's criticism and review.

Schott's letter of defense, written on October 20, 1897, was a personal statement of his standing in the Survey and a revelation of the suddenness of Duffield's move against him. "Up to yesterday," Schott began, he had enjoyed the same confidence with the present superintendent accorded him by six preceding superintendents. "Only the other day," the present superintendent had asked him to prepare an abstract of the standard longitude system of the United States. Thus, the superintendent could hardly have an opinion of the computing division, since he had never acquainted himself with its work. Schott also referred to his publications, which in a bibliography of 1902 occupied four and one half pages; no one in the nineteenth-century Survey came even close to Schott's total.[52]

The best that could be said about the trouble for Schott and the other two was its brevity. There was time, after Duffield showed his hand in mid-October, for Senator Henry Cabot Lodge to term the situation outrageous, for Hubbard to write the superintendent and accuse him of being an enemy of science, and for Mendenhall to call Duffield insane. Then, at the end of October, President McKinley nominated Henry Smith Pritchett of St. Louis as superintendent. Six months later, Secretary of the Treasury Lyman J. Gage said that he considered the case of the three assistants closed.

In upholding their side of the partisan dialectic over science, the Republicans were curious or enthusiastic about the new knowledge and its cultivation by the government. They adjusted realistically to the rapid change in the second half of the nineteenth century, and looked to an open future vis-à-vis the course of events. They were progressive. The Democrats were the ones to fight modern science, rather than accept it—to abolish government bureaus just when the great age of these bureaus was beginning. They were nostalgic in wishing to return to a bygone political age and old-fashioned in their religious attitude toward physical events, which scientists were now interpreting within a naturalistic framework. They were also utopian, for they seriously discussed the millennium: when peace would be forever; when the rule of law, based on public opinion, would make police unnecessary; and when patriotic spirit, rather than armaments, would guarantee national security. The redeeming feature of this Democratic vision was the commitment to free trade during the struggles over the tariff.

Confrontation of the Hydrographic Office and the House of Representatives in 1900

6

While the Coast Survey floundered under the hapless Duffield, the Hydrographic Office continued to advance as it had in the eighties. Commander Sigsbee, inventor and explorer, was now the hydrographer, and his regime from 1893 to 1897 was almost the mirror image in spirit and purpose of Bartlett's headship. Sigsbee stressed the immediately useful service performed for the mariner, telling one Washington scientist that the Hydrographic Office often published reports which were neither exhaustive nor absolutely accurate, but were good enough to bring the seafarer safely into port. The reward for being practical was popularity at home and abroad. "This Office," asserted Sigsbee, "is nearer the people than any other branch of the Navy Department"; and the American consul at Liverpool reported that "shipmasters of all nations" frequenting that port appreciated the efforts of the Hydrographic Office to improve navigation at sea.

A new note in the thinking of the Hydrographic Office during the 1890s was the insistence that maps and charts be ready for "localities where American men-of-war were likely to be hurriedly sent for the protection of American interests." Thus, Sigsbee ordered a new chart compiled for Cuba in 1896, in anticipation of an American naval demonstration there, and the branch office at San Francisco, also sensitive to nationalistic rivalries, constructed a multicolored map showing the English, French, and German claims in the Pacific.[1]

For Sigsbee, the monthly pilot chart of the Atlantic Ocean continued to be the most honored and remarkable feature of the Hydrographic Office. Over a thousand sea captains, mostly British and German, funneled information to Washington, where chartmakers used blue and red coloring to communicate weather trends and sea dangers, and put down distances and directions in black. Atlantic navigators not only consulted the pilot chart of the Hydrographic Office, but many of them, according to Sigsbee, plotted their course tracks on it. A pilot chart of the Pacific was the obvious next step, and Sigsbee began this Pacific series in 1894— admitting, however, that for lack of observers many years would pass before this new issue could come up to the Atlantic publication. This chart provided notes on the fishing banks of the North Pacific, typhoon warnings in the Philippines, the best equatorial crossing for sailing ships, the drift of currents (learned from bottles allowed to take their natural course across the Pacific), and "the average storm track of the North Pacific," deduced from ten years of observations previously collected by the Weather Bureau.[2] Another publication which received high praise for its relevance and elegance was a new circumpolar chart in 1896, entitled "The Arctic Regions with the Tracks of Search Parties and the Progress of Discovery." The speedup in the frequency of these northern explorations inspired Sigsbee to prepare this chart, which he called the most valuable and ambitious publication so far attempted by the Hydrographic Office. He carried his account back one hundred and fifty years, and Peary, who had already begun those explorations of northern Greenland that would prepare him for his dash to the pole, wrote to congratulate the commander and ask for a copy.[3] Another production which showed the outward-looking and up-to-date view of the Hydrographic Office was a submarine cable chart, set in a global context and showing, in four colors, not only the cables of the world but also the coaling, docking, and repair stations. One line drawn on this chart was the route along the sea bottom of the Hawaiian cable, a route which the Hydrographic Office had surveyed in 1892.

Like Bartlett, Sigsbee strove to better the scientific surveying on Mexico's Pacific coast. The presence of a full-time scientist on the Washington staff aided him in his concern. This was the civilian George W. Littlehales, a graduate of Annapolis, who was chief of the division of chart construction and later chief of the division of research. Littlehales also earned a degree in civil engineering at Columbian University; and in the twentieth century he became professor of nautical science in the renamed George Washington University. He would publish some one hundred papers on oceanography, surveying, and terrestrial magnetism. Littlehales it was who introduced the measured baseline into the surveying of Baja California; he also ordered further work in lagoons and other inner waters previously bypassed. As an honest scientist, Littlehales had to admit the limitations of his measured baseline, which Woodward of the Coast Survey had pounced on so effectively during the hearings before the House Naval Affairs Committee in 1893.

Sigsbee knew that the Hydrographic Office had a long way to go before it could equal the Coast Survey. In 1894, the surveying vessel in Baja California was the USS *Thetis,* with naval officer Charles T. Hutchins in command. Early in the year, Hutchins told the commander that the two theodolites which had come were not suitable for scientific work. Hutchins said that he could use a sextant, surveyor's compass, and "ordinary base line (Navy style)," but this, he thought, would reflect seriously on the navy. Later in the same year, he showed surprise at the number of "old trash instruments" aboard the *Thetis;* and at the end of the year Sigsbee informed Hutchins that the contour lines "drawn at the different stations by the main and secondary triangulators" had no "pretense to accuracy." They could be depended upon within one or two hundred feet in the mountains and "within a very few feet along the coast."[4]

The new geographical area which the Hydrographic Office occupied was the Great Lakes region, where, as commerce grew, the lake fleet increased in number, size, and draft. Politically, the beckoning opportunity was a large interior population which the navy had little or no rapport with; also, there was the chance of aggrandizement against other public sciences. The congressional authorization for lake surveys, as an addendum to ocean surveys, came in 1892, and Sigsbee presided over the burst of activity which followed. As always with the Hydrographic Office, a good part of the work was republication of other people's charts: eighteen of Canadian shores from a listing of the British Admiralty, six on American harbors by the Corps of Engineers, and nine others by the same army engineers within the U.S. Lake Survey. The most original charts by the Hydrographic Office resulted from the surveying by the USS *Michigan* on the Erie, Cleveland, Detroit, and Chicago waterfronts, and in important channels and streams connecting the major bodies of water. Sigsbee prepared and issued a pilot chart of the Great Lakes, carrying information which the Office was always trying to get across to the maritime world: location of lighthouses, harbors of refuge, weather and storm-signal stations; rules for using oil in storms; distances between ports and depths of water in canals; and knowledge of wrecks, buoys, and obstructions. Of course, there were sailing directions and notices to mariners. To facilitate this publishing and surveying program, Sigsbee secured permission from Congress to establish new branch hydrographic offices in Buffalo, Cleveland, Chicago, Sault Ste. Marie, and Duluth.

The army engineers were very much on Sigsbee's mind as he led his Hydrographic Office into the Great Lakes region, for the engineers directed the established operation there—the U.S. Lake Survey. The commander was reluctant to engage in public controversy with his military colleagues, and advised his branch offices not to be quarrelsome, either. At the same time, he did not hesitate to claim that the navy could do better than the army in coastal surveying. He had to admit that the army charts were popular, but this was because the "Lakes people" knew no other kind. His own preference for naval control was not based on scientific grounds but rather on the authority of the navy in nautical affairs. "The claim of this office," Sigsbee wrote to the Cleveland branch in 1894, "is that it knows far better than soldiers . . . what to do for sailors," and he wondered why the army engineers did not have "the courtesy" to hand over "at once" all management of nautical affairs in the Great Lakes region.[5] There was no confrontation between the Hydrographic Office and the Corps of Engineers while Sigsbee was hydrographer—if only because the Corps remained officially calm. Theirs were the standard charts for mariners on the Great Lakes, and one of their number spoke contemptuously of the "local examinations" by the Hydrographic Office "in a few localities."[6]

In the late nineties the Coast Survey had time, after Duffield's departure, to climb out of its political abyss and prepare for the opportunities and rivalries that soon appeared. Pritchett, the new superintendent (who was 40 years old), had worked at several American observatories, and two years before coming to Washington had taken the doctoral degree in astronomy *summa cum laude* at the University of Munich. He stayed only three years with the bureau, but in that short time did much to bring it out of its cyclical decline.

In science at home, Pritchett turned the Coast Survey toward the measurement of terrestrial magnetism, a longstanding activity of the bureau, but not attempted heretofore on a large scale. Pritchett's goal was a magnetic survey at every county seat in the United States, to help land surveyors and to win sorely needed popularity for the Coast Survey. At every county seat that was surveyed, the Coast Survey assistant established a true north and south line, or meridian, and sometimes marked this line with stone piers, several hundred feet apart, whose astronomical positions were located by observations of the sun. Having the true meridian of the site, the assistant could then observe for magnetic elements, that is, for the direction and intensity of magnetic lines of force. Above all, the assistant wanted to know the horizontal declination or variation of the compass needle from true north. In rediscovering old boundary lines, whose markings had disappeared and whose locations were often in litigation, the land surveyor needed the declination of the needle from the true meridian as it pointed along the magnetic meridian to magnetic north, for usually the original survey had been run with a compass and the results recorded in magnetic bearings. Now that the angular departure of the compass from the true meridian had changed, these older magnetic bearings could not be used to rerun the original survey. If, however, the surveyor knew the declination of the needle at the time of the original survey, and had the present declination from the Coast Survey, he could rerun the lines of the original survey and record them this time as true bearings. Before many years had elapsed in the twentieth century, the Coast Survey had gathered a "large number of new, reliable, and well-distributed determinations"[7] of the magnetic elements on the earth's surface. The bureau then constructed magnetic maps, and the one most in demand was an isogonic chart, giving the lines of equal magnetic declination for the continental United States.

Early in Pritchett's campaign, the Paris Academy of Sciences had awarded Schott a prize for his work in terrestrial magnetism. Schott, on the verge of retirement after surviving with anxiety the Survey's troublesome years, was the author of the successive editions during the nineteenth century of the Coast Survey publication on the secular variation of magnetic declination in the United States.

Pritchett faced a new experience as superintendent of the Survey: formidable public criticism of some of its science. The criticism, originating among civil engineers, focused on the leveling work, whereby heights were determined as part of the network of mapping controls. The Coast Survey assistant took horizontal sightings from place to place with a level instrument to find the ascent or descent; benchmarks then recorded the elevations, which were interconnected through reference to the same surface, or mean sea level. What precipitated the issue of the accuracy of this civilian leveling was the completion of several large circuits of lines of level at the end of the century by both the Coast Survey and the Corps of Engineers. The ultimate test of the accuracy of these lines of level over great distance was the error of closure, and as it turned out, the errors were less for the Corps of Engineers than for the Coast Survey. At St. Louis, for example, a Coast Survey line of level from Mobile and a line from Sandy Hook closed with an error of five feet; also within St. Louis, a line by the Corps of Engineers from the Gulf of Mexico and lines from two other Corps circuits closed with a divergence of only one foot.

Pritchett was quick to organize a committee on leveling practice, which, after meeting for several hours almost every workday between November 1898 and December 1899, recommended that the bureau's method of leveling be abandoned and the instrument itself be modified. The committee acknowledged the "much higher degree of accuracy of the Corps of Engineers leveling,"[8] and ascribed the inferiority of the Coast Survey work to a systematic temperature error, which the military had avoided.

Above all, Pritchett associated his bureau with a powerful event of the national life, the Spanish-American War, which increased many times the demand for Coast Survey charts from the Hydrographic Office, from other executive agencies, and from the "war room of the White House."[9] Imperialism gave the Coast Survey more opportunities for expansion than had come its way since the bright years just after the Civil War. Early in August 1898, the Navy Department asked for the mapping of the south side of Puerto Rico, and soon Coast Survey parties were measuring a baseline on the island, developing triangulation, and working up the topography and hydrography of San Juan Harbor. In Hawaii, the Coast Survey signed an agreement with the government of S. B. Dole, whereby W. D. Alexander, the surveyor-general of the Islands, and his staff were incorporated into the mainland organization. In 1899 the USS *Pathfinder,* a vessel "of considerable power and coal capacity,"[10] sailed for Honolulu to consult with President Dole as to where to begin.

Congressional approval of entrance into the new American empire came in the Sundry Civil Act of March 3, 1899, which authorized the Survey to work in the Atlantic on "coasts of outlying islands under the jurisdiction of the United States," and in the Pacific on coasts "under the jurisdiction of the United States."[11]

Concurrently, a reorganized Hydrographic Office was launched into the new empire. In a series of moves between 1897 and 1899, Commander Royal B. Bradford secured the headship of the Bureau of Equipment (which coaled the fleet); managed, with congressional permission, the transfer of the Hydrographic Office from the Bureau of Navigation; had the appropriation for ocean and lake surveys raised from $14,000 to $100,000; gained authorization from Congress in 1898 to construct "a series of charts of the coasts and waters between the state of Washington and the territory of Alaska" and, even more important, in 1899, to survey "the imperfectly known parts of the coasts and harbors of the Philippine Archipelago." Secretary of the Navy John D. Long joined in urging that the hydrography of the Coast Survey be handed over to naval supervision.[12]

In government circles, Bradford was reputed to be an imperious administrator. Had not Secretary of the Treasury Gage complained to Congress that his department had been given ten days' notice, in the middle of the quarantine season, to remove a public health station from the Dry Tortugas Islands, where Bradford was preparing to develop a coaling facility—his bureau, after long negotiations, having persuaded the War Department to transfer this location in the Gulf of Mexico to the Navy Department?[13] Also, Bradford's position in the Line Officer's Association gave him political clout. The Coast Survey experienced the pressure of this man's desires when he had called for, and passed on, complaints about errors on its charts. Commodore M. R. S. Mackenzie of the USS *Prairie* charged the bureau with "culpable carelessness" for giving sixteen feet as the amount of water in one place when actually the depth was twenty feet. Mackenzie also found a reversed bearing, as if the sighting had been made from the land to the sea, when what was needed, and supposedly communicated, was the sighting from the sea to the land. Pritchett thanked the commodore for his letter, although he thought some of Mackenzie's expressions betrayed a "degree of feeling the cause for which I am unable to understand."[14]

Early in 1900 Bradford, now an admiral, shifted the locus of his campaign to Capitol Hill when he submitted desirable clauses to the House Committee on Naval Affairs for the Naval Service Appropriations bill, where the scientific duties of the Hydrographic Office were listed, along with the money to carry them out. Not only did these clauses repeat the novel places in the Caribbean and the Pacific where the Hydrographic Office could go, but they now carried language broad enough to include the coast of the United States. The Hydrographic Office was authorized to continue the investigation and charting of "reported obstructions to navigation in the United States water of the Great Lakes"; it could spend money for surveys "required under the regulations of the government of the Navy"; and perhaps it could even organize a civilian corps, for one of Bradford's clauses authorized the hiring of vessels and the compensation of "persons employed in field work."[15] Pritchett, who made it a point to communicate with the naval committee, interpreted Bradford's emanations as a proposal for a "second coast survey."[16] The Office, he said, was seeking to transform itself from a bureau of information into a department of surveying.

In March, the Hydrographic Office had a pamphlet printed for the use of the naval committee, full of familiar arguments from the past twenty years. Maritime nations did their best marine surveying in naval departments; naval officers knew what should go on a mariner's chart, and were the most skillful in obtaining the hydrographic data. For sixty years, naval officers had done the hydrographical work for the Coast Survey, which had a penchant for doing "unnecessary" and "outside" work, not needed on a mariner's chart. After ninety years, the bureau had not yet completed the American coast—and twice as much coastline had been added, in Alaska and the new island possessions. If the two organizations were consolidated, naval officers would provide the needed charts in five or ten years.[17]

When he came before the House Appropriations Committee about the annual budget, Pritchett had his chance to answer the pamphlet, insisting again that the Hydrographic Office did not make original charts; it only collected information. Thirteen percent of their charts were based on original surveys by the Navy Department. He challenged the confident authority of naval officers in maritime commercial affairs; they were deep-sea sailors who had "very little in common" with the coastwise fleet of merchant vessels, which used Survey charts. He remarked on the chronic inability of regular naval vessels to stay with their scientific work. The USS *Bennington,* assigned to surveying at Guam, had been called away after a few weeks for other duty.

Pritchett also generalized about the five hundred naval officers, who had served two-year terms with the Coast Survey since the

Civil War. Some of these officers had been among the most skillful hydrographers who had ever worked for the Coast Survey; a still larger number had acquired a certain knowledge of the subject, but the great majority of the naval officers were not valuable manpower for sustained surveying. The present age, Pritchett went on, was for specialists, and the professional engineer would do hydrographic surveying more quickly and economically than the naval officer who regarded this kind of work as incidental to his career. With little or no training in surveying or instruments, they could not be put aboard ships and, in three or four weeks, made as good surveyors as trained engineers. Concluding, Pritchett did not think the efforts of naval officers to control the Coast Survey, the Revenue Cutter Service, the Lighthouse Service, the Marine Hospital Service, and other technical bureaus were creditable "either to their good judgment or to their appreciation of the conditions of modern professional life."[18]

After Pritchett's appearance before the House Committee on Appropriations early in April, the Coast Survey faded into the background while the Hydrographic Office, attempting to apply political pressure in behalf of its program, raised a storm of protest in the House.

The method of the Hydrographic Office for securing its legislative program involved the seventeen branch hydrographic offices. Right from the beginning, one of their purposes had been to strengthen the public standing of the parent bureau, and sometimes even to challenge or undermine the local position of rival organizations. In 1900, these offices were transformed into high-powered lobbying outfits under the direction of Commander Chapman Coleman Todd, who had become hydrographer in January and who worked closely thereafter with Admiral Bradford. From February to May, as the opposition to the Hydrographic Office grew in Congress, Commander Todd sent a steady stream of letters and circulars to naval officers at the branches, which required them to communicate with chambers of commerce, marine institutions, exchanges, and boards of trade. The naval officers were to urge these associations and corporations to send telegrams to members of Congress, praising the work of the Hydrographic

Office and asking liberal appropriations for it. To pay for some of the telegrams sent by organized groups, branch offices provided government funds.[19]

As the legislative situation became clearer, Todd focused his campaign on the House Appropriations Committee. He advised his subordinates to reach these people through their friends, rather than directly. "Stiffen his backbone," he wrote one branch officer; "keep them up to their work," he wrote to another. He also wanted the branch offices to find out all they could about the sentiments and reasoning of the politicians in opposition. Todd did not hesitate to argue that the navy or the Hydrographic Office, rather than Congress, should have the power of decision in this matter of hydrographical surveys, for they were the true guardians of the maritime interests and the public good. Naval knowledge and experience justified opposition to "ill-informed legislation"; congressmen did not appreciate the needs of the Hydrographic Office, or were too busy to learn the details of measures.

As the political tide turned against him in the House of Representatives, Todd sharpened his statements. Failure to let the navy do the surveying in the new territories would be "a direct menace to the Fleet." He began telling his aides to look for "covert influences that may be attacking us beneath the surface." And on April 20, he charged "a combination" of the Corps of Engineers, the Coast Survey, and the chairmen of the Rivers and Harbors Committee, the Insular Committee, and the Appropriations Committee to eliminate the ocean and lake surveys of the Hydrographic Office. Members of the House were now displaying "political cowardice," or putting "their hands in the public crib," or issuing "twisted" statements to "hoodwink" their colleagues.[20] At this point the navy came closest to that unrepublican conduct which Treasury chiefs had charged it with two decades before, at the time of Chandler's attempted coup.

Four times between February and June 1900 the House of Representatives, while passing on three appropriation bills, earnestly debated what to do about the Hydrographic Office. The dominant sentiment about the agency was dislike or anger. Indeed, not since the trouble with the Geological Survey in the early nineties had legislators shown such sustained and intense feelings against a science organization of the government. And rarely in peacetime have the behavior and power of the military been so frankly and passionately debated as they were in 1900. The leadership in the House came from four Republicans and one Democrat, all of whom were to have an influential future.

The initial action in Congress was not controversial among the politicians. On February 14, 1900, Representative James A. Hemenway, Republican of Indiana (and later senator), in reporting the Legislative, Executive, and Judicial Appropriations bill offered, in a matter of fact way, an amendment to the appropriation for civilian salaries in the Hydrographic Office at Washington. This amendment, which was adopted without a breath of a protest, forbade expenditures "for personal services" by the Hydrographic Office in the District, except as authorized under the heading "Navy Department" within the Legislative, Executive, and Judicial Appropriations Act.[21] Hemenway justified his amendment as a healthy reaction to the freedom that Admiral Bradford had taken with several lump-sum items in the budget of the previous year. He had doubled the $40,000 allocation by Congress for salaries by transferring money from one fund to buy copper plate, from another fund to manufacture charts, and even from the authorization to make ocean and lake surveys, which was in another appropriation act altogether.

Members listened without comment as Hemenway assured them that they would "at once recognize the necessity" for his amendment. If the Hydrographic Office could use lump-sum appropriations, not earmarked for salaries, for the purpose of creating or maintaining positions, then Congress would have no way of knowing the number of persons employed in the Office or the amount paid each employee. Hemenway was positive that Congress desired to know "at all times" who was employed in the Hydrographic Office and how much each employee was paid.[22]

Two months later, on April 19, the Naval Service Appropriations bill, with its authorization of power and money for the Hydrographic Office to do ocean and lake surveys, reached the floor of the House. Chairman Cannon reported this bill from the Appropriations Committee with an amendment striking out the twenty-three lines, sponsored by the Naval Affairs Committee, which set forth all the broad powers at home and abroad that Admiral Bradford and Commander Todd had asked for. Also, the customary designation, "ocean and lake surveys," which had appeared in Naval Service appropriations since 1892, was now cut back to "ocean surveys," the word "hydrographic" was omitted, and the sum of $100,000 secured in 1899 was reduced to $10,000. In Committee of the Whole, the House accepted Cannon's crushing change, 111 to 41.[23]

Cannon was an expert on scientific agencies of the government, because he had dealt with them for so many years in the Appropriations Committee, where more than once he had praised the Coast Survey. Recently, he had informed the New York state chamber of commerce that he would not consider "a complete coast survey" in the Navy Department when there was a "long established" Coast Survey in the Treasury.[24] Before the House, he said he was protecting the navy from "wild schemes" to absorb other services, including even the Weather Bureau. His statement was greeted with "loud applause on the Republican side,"[25] and a voice was heard to exclaim amid laughter: "That settles Dewey's canvass." (There had been talk of the heroic admiral as a candidate for the presidency.) Cannon saw no sense, he told the House, in agonizing about putting naval officers on civil duty when the navy could not find enough of them to man its own fleet.

Several representatives wondered what the Hydrographic Office was doing in the Great Lakes, where army engineers had been mapping for sixty years. William H. Moody, Republican of Massachusetts and soon to be a Cabinet member and justice of the Supreme Court, introduced a new word, "militarism," into the exchange between the civilians and the military about the control of government science. Moody said he refused to change a "great department of the Government" from civilian to military control; the danger of militarism lay in the increase of its activities. And Thomas C. McRae, Democrat of Arkansas (and later governor of his state), urged resistance to "the encroachments of the military upon civil jurisdiction."[26] The House gave assent with applause. Representative George E. Foss of Illinois, a member of the Naval Affairs Committee, spoke for the Hydrographic Office and drew applause when he said that if naval officers were responsible for the safety of the fleet, then, out of common decency and fairness, they should not be denied the "right to make the surveys for the uncharted seas."[27]

On May 4, debate was renewed, this time over the Sundry Civil bill and the appropriation for the Coast Survey. Alston G. Dayton of West Virginia, chairman of the House Naval Affairs Committee, moved to eliminate the new authority that had been granted the Coast Survey the previous year to survey any coasts under the jurisdiction of the United States.[28] One of Cannon's answers in opposition was to stress the unavailability of naval officers for coastal surveying in the territories. "How, in the name of all that is good, will there be any [officers] to spare, if you make some new law and put the Coast Survey on the Navy?" he asked. He remembered that when the Spanish-American War was over his committee had asked the secretary of the navy to transfer some of the numerous yachts which had been bought for the emergency to the Revenue Service, or to the Lighthouse Service, or to the Coast Survey. The answer came back from the secretary that not one single ship could be spared. Cannon claimed to be as proud as any man of the army and the navy, and he was ready to do the two services great honor, "for they are the peers of any army and navy . . . in the tide of time"; but he intended to limit the two services to their military role. Echoing Representative Moody's linguistic innovation, he told the House he did not "believe in bringing the Navy into everyday affairs of civil life. Such action is militarism and I am against militarism." Applause followed.[29]

On this same day of May 4, Hemenway revealed some of the animus behind his amendment in February to the Legislative, Executive, and Judicial bill limiting the discretion of the Hydrographic Office in its expenditure of appropriated funds. He reminded the House that two of the persons paid by the Hydrographic Office from a lump-sum appropriation were retired naval officers who had passed Civil Service examinations. "Now, gentlemen, catch that statement," Hemenway went on. Who was passed by the board of naval officers administering the Civil Service examinations "when civilians were contending for the places that retired naval officers wanted?" The House applauded, and Hemenway charged his audience that if they wanted militarism in this country, "if you want this whole thing controlled by the Army and Navy, you follow the Committee on Naval Affairs."[30] The House refused Dayton's amendment.

Before the final debate in the House on June 6, Cannon brought to the point of decisive action a correspondence with Secretary John D. Long of the Navy Department. Todd's public campaign for congressional support finally got on the representative's nerves, for letters had been coming in from all over the country, sent by maritime associations and boards of trade, "telling us," as Cannon later related, "not to cripple the Navy."[31] What particularly irritated Cannon was the wonderful similarity of these letters, as if "some central intelligence" was inspiring them. On April 21, two days after the House had gutted the authorization in the Naval Service bill for the Hydrographic Office in ocean and lake surveys and other activity, Cannon wrote to Secretary Long for the Committee on Appropriations, asking for copies of all telegrams and letters since the beginning of February, "written by the Navy Department, or any of its bureaus of officers"[32] to chambers of commerce, boards of trade, corporations, and individuals outside of Washington, concerning appropriations and legislation affecting the Hydrographic Office, or its ocean and lake surveys. Cannon also wanted to know the authority for the sending of any such telegram and letters, and what government funds were used to pay for them. The secretary replied, on April 30, that "it does not appear that any letters or telegrams have been sent by the Department." He based his statement on a letter from Commander Todd to Admiral Bradford of April 25, in which the commander reported that "a careful examination of the files of this office show that no letters or telegrams have been sent."[33] At this time, neither Secretary Long nor Representative Cannon knew that Todd on the same day, April 25, had written a *memorandum* to Admiral Bradford, which was more honest than his *letter* to the admiral. Todd admitted that he had kept the branches informed of the progress and results of legislation and appropriations relating to the Hydrographic Office and its ocean-lake surveys. The liaison was maintained, Todd told Bradford, so that "organized bodies having an interest in hydrographic matters" could take proper action. Whatever had been done by the Hydrographic Office, Todd insisted, was "in the interests of this office, in the interests of the Department, and of the country."[34]

Two weeks later, on May 14, Cannon again communicated with Secretary Long, because the representative had come into possession of a faulty copy of the circular sent from Todd to the branch office at Port Townsend, Washington, on April 20, which reported the 90 percent slash of ocean surveys in the House on April 19 within the Naval Service Appropriations bill, and charged "a combination" of government science bureaus and House committee chairmen against the Hydrographic Office. Cannon asked Long for the complete copy of this April circular, and Long replied the next day, May 15. The circular letter of April 20 had been sent, Long wrote, "without the knowledge of the Department," and had just been brought to the secretary's attention. Because the hydrographer had written on April 25 that no letters had been sent, and because the letter of April 20 had been in violation of naval regulations, Secretary Long informed Cannon that he was suspending the hydrographer from duty, pending the action of the department in the matter.[35]

In the first week of June, the Naval Service Appropriations bill returned from the Senate with the $100,000 restored "for hydrographic surveys." Influential and experienced members, like Lodge, Hale, and Chandler (now a senator), were so confirmed in their support of the navy that they held the Coast Survey to be the aggressor. "It is an attempt," said Senator Lodge, "to take from the Navy its hydrographic surveys and throw them into the Coast Survey, building up another great department with, as the senator from New Hampshire [Chandler] said, another little navy." The Hydrographic Office "was most excellently managed," said Hale. These three men were on the defensive about the conduct of Commander Todd, and they did not insist on the broad powers originally proposed by the naval officers and supported in the House by the Naval Affairs Committee. But they lauded their conferees for standing with "absolute firmness" on the ocean and lake appropriation.[36]

Along with the cost of naval armor, this issue became the great sticking point between House and Senate during the first week in June, as each body refused to yield and the agreed time for adjournment came nearer and nearer. On May 29, the House organized its conference committee of three managers, including Dayton and Foss of Naval Affairs, and instructed them—through a motion by Cannon, which passed 114–70—to stick with the word "ocean" as indicative of the kind of survey the Hydrographic Office could do, and not to yield on the other two key words, "lake" and "hydrographic." The House agreed to raise the appropriation from $10,000 to $20,000. In conference, the managers on behalf of the Senate came down to $50,000 on the appropriation, and agreed to elimination of the word "lake." The upper house stood fast, however, on the other disputed word, "hydrographic." The managers for the House returned to their colleagues and recommended acceptance of the compromise. A number of articulate representatives reacted fiercely, charging their managers on the conference committee with betraying the House.[37]

When the House debated the conference report on June 6, Cannon's speech was the main event and the exciting climax of the continuous discussion since February. It was no longer, he began, a question of the best scientific service to be obtained. Rather, it involved a fundamental choice by the American political community between the civilian and the military. Cannon was effective because he was so angry about being lied to by officers in the Navy Department. He detailed the story of his correspondence with the secretary of the navy, beginning with the first letter of April 21, asking for copies of Hydrographic Office communications to persons, corporations, and boards of trade. The answer came back, said Cannon. "There is nothing! nothing! nothing! I knew that was a falsehood. . . . That is strong language." Loud applause greeted him. Then he described the remarkable resemblance of the letters which descended on him, and laughter rose when he cried,

"I know a round robin when I see it." There was more loud applause when he read the information from Secretary Long's letter of May 15, saying that Todd had been suspended as hydrographer. Cannon characterized the contest as one to decide "whether this House . . . close to the people, was stronger than a few men connected with the Navy and in bureau positions in the Navy Department."[38] Loud applause rose again, and also at the end of the twenty-minute speech.

Hemenway and Moody, both on the Appropriations Committee, won applause, too. Like his colleagues, Hemenway wanted to confine naval officers to fighting, the business "for which we educate them . . . we are proud of them for their fighting qualities," he continued. But they should not "reach out and grasp duties that belong to civilians in this country." Moody escalated his rhetoric by linking the dislike of the military to the dislike of bureaucracy. He wondered which was bigger: "A coterie of naval officers . . . or the House of Representatives." The House was maintaining a policy decided fifty years ago. "Are you going to get down in the dirt to these bureau officers?" he asked bitterly. Theodore E. Burton of Ohio, Republican chairman of the Rivers and Harbors Committee and afterward senator, said that "a bureaucrat" in the Navy Department had sent out letters charging him with making "a combination." Denying this charge, "Busy, Brainy Burton," as the *New York Times* called him, said that it was "time for the House to assert its prerogative"; "we know something about this subject," he exclaimed. The representatives should insist on "fair dealing": let those who sought "to influence legislation come before the public and act in the light and not in the dark." Loud applause showed House approval.[39]

The House rejected the conference compromise, 131–83, and assented to a reconstitution of its conference committee, with Cannon, Moody, and John F. Shafroth of Colorado the new members. This last-minute change seemed a useless step, for the next day, June 7, when Congress adjourned, the House, with Dayton supported and Cannon overruled, voted to recede from its position and to concur with the Senate, that body having meanwhile returned to its original position, expressed in the wording sent to the House at the end of May.[40] Thus the appropriation for the Hydrographic Office in the Naval Service Appropriations Act, approved as law on June 7, carried the heading "Ocean and Lake Surveys" and, thereunder, "for hydrographic surveys . . . one hundred thousand dollars."[41]

The restoration of the navy's money on June 7 and the reinstatement of Todd as hydrographer on June 8 no doubt inspired the later claim by the *New York Tribune* of "a complete victory of the Navy."[42] However, this interpretation has to be qualified somewhat because of what happened on June 9, when Congressman Burton, following through on his remarks of three days before, wrote to Secretary Long. Burton insisted that the charge of his participating in "a combination" against any appropriation which the Hydrographic Office benefited from was "absolutely without foundation," and he demanded "a prompt apology" and an outgoing letter disowning the circular of April 20. Secretary Long passed Burton's letter along to Todd, with the hand-written notation that the commander will "answer this letter today." If he had any reasons for making the charge against "Mr. Burton," he would give them; otherwise, he was to make "a proper disclaimer." Todd replied to Secretary Long that he had "no desire to do any injustice to Mr. Burton"; and he regretted that "Mr. Burton should take the view of the case as set forth in his letter." The commander agreed that "it would be an act of justice to Mr. Burton" if a letter was sent to the branch offices, and from there to such bodies as may have been approached, saying that Mr. Burton did not have anything to do with any combination against the Hydrographic Office.[43]

For decades, the legislative wording of the scientific duties for the Hydrographic Office and the Coast Survey did not change in the Sundry Civil and the Naval Service Appropriations Acts. Gradually, however, movement within the Executive branch ratified the thrust of the angry sentiment in the House. An early attempt at collaboration ended in a stalemate. Ordered by President McKinley to try to reach an agreement, the three Cabinet secretaries of Treasury, Navy, and War appointed a working committee of Superintendent Tittmann (Pritchett's successor), Admiral Bradford, and John M. Wilson, chief of the Corps of Engineers. After several "stubborn conferences" in December 1900, the three officials agreed to retain the wording for the ocean and lake surveys in the legislation of 1900.[44]

On his own, Tittmann sent a party of men, under one of the Survey's engineers, to the Philippines, where a branch office was established at Manila, something the Hydrographic Office did not have authority to do. In 1901 the U.S. Philippine Commission placed the Coast Survey under the control of the Department of Commerce and Police in the Philippines,[45] which was approved by Congress the following year. In November 1901, the Survey vessel *Pathfinder* arrived at the island of Luzon to go to work. By then, as many Coast Survey vessels were engaged in the Philippines as had been working in the continental United States before the Spanish-American War.

Still trying, even after the House demonstration, Bradford and Todd could not persuade the navy to commit itself to a long-term program of surveying in the Philippines, for the reason that Admiral Arent S. Crowninshield, chief of the Bureau of Navigation, which in those days was responsible for the movement of naval personnel, insisted that no naval officers be assigned to scientific surveys anywhere in the government. Then, late in 1902, Representative Moody resigned from the House to become secretary of the navy, and a thirty-year naval attitude toward the Coast Survey began to wind down. Moody communicated his disapproval to Admirals Bradford and George C. Remey (of the Asiatic squadron) of their "zealous efforts" to execute scientific surveys.[46] He also wrote a letter to the secretary of commerce (where the Coast Survey was now domiciled), asking for the charting of various harbors in Alaska, the Aleutians, Puerto Rico, and the Philippines for the navy's use, and urging the augmentation of Coast Survey resources for this broad program.[47] Even after Moody had moved to the Supreme Court, the navy turned over to the Coast Survey for publication a survey by a naval officer of a major river in the Philippines. Secretary Hunt's announced principle in 1881 that naval surveys in territorial waters should be sent to the Coast Survey for publication came to fruition in the territory of the Philippines.

Thus did Cannon and the House clinch their victory over Admiral Bradford and his Hydrographic Office, thereby reaffirming civilian supremacy over the military in government science, although a popular, imperialistic war had given this same military, and the nation at large, new heroes and glory.

To make the year 1900 even more definitive, the final divorce occurred of naval personnel from hydrographic work within the Coast Survey. In 1898, at the beginning of the Spanish-American War, the navy, following the precedent of 1861, withdrew all its officers from Coast Survey duty—never to return. Even with the officers gone, the petty officers and crews of many of the Coast Survey vessels were still naval personnel. So Pritchett worked, in the spring of 1900, to place the expenditures for the pay and subsistence of naval crews in Coast Survey vessels in the Sundry Civil bill. And in May, Cannon spoke for this switch in expenditures, even as he was defending the bureau against hostile amendments from the Naval Affairs Committee. After passage of the Sundry Civil bill, Pritchett arranged with Secretary Long to transfer all naval personnel on Coast Survey ships to Coast Survey jurisdiction. On July 1, 1900, when the new Sundry Civil Act went into effect, several of the ships manned by navy crews were en route to Alaska, others were returning from Puerto Rico, but by November the crew of the last vessel arriving from Alaska had been transferred to the civilian bureau, and in December 1900 the Navy Department closed its enlistment records for the sailors on Coast Survey ships.[48]

For the first time in its history, the Coast Survey was a completely civilian outfit. To take the place of the naval officers, Pritchett was authorized to hire thirty new assistants, which more than made up for the losses under Duffield.

In the nineteenth-century search for knowledge, the Coast Survey was better than the Hydrographic Office. It entered seriously into more scientific disciplines and connected its practical work with broad, theoretical studies in geodesy. The determination to make the most accurate measurements possible of line and arc on the face of the globe encouraged good and painstaking instrumentation, which rounded out the professional character of the Coast Survey scientific practice. Although on the frontier of advancing nineteenth-century science, astronomers and geodesists in and out of the Survey were traditional in their social ideals, as determined as the Founding Fathers to be free of military control and power. It remains to ask whether the Coast Survey should have devised further means to reach the mariner more quickly or systematically. Certainly the assistants were sensitive and deeply helpful to their maritime constituency. Had they gone in, like the Hydrographic Office, for institutionalized, day-to-day contact with seafarers, this would inevitably have cut into the production of charts, which always lagged behind expectations, given the resources Congress was willing to allot. And salesmanship was not something these scientists and engineers wanted much to do with.

There was plenty of scientific talent in the emerging new navy, with the officers doing best at technology. In their maritime research they were Baconian, for they emphasized the collection and distribution of facts, which was quicker and cheaper than Coast Survey science and appealed, therefore, to congressmen who prided themselves on their frugal and practical attitude toward government expenditure. Why, then, did the navy fail in its attempt to take over the Coast Survey, after the glorious victories at sea? Victories which might be considered a counterweight to the pervasive prejudice against the military in republican America?

To begin with, the criticisms of the civilian agency were essentially superficial. To propose the distribution of knowledge more quickly and clearly was enough, perhaps, to cause uneasiness among the defenders of the Coast Survey about their position, but hardly constituted a threat to overthrow it. Then there was the isolation of the navy, which had little or no network of supporters in academe or within the government. Absence of naval protagonists in the National Academy of Sciences was a serious weakness, especially when that body was called upon for opinions. Because of the code they lived by, naval officers had less freedom in approaching Congress, where scientists had lobbied feverishly ever since the Civil War. When bureau members of the Navy Department *did* solicit the politicians, their techniques seemed reckless or arrogant. The branch hydrographic offices, which in the beginning were a sensible and successful attempt to close the gap between the naval officer and the merchant captain or sailor on coasting vessels, soon degenerated into a political machine, contemptuous of democratic practice and childish in its conspiratorial view of American politics.

The struggle between the military and the civilian entities was most uneven in 1900: one capable bureau chief against five extraordinarily able House members, three or four of whom were on the threshold of advanced careers in politics or business in the early twentieth century. The result was the most serious defeat for the military in nineteenth-century government science since the ouster of the Corps of Engineers from territorial research twenty years before.

7 Reverberations in the Twentieth Century

Essentially, the story of scientific rivalry has ended. The intensive method toward the course of events no longer applies; the meaning and lessons can now be educed. However, an epilogue makes a fitting complement to the central study. Twentieth-century happenings extend the known trends concerning the two agencies, or change their direction. A face-to-face confrontation occurred once more during a congressional inquiry. And each organization pursued enough new science, so that a brief review of developments is required to connect the nineteenth-century work with present-day activity. Then, today's reader will not feel uneasy because of any gap in his or her knowledge between the two centuries. There is a major revision of one scientific finding.

A strengthening of the Coast Survey was one consequence of the founding of the Department of Commerce . . . in 1903. For two generations, those advocating the transfer of the Coast Survey to the navy had asserted the misplaced location of this maritime bureau in the Treasury Department. When, therefore, business interests moved at the beginning of the century to establish a Department of Commerce in their favor, the Coast Survey, under Superintendent Tittmann, won the support of the House for incorporation into the new department, and although some senators still wished to place the Coast Survey in the Navy Department, the

House had its way; and for the first time in its history the Coast Survey, as a science bureau for the benefit of maritime interests, had a comfortable location in the government.[1] Nineteenth-century arguments about the unseemliness of its departmental status vanished.

During World War I, a new and permanent feature of the Coast Survey contributed in an ironic way to the theme of the military versus the civilian in government science. Tittmann's successor, Ernest L. Jones, in desperation about the low Coast Survey salaries, which were, he said, "starving" the government's "intellectual workers,"[2] found a way to improve these salaries by securing new status and titles for his scientists. In February 1917, Superintendent Jones proposed calling them engineers rather than assistants, and his idea became law several months later in the Sundry Civil Act. In May 1917, the Naval Personnel Act authorized the president of the United States to appoint the field officers of the Coast Survey, who were designated in this Act as hydrographic and geodetic engineers. The same Personnel Act made the Coast Survey one of the six commissioned forces or services of the government for the duration by saying that these Coast Survey engineers, when serving with the navy or with the War Department, should rank as lieutenant, captain, or colonel and receive the corresponding salaries.[3]

After the war, Jones persuaded Congress to extend and perpetuate this militarized style and standing in the peacetime Coast Survey. If Coast Survey personnel, he argued, could go into the army and navy in large numbers and do the work of the ranks they held there, along with the corresponding salaries, they deserved the same ranks and salaries when they came back into the Coast Survey.[4] Finally, in 1937 the director of the Coast Survey (Jones had fathered the name change from superintendent) received the title, rank, and salary of rear admiral, as chiefs of bureaus did in the navy.[5]

On one occasion during the 1920s, the hard-pressed hydrographer of the Navy Department sneered at this change of status of Coast Survey scientists as an example of civilian hypocrisy. For decades, these scientists had expressed moral disdain toward military organizations, yet financial exigency caused these same civilians to desert their republican principles and put on some of the form and trappings of the military order. An important consequence of military rankings for Coast Survey history was that Coast Survey officers could now receive pensions, and the informal practice of keeping superannuated persons in positions, which had so exercised Cleveland Democrats, could be discontinued. One of the first retiring assistants to take this income for old age was Pratt, who had held on through the ordeal of Cleveland Democracy to serve forty-nine years with the Coast Survey.

A train of events in the 1920s caused the Hydrographic Office to have the feeling of the Coast Survey in the nineteenth century that the very survival of the organization was at stake. After the war, Congress had established a joint committee to inspect the operations of the Executive branch, and authoritative persons appeared before this committee in January 1924 to urge that the Department of Commerce preside over a consolidation within its jurisdiction of the Coast Survey (already there) with the Hydrographic Office from the navy and the Lake Survey from the War Department. William F. Willoughby, of the Institute for Government Research, asserted that there was no necessity for three hydrographic offices; here was "the most striking duplication in the Government," he said. Another witness testified that a vessel built on the Great Lakes for delivery at New York had to go to three departments for its charts. In five principal ports of the United States, the Coast Survey and the Hydrographic Office operated separate offices for contact with maritime interests; furthermore, each had its own printing plant. Willoughby thought that the Coast Survey could collect charts of foreign waters for the navy. If the navy wanted special surveys, it could apply to a Coast Survey board where there would be naval representation. He accused both the army and the navy of wanting to be independent of "every other service of the Government." A formidable witness against the Hydrographic Office was Secretary of Commerce Herbert Hoover, who would be for the Hydrographic Office in the twentieth century what Randall had been for the Coast Survey in the nineteenth century. Hoover knew that the Hydrographic Office made some original surveys, but dismissed them as of little consequence. If the goal was efficiency and economy, then the two services should be consolidated and a long controversy ended. Congress, he said, had considered eleven times the removal of the Coast Survey to the navy.[6]

The strategy of Captain and Hydrographer Frederic B. Bassett and Secretary of Navy Edwin Denby before the joint committee was to concentrate on what the Hydrographic Office was good at, namely, the printing and distributing of charts, directions, and notices. The U.S. government issued 3,400 of the 4,500 charts needed to navigate the waters of the earth; 2,700 of the American charts came from the printing and engraving plant of the Hydrographic Office, the great majority being reproductions of charts of other governments. Captain Bassett stressed the distribution of these charts to naval vessels; there were forty-eight different portfolios for naval vessels going on station. And the secretary of the navy would trust no other agency of the government than the Hydrographic Office to distribute these charts properly to the men-of-war. The Hydrographic Office went to great trouble to eliminate errors from its printing. It corrected Coast Survey sailing directions for American waters, and two nautical experts visited the Government Printing Office every Tuesday to read proof for half a day. The Department of Commerce showed no such carefulness, asserted Bassett.[7]

Director Jones of the Coast Survey spoke with irritation during his testimony. He said that the controversy about consolidation was not pleasant, and he had kept out of it for three years because he did not wish to make propaganda or discredit another bureau. What had brought him into the fray was the republication by the Hydrographic Office of some of the materials of the eighties and nineties, which expressed the confident wish to absorb the Coast Survey. What particularly irritated Jones was the contention that the Coast Survey was not an organization of seamen and navigators, and therefore should not have the responsibility of making charts. Jones said that most of the one hundred and forty-one commissioned officers in the Coast Survey held unlimited licenses as masters of ocean-going vessels. He compared the *Notices to Mariners* of both organizations; 90 percent of the notices from the Hydrographic

Office were from previously published sources whereas over 80 percent of the materials published by the Coast Survey originated in new hydrographic surveys. Who here was in contact with the mariners? he asked. If the navy did not choose to talk much about its original surveying, Jones did. Like his predecessors, he held no high opinion of it: a few soundings and a running sketch of the shoreline in remote places such as the Gulf of California. Since these surveys were without fundamental controls through triangulation, they were not true, accurate surveys. Twenty-eight different naval vessels had surveyed Haiti, and the result had been uncoordinated, unconnected surveys, based on no system of triangulation. He charged that the navy used their survey ships as training schools, a practice which made the surveying work expensive, inefficient, and potentially very harmful to the mariner, who had to rely on an amateur product for his safety. Whatever its natural talent, the navy was not organized to do serious surveying. Jones also testified that he had "repeatedly" heard naval officers state that "they dare not become specialists . . . at the expense of general efficiency," for low marks in general efficiency were "an impassable barrier to the attainment of the highest goal in the naval service," fleet command or chief of naval operations.[8]

Fundamentally, the reaction of the joint committee was an answer to the outcries of Willoughby and Hoover about efficiency. Given the friction or antagonism between the Hydrographic Office and the Coast Survey, what good would it do to put the two together? the committee asked. Senator Pat Harrison of Mississippi sensed "stronger feeling" in this matter than in anything else which had come before the committee.[9] Agreeing with the navy's instinctive reaction that commanding officers should be able to go to fellow officers for their charts, the committee decided to let the navy retain its own distributing apparatus.

Herbert Hoover was more stubborn. As president, he issued reorganization orders, late in 1932, bringing the Lake Survey and the Hydrographic Office into the Department of Commerce, where the Coast Survey was. However, a Democratic Congress refused, in January 1933, to approve this organization.

During the first decades of the twentieth century, the science of the Hydrographic Office was routine; original research was slight. Money and personnel did not increase, and lake surveys were abandoned after 1900. The annual reports dwelt with conviction on the pilot charts of the North Atlantic and the North Pacific, with their graphic information on latitude, longitude, winds, currents, storms, sailing and steamship routes, lines of equal variation of the compass, and so forth. The backs of these charts continued to be utilized for articles on special subjects. Less regularly, such charts appeared on the South Atlantic, South Pacific, and Indian Oceans. The *Notices to Mariners* were a heavy printing expense, and several volumes on sailing directions for Asia appeared. The new surveying concentrated on West Indian and Caribbean waters, and coastal charts were prepared for parts of Cuba, Santo Domingo, Central America, and the approaches to the Panama Canal.[10]

The remarkable change for the Hydrographic Office during the past fifty years has been its willingness to make alliances with modern science through research in oceanography. For example, in 1933, the year of Herbert Hoover's failure to abolish the Office, the hydrographer announced "a dynamic ocean survey," by which he meant an unusual combination of research studies aboard a naval vessel: the measurement of gravity, the determination of depth by sonic soundings, and testing for the chemical content of water and the flow of current. The Office broke its long isolation from American civilian scientists in 1935, when it revealed that it was consulting with two representatives from an oceanographic laboratory located at the University of Washington, and the next year a professor of biology joined one of the surveying ships. In 1939 the Office prepared a bathymetric chart of the Caribbean as part of the final report of the Navy–Geophysical Union Gravity expedition. During World War II, innovative research was directed toward predicting ocean waves so that landing craft could be more safely operated. And using submarines, the Office investigated the phenomenon of temperature, when sea-water readings rose, rather than fell, as depth increased.

Given the favorable attitude toward research in the Navy Department after World War II, the Office was able to continue its contributions to the science of oceanography. In 1949, two vessels were specifically designated to conduct oceanographic surveys, an action which Captain Bassett had recommended twenty-five years before. Aerial magnetic surveys of oceans were begun, and in one year six sea-gravity meters were kept in continuous operation. The Gulf Stream and Point Barrow in Alaska became foci of research, and the Office had contracts with the Office of Naval Research, the Scripps Institution, and the Woods Hole Oceanographic Institution.

After Sputnik, funds flowed freely for oceanographic research. In 1961, the Assistant Secretary of the Navy for Research and Development ordered the hydrographer to establish a national oceanographic data center. In 1962, the Hydrographic Office became the U.S. Naval Oceanographic Office. In 1964, an Oceanographic Instrumentation Center rose within the Office, and in 1965 a contract with private industry provided for the sampling of sea floor and water masses to define physiographic provinces beneath the Atlantic and Pacific. Other activity in 1965 and 1966 illustrates how far the Oceanographic Office had come from nineteenth-century days, when the science of geodesy had been treated so cavalierly. Preparing for missile ranges in the Southwest Pacific, the Office worked on a geodetic survey and planned for accurate geodetic positioning of transmitters, monitor stations, and calibration sites. Four geodesists and six oceanographers from the Office were among those at Palomares, Spain, in 1966, after a nuclear bomb had been lost.[11] In the mid-eighties, the Office possessed twelve ships, worked with a budget of $175 million, and supported the research of nearly 500 scientists. Its pristine function, chart production and distribution, had been transferred in 1972 to a central organization in the Department of Defense, the Defense Mapping Agency.

In the twentieth century, the Coast Survey won wide acceptance for its product, as the airplane and the motorboat entered American life, inspiring a large demand for accurate charts to navigate the airways and to travel the intercoastal and inland water routes. What had often been challenged in the nineteenth century was now taken for granted: resurveys must be made. The entrances to Chesapeake and Delaware Bays needed new charts every ten years, and interior harbors required examination every fifty years. The Coast Survey finally bowed to the criticism by naval officers of unnecessary topographical detail; in 1930, the bureau announced that it would no longer revise all the topography on its sheets, only the important features, and eliminate the rest.[12] A satisfying experience came in 1936 with the survey of the Hudson submarine canyon off New York City, whose true form and size had never before been determined.

The first technological change was in the sounding for depth in coastal waters. The dropping of a lead weight at the end of a line had been the traditional way, but this method had the fatal weakness of missing rocks or bouncing off them, especially in Maine waters and in southeast Alaska, where many boulders or pinnacles lay just beneath the surface. In 1904, borrowing from French practice, the Coast Survey introduced a new device to discover these hidden, treacherous dangers. This was a long wire line, held taut between two vessels headed in the same direction and then moved along horizontally, so as to sweep areas just below the surface of the water. Visible buoys, attached to the wire line, were pulled beneath when a hidden rock was met. So many underwater obstacles were discovered by this wire-drag method, as it was called, that after two decades the head of the Coast Survey was led to testify publicly that nineteenth-century hydrographic surveys, whether naval or civilian, had not fulfilled their mission to measure depths of water.[13]

In 1910, Leland P. Shidy directed the construction of a second tide-predicting machine to replace what he called the overdelicate and mechanically crude invention of Ferrel's; and after 1929, the field forces of the Coast Survey used Bilby's steel tower for distant sightings.

In gravity studies, Survey technicians were under strong pressure to speed up their measurement of relative gravity, for they were satisfying only a small number of the legitimate requests for data. The result was the replacement in 1930 of the Mendenhall pendulum with the Brown gravity apparatus. The Brown apparatus did away with the chronometer, which for Mendenhall provided the time at the beginning and end of the pendulum swing, an interval which must be determined with the utmost accuracy if g, the acceleration of a freely falling body, was to be accurate. Of course, the error of the chronometer had to be found—that is, its rate of gain or loss—and this operation doubled the number of observations at a given station. The Brown apparatus introduced a device for recording the pendulum oscillations on a chronograph which also carried radio time signals. With this dual record, the observer could make comparisons of time and position for the pendulum without another instrument. During the 1930s, there were three times as many determinations of relative g as in the previous forty years.

The next change came in the 1950s, when the gravimeter disposed of the pendulum for most land observations. The gravimeter operated on the principle that if a weight hung from a spring, the extension of the spring would vary as g. Thus values for g are obtained through measurements of varying lengths of the spring.[14]

Geodetic science, so often attacked in the nineteenth century, now rose to new influence and appreciation. Railroads, oil companies, hydroelectric plants, states, counties, and cities all needed the Coast Survey's triangulation and leveling data; and so did projects in irrigation, drainage, and flood control. After the completion of the transcontinental triangulation and leveling along the thirty-ninth parallel at the end of the nineteenth century, the Coast Survey went on to build other trunk lines along parallels and meridians. By the Depression Decade, the bureau was beginning to fill in the national network with shorter and intermediate lines. The scientific objective, continually elaborated to introduce more control stations, has been the emplacement every few miles of a permanently marked point whose geographical position and elevation are stated authoritatively.[15]

After World War II, electronic surveying transformed geodetic triangulation. One electronic device, the tellurometer, uses a modulated, continuous radio signal for measuring distances; the geodimeter measures distance by the travel between points of transmitted light rays. A good example of the use of electronics came in the 1950s, during the work in Alaska, when a geodetic connection was accomplished between islands in the Bering Sea and the continental mainland by the method called trilateration, which involves the determination of huge distances by measuring the sides of huge triangles, with the computation of angles coming afterward. Through this electronic trilateration, the Bering Sea islands were positioned correctly in relation to the geodetic framework on the American continent.[16]

Data and sample collecting increased significantly after 1959, when the National Academy of Sciences recommended movement along that line. Continual reorganizing has shifted the Coast Survey about within the Department of Commerce, first to the Environmental Science Services Administration in 1965 and then in 1970 to the National Oceanographic and Atmospheric Administration, to become in 1982 the National Ocean Service (including the National Geodetic Survey). A major objective is the confinement of tanker mishaps and oil spills; a more modest goal is the defense of the marine sanctuary where lies the USS *Monitor*. For research in the eighties, the National Ocean Service has twenty-three ships (half oceanographic and half coastal), six hundred scientists, and a budget above $150 million.

Notes

1: The Expansion of the Coast Survey after the Civil War

1. *Congressional Globe,* 37 Cong., 2nd Sess., January 8, 1862, p. 238.
2. The sources for this Civil War summary were U.S. Coast and Geodetic Survey, *Military and Naval Service of the United States Coast Survey, 1861–1865* (1916), and the annual reports of the superintendent for the years 1861–64.
3. *Report of the Superintendent of the United States Coast Survey . . . during the Year 1867,* p. 1.
4. Ibid., pp. 2, 4.
5. G. F. Edmunds to Benjamin Peirce, August 12, 1870, Records of the Coast Survey, Superintendent's File, Congress, Army & Navy, 1867–77, National Archives. For the comments in the House during February 1868, see *Congressional Globe,* 40 Cong., 2nd Sess., 1868, pp. 1457–58.
6. J. E. Hilgard to Benjamin Peirce, July 18, 1870, Records of the Coast Survey, Superintendent's File, Assistant in Charge, 1867–76.
7. *Report of the Superintendent of the U.S. Coast and Geodetic Survey . . . during the Fiscal Year Ending with June, 1882,* p. 8.
8. For the quotations in this paragraph, see C. S. Peirce, "Measurement of Gravity at Initial Stations in America and Europe," *Report of the Superintendent of the United States Coast Survey . . . for the Fiscal Year Ending with June, 1876,* p. 202; *Report of the Superintendent of the United States Coast Survey . . . during the Year 1867,* Appendix 9, p. 141; Benjamin Peirce to C. P. Patterson, November 9, 1870, Records of the Coast Survey, Superintendent's File, Hydrographic Inspector, 1867–74; *U.S. Statutes at Large,* XVI, 508. Historians have long recognized the merit of Peirce's transcontinental move.
9. C. A. Schott, "The Pamplico-Chesapeake Arc of the Meridian and Its Combination with the Nantucket and Peruvian Arcs, for a Determination of the Figure of the Earth from American Measures," *Report of the Superintendent of*

the United States Coast Survey . . . for the Fiscal Year Ending with June, 1877, pp. 84–95.

10. C. A. Schott, "Comparison of Local Deflections of the Plumbline in Latitude, Longitude, and Azimuth, at Stations of the Oblique Arc along our Atlantic Coast, as Developed on Bessel's and Clarke's Spheroids," *Report of the Superintendent of the U.S. Coast and Geodetic Survey . . . during the Fiscal Year Ending with June, 1879,* p. 110.

11. Schott, "Pamplico-Chesapeake Arc of the Meridian," *Report of the Superintendent* (1877), p. 86.

12. Ibid., p. 94.

13. Mansfield Merriman, *A Textbook of the Method of Least Squares* (1884), p. 1.

14. C. S. Peirce, "On the Theory of Errors of Observations," *Report of the Superintendent of the United States Coast Survey . . . during the Year 1870,* pp. 204, 201.

15. Merriman, *Textbook of the Method of Least Squares,* p. 4.

16. J. F. Hayford, "Determination of Time, Longitude, Latitude, and Azimuth," *Report of the Superintendent of the U.S. Coast and Geodetic Survey . . . July 1, 1897, to June 30, 1898,* p. 266.

17. *Report of the Superintendent of the Coast Survey . . . during the Year 1860,* p. 26; *Report of the Superintendent of the Coast Survey . . . during the Year 1854,* p. 70.

18. See Mansfield Merriman, *The Figure of the Earth: An Introduction to Geodesy* (1881), pp. 48, 57, and *A Textbook of the Method of Least Squares,* pp. 17, 22, 38, 181–82.

19. Benjamin Peirce to George Davidson, November 7, 1868, Records of the Coast Survey, Superintendent's File, George Davidson, 1866–75.

20. P. C. Johnson to George Davidson, October 5, 1872, in ibid., Assistants I, J, K, 1866–75.

21. *Report of the Superintendent of the U.S. Coast and Geodetic Survey . . . during the Fiscal Year Ending with June, 1881,* p. 186; *Report of the Superintendent of the United States Coast Survey . . . during the Year 1865,* p. 221.

22. The following three paragraphs on Assistant Bache are based upon Records of the Coast Survey, Superintendent's File, Assistants B, No. 1, 1866–75.

23. R. M. Bache to Benjamin Peirce, March 13, 1872, to C. P. Patterson, November 19, 1874, to Governing Board, Sheffield Scientific School, January 14, 1876, in ibid.

24. *Boston Daily Advertiser,* March 27, 1879. In 1876 Eliot had written more critically to the superintendent about the first volume of the *Coast Pilot.* He urged shorter and clearer sentences for the benefit of the "common coaster," and thought that the "Pilots," more than charts, would "attract to the Coast Survey the good will and good opinion of our maritime population." C. W. Eliot to C. P. Patterson, April 22, 1876, Records of the Coast Survey, Superintendent's File, Assistants A–D, 1876.

25. A. F. Rodgers to Benjamin Peirce, March 12, 29, 1867, to C. P. Patterson, December 1880, in ibid., Assistants R, 1866–75, Assistants R–Z, 1880.

26. A. F. Rodgers to W. W. Duffield, April 24, 1895, H. M. Hamilton to A. F. Rodgers, November 29, 1897, in ibid., Assistants R–Z, 1895–97.

27. *Report of the Superintendent of the United States Coast Survey . . . during the Year 1866,* p. 40.

28. Henry Mitchell, "On the Circulation of the Sea through New York Harbor," *Report of the Superintendent of the U.S. Coast and Geodetic Survey . . . during the Fiscal Year Ending with June, 1887*, pp. 409–32.
29. C. H. Boyd to F. M. Thorn, July 3, 1888, Records of the Coast Survey, Superintendent's File, Assistants A–C, 1888.
30. Stehman Forney to H. S. Pritchett, August 14, 1900, in ibid., Assistants A–F, 1900.
31. William Eimbeck to F. M. Thorn, September 30, 1888, in ibid., Assistants E–H, 1888; to T. C. Mendenhall, June 29, 1894, in ibid., Assistants A–N, 1894.
32. J. F. Pratt to F. M. Thorn, August 13, 1887, in ibid., Assistants N–Q, 1887; G. A. Fairfield to the Superintendent, January 4, 1893, in ibid., Office, 1894; *Report of the Superintendent of the U.S. Coast and Geodetic Survey . . . during the Fiscal Year Ending with June, 1879*, p. 56.
33. F. W. Perkins to W. W. Duffield, August 15, 1895, Records of the Coast Survey, Superintendent's File, Assistants G–P, 1895; *Centennial Celebration of the United States Coast and Geodetic Survey, April 5 and 6, 1916*, p. 84.
34. *The Fisheries Exhibition Literature*, vol. XII (1884). *Official Catalogue and Awards of the International Juries*, p. 407.
35. William Ferrel, "Maxima and Minima Tide Predicting Machine," *Report of the Superintendent of the U.S. Coast and Geodetic Survey . . . during the Fiscal Year Ending with June, 1883*, Appendix 9, pp. 247–51.
36. F. M. Thorn to Secretary of the Treasury, September 24, 1885, General Records, Treasury Department, Solicitor Correspondence, July 3, 1885–March 8, 1886, National Archives.
37. Clipping from *Portland Argus*, November 7, 1882, in Stephen Berry to J. E. Hilgard, November 7, 1882, Records of the Coast Survey, Superintendent's File, Miscellaneous Correspondence, A–Z, 1882; E. M. Wallace to F. M. Thorn, January 15, 1886, in ibid., Applications and Testimonials, 1886.
38. *Revised Statutes of the United States* (1878), Sections 170, 1764, 1765.
39. I am indebted to William F. King for materials from his Chapter XI in "George Davidson: Pacific Coast Scientist for the U.S. Coast and Geodetic Survey, 1845–1895" (1973) (University Microfilms Order No. 74-965).
40. C. O. Boutelle to George Davidson, May 23, November 13, 1884, August 14, 1885, J. S. Lawson to George Davidson, July 2, 1884, E. F. Dickens to George Davidson, March 27, 1885, C. A. Schott to George Davidson, August 25, 1885, George Davidson Papers, Bancroft Library, University of California, Berkeley.

2: The Emergence of the Hydrographic Office

1. F. L. Williams, *Matthew Fontaine Maury: Scientist of the Sea* (1963). Chapter X was very helpful here.
2. The Hydrographer to W. D. Whiting, May 18, 1891, Records of the Hydrographic Office, Press Copies of Letters Sent, 1866–85, National Archives. H. L. Burstyn in his *At the Sign of the Quadrant* (1957) and J. F. Campbell in *History and Bibliography of the New American Practical Navigator and the American Coast Pilot* (1964) explain what the copyright issue was mainly about.

3. For Admiral Davis and his part in the launching of the Hydrographic Office, see *Senate Report No. 85,* 38 Cong., 1st Sess., p. 4.

4. D. C. Johnson to Chief of the Hydrographic Office, September 8, 1882, Records of the Hydrographic Office, General Letters Received, 1867–85.

5. *Annual Report of the Secretary of the Navy for the Fiscal Year Ending June 30, 1880,* p. 120.

6. *U.S. Statutes at Large,* XVII, 148; R. H. Wyman to Daniel Ammen, May 24, 1872, Records of the Hydrographic Office, Press Copies of Letters Sent, 1866–85. See also *Report of the Secretary of the Navy for the Year 1872,* p. 88.

7. *Report of the Secretary of the Navy for the Year 1876,* p. 95.

8. Henry Cummings, *A Synopsis of the Cruise of the U.S.S. Tuscarora from the Date of Her Commission to Her Arrival in San Francisco, September 21, 1874,* pp. 22, 50.

9. Records of the Hydrographic Office, Letters Sent and Received, 1885, No. 113.

10. J. R. Bartlett to J. G. Walker, June 29, 1885, in ibid., 1895, No. 793; L. E. Bixler to J. R. Bartlett, January 24, 1886, in ibid., 1886, No. 317.

11. *Science,* XII (August 10, 1888), 65. Bartlett also initiated another monthly series, the meteorological charts, which gave the permanent climatic conditions for every 5 degrees square of the ocean; winds were a major category in these charts.

12. *U.S. Statutes at Large,* XXIII, 184.

13. W. L. Field to J. R. Bartlett, April 11, 1885, Records of the Hydrographic Office, Letters Received from Hydrographic Branch Officers, 1883–85, New York.

14. W. P. Ray to J. R. Bartlett, November 1, 1884, in ibid., New Orleans.

15. Liverpool Underwriters' Association to J. R. Bartlett, January 14, 1886, Records of the Hydrographic Office, Letters Sent and Received, 1886, No. 144; John Worthington to J. R. Bartlett, June 22, 1885, in ibid., 1885, No. 877.

   Through branch offices, Bartlett undertook another public service to increase the influence of his organization. He entered the field of time signaling in Philadelphia, Baltimore, New Orleans, and San Francisco. The Naval Observatory provided the time, Western Union the connection to the cities, and the Hydrographic Office the supervisor and signal mechanism for dropping a timeball from high and visible places. Jewelers, railroad companies, and the general public used the service. The greatest difficulty was technical: getting the iron ball to drop when it was supposed to. In San Francisco, the timeball failed so often in the summer of 1885 that this service by the Hydrographic Office became an object of ridicule. Although there is good material here for a separate study, the need to keep moving ahead with the main narrative precludes further consideration of time signaling.

16. For Captain Wharton's statement, see Everett Hayden, "The Pilot Chart of the North Atlantic Ocean," *Journal of the Franklin Institute,* CXXV (June 1888), 451.

17. Records of the Hydrographic Office, Letters Sent and Received, 1886, No. 2776.

18. Ibid., 1885, Nos. 1286, 1517, 2676; 1887, No. 4662.

19. Ibid., 1887, No. 3784.

20. W. S. Secombe to J. R. Bartlett, March 28, 1887, in ibid., 1887, Nos. 5645, 1472.
21. R. E. Peary to J. R. Bartlett, October 27, 1885, in ibid., 1885, No. 1321.
22. The account here is based on Records of the Coast Survey, Office of the Inspector of Hydrography, Letters Received, 1879–98, passim.
23. C. P. Patterson to C. D. Sigsbee, June 8, 1878, Records of the Hydrographic Office, Letters Sent and Received, 1895, No. 1774a.
24. *Report of the Superintendent of the U.S. Coast and Geodetic Survey . . . during the Fiscal Year Ending with June, 1884,* Appendix 17, p. 619.
25. *American Journal of Science,* CXXXV (June 1888), 497.
26. C. D. Sigsbee, *Deep Sea Sounding and Dredging: A Description and Discussion of the Methods and Appliances Used on Board the Coast and Geodetic Steamer Blake* (1880), pp. 78–80, 159–60.
27. Thomas A. Edison to C. P. Patterson, October 15, 1880, Records of the Coast Survey, Superintendent's File, Miscellaneous Correspondence A–L, 1880; W. N. Mosely to C. P. Patterson, October 2, 1880, in ibid., M–Z, 1880.
28. J. E. Pillsbury, "The Gulf Stream: A Description of the Methods Employed in the Investigation and the Results of the Research," *Report of the Superintendent of the U.S. Coast and Geodetic Survey . . . during the Fiscal Year Ending with June, 1890,* pp. 461–620.

3: The Naval Challenge to Civilian Science and the Congressional Response

1. J. E. Hilgard to Benjamin Peirce, November 5, 1868, Records of the Coast Survey, Superintendent's File, Assistant in Charge, 1867–76.
2. For the quotations in this paragraph, see *National Republican,* January 24, 1872, and *Boston Evening Journal,* January 24, 1872.
3. C. P. Patterson to Benjamin Peirce, October 2, 6, 1869, Records of the Coast Survey, Superintendent's File, Hydrographic Inspector, 1867–74.
4. Ibid., Departments, Congress, Army & Navy . . . 1881, under "Navy Department."
5. L. B. Richardson, *William E. Chandler, Republican* (1940), p. 365.
6. "The Joint Commission to Consider the Present Organization of the Signal Service, Geological Survey, Coast and Geodetic Survey, and the Hydrographic Office," *Senate Misc. Doc. No. 82,* 49 Cong., 1st Sess., p. 68. Hereafter referred to as Record and Hearings of the Joint Commission.
7. See *Annual Report of the Secretary of the Navy for the Year 1882,* pp. 27–40, for Chandler's proposals.
8. *Congressional Record,* 47 Cong., 2nd Sess., January 2, 1883, p. 737.
9. *Annual Report of the Secretary of the Navy for the Year 1882,* p. 244; see ibid., pp. 236–398, for all the supporting materials from naval officers.
10. *Reports in Regard to the Transfer of the Bureaus and Divisions of the Merchant Marine in the Treasury Department to the Navy Department* (1883), pp. 10, 13, 14, 18, 46, 53. The location of these agencies in the Department of the Treasury illustrates its role in originating new governmental work during the

nineteenth century. To follow up on their histories would risk losing the coherence and thrust of the narrative.

11. *Congressional Record*, 44 Cong., 1st Sess., June 22, 1876, p. 4051; ibid., 53 Cong., 2nd Sess., May 11, 1894, p. 4622.

12. Ibid., 52 Cong., 1st Sess., May 10, 1892, p. 4139.

13. Ibid., 46 Cong., 2nd Sess., May 24, 1880, p. 3733; 45 Cong., 2nd Sess., June 11, 1878, p. 4447; 52 Cong., 1st Sess., July 9, 1892, p. 5956; 44 Cong., 2nd Sess., May 10, 1876, p. 1631.

14. See the nostalgic statement of Fernando Wood, Democrat of New York, in the *Congressional Globe*, 42 Cong., 2nd Sess., January 23, 1872, p. 540; see also S. S. Cox, Democrat from the same state, expressing much the same sentiment, in ibid., 3rd Sess., February 21, 1873, p. 1586.

15. *Congressional Record*, 45 Cong., 2nd Sess., May 2, 1878, p. 3099.

16. Ibid., 47 Cong., 2nd Sess., February 21, 1883, p. 3086.

17. *Congressional Globe*, 42 Cong., 3rd Sess., February 21, 1873, p. 1589.

18. For Beck and Blount, see *Congressional Globe*, 42 Cong., 3rd Sess., February 19, 1873, p. 1493, and *Congressional Record*, 46 Cong., 2nd Sess., May 25, 1880, p. 3765.

19. For McMillin and Maginnis, see T. G. Manning, *Government in Science: The U.S. Geological Survey, 1867–1894* (1967), pp. 49, 207.

20. *Congressional Record*, 52 Cong., 1st Sess., May 12, 1892, p. 4239; ibid., 43 Cong., 1st Sess., April 18, 1874, p. 3177. Although states' rights doctrine informed Democratic thinking in the late nineteenth century, there is no evidence that it affected party science policy in Congress.

21. L. W. Busbey, *Uncle Joe Cannon* (1927), p. xvii. For decades, historians have justly targeted Cannon for his conduct as Speaker of the House. I have surveyed his earlier House career on the floor and in committee.

22. For Holman's words or ideas in this paragraph, see *Congressional Globe*, 40 Cong., 2nd Sess., February 12, 1868, pp. 1136, 1137, 1138; 42 Cong., 3rd Sess., February 18, 1873, p. 1460. See also *Congressional Record*, 52 Cong., 2nd Sess., January 31, 1893, pp. 1010–11.

23. *Congressional Record*, 44 Cong., 1st Sess., June 22, 1876, p. 4078; ibid., 43 Cong., 1st Sess., December 17, 1873, p. 274; W. H. Barnes, *History of Congress, The Forty-first Congress of the United States, 1869–1871* (1872), p. 296; *Congressional Globe*, 43 Cong., 3rd Sess., February 24, 1873, Appendix, p. 158.

24. *Congressional Record*, 45 Cong., 2nd Sess., April 30, 1878, p. 2982. For a statement of the rule and its effect, see ibid., 46 Cong., 2nd Sess., April 8, 1881, p. 2236. The Forty-ninth Congress changed this rule so as to prohibit legislation within an appropriation bill, whether it reduced or increased expenditures.

25. On Herbert's query about the evidence for glaciers, see Record and Hearings of the Joint Commission, p. 648. Kevles has called the attention of historians to Herbert as a man of principle and a gentleman.

26. *United Service Magazine: A Monthly Review of Military and Naval Affairs*, XI (November 1884), 542.

27. Manning, *Government in Science*, p. 43n.

28. *Congressional Record*, 45 Cong., 1st Sess., November 8, 1877, pp. 300, 301.

29. *Congressional Record,* 45 Cong., 2nd Sess., June 11, 1878, p. 4448; ibid., 56 Cong., 1st Sess., March 27, 1900, p. 3367.
30. The Lowry Letters, Library and Information Services Division, National Oceanic and Atmospheric Administration, Rockville, Maryland.
31. C. A. Young to Robert Lowry, June 16, 1884; ibid., passim.
32. *Engineering and Mining Journal,* 39 (1885), 152, 153, 169–70, 205–206, 223–34.
33. L. M. Haupt to Robert Lowry, June 16, 1884, J. T. Gardiner to Robert Lowry, July 1, 1884, D. D. Porter to W. H. Hunt, February 22, 1882, to Robert Lowry, June 16, 1884, Lowry Letters.
34. "The Late Attacks on the Coast and Geodetic Survey," *United Service Magazine: A Monthly Review of Military and Naval Affairs,* XI (October 1884), 345–64; ibid. (November 1884), 530–59.
35. See R. C. Cochrane, *The National Academy of Sciences: The First Hundred Years, 1863–1963* (1978), pp. 144–49; A. Hunter Dupree, *Science in the Federal Government: A History of Policies and Activities to 1940* (1957), Chapter XI; D. J. Kevles, *The Physicists: The History of a Scientific Community in Modern America* (1979), pp. 51–59; Manning, *Government in Science,* pp. 123–26.
36. For the three quotations in these two paragraphs see, successively, W. E. Chandler to R. T. Lincoln, September 23, 1884, M. C. Meigs to R. T. Lincoln, October 13, September 25, 1884, Records Series, 1863–1913, Archives of the National Academy of Sciences; see also R. T. Lincoln to M. C. Meigs, September 24, October 11, 1884, in ibid., and Simon Newcomb to O. C. Marsh, September 19, 1884, O. C. Marsh Papers, Sterling Memorial Library, Yale University. No doubt Meigs was also thinking of another civilian-military conflict: the geologists against the Corps of Engineers in 1879 at the founding of the Geological Survey.
37. Record and Hearings of the Joint Commission, p. 86.
38. J. D. Dana to C. P. Patterson, December 18, 1875, Records of the Coast Survey, Superintendent's File, State Surveys, 1867–87, under "Connecticut."
39. For this opinion of Meigs, see his handwriting on a Dana letter to him: J. D. Dana to M. C. Meigs, September 12, 1884, Weather Bureau Records, Signal Division Series, 1870–91, No. 2036, National Archives.
40. Record and Hearings of the Joint Commission, pp. 71, 72, 75.
41. For the quoted words of Bartlett, see ibid., pp. 76, 81; see also J. R. Bartlett to W. B. Allison, December 24, 1885, p. 887.
42. Records of the Hydrographic Office, Letters Sent and Received, 1885, No. 1408; 1886, No. 2019; 1887, No. 3316.
43. Record and Hearings of the Joint Commission, pp. 150, 82, 362, 142. Director Powell made Hilgard's position easier by refusing to go along with the plan of Democratic politicians and naval officers to transfer the geodetic work of the Coast Survey to the Geological Survey. Powell testified that all parts of the Coast Survey were valuable and should be continued.

    The relation of the Geological Survey to the Coast Survey, whether in cooperation or in rivalry, fascinated scientists a hundred years ago, and has attracted the attention of several historians today, including Dupree, Kevles, and Reingold. A complete history of the Coast Survey would give this relationship much attention; my objective has been more circumscribed: to interrelate the histories of the Coast Survey and the Hydrographic Office.

4: The Ordeal of the Coast Survey under Cleveland in the Eighties

1. *Baltimore Sun,* July 18, 1885; *New York Sun,* May 17, 1886.
2. B. A. Colonna to George Davidson, August 1, 1885, Davidson Papers; see also *Washington Evening Star,* July 24, 25, 1885.
   On Wednesday, July 22, Hilgard had had an interview with Secretary of the Treasury Daniel Manning and returned to the Coast Survey office with the news that the interview was satisfactory. However, Colonna reported him as being "sick all day." B. A. Colonna to George Davidson, July 22, 1885, Davidson Papers.
3. John Rodgers to C. P. Patterson, February 13, 1879, Records of the Coast Survey, Superintendent's File, Departments, Congress, Army & Navy . . . 1879.
4. *Washington Post,* August 7, 1885; *New York Evening Post,* August 7, 1885. For the Thorn report, see "Report of the Commission to Investigate the United States Coast and Geodetic Survey," *Hearings before the Committee on Naval Affairs, U.S. House of Representatives* . . . (1894), pp. 195–202. Hereafter referred to as the Thorn Commission Report.
5. Thorn Commission Report. In August, Hilgard sent the Coast Survey $50 to cover the sale of the black mare.
   After being summarily dismissed in July, Saegmuller was allowed to resign in October. He showed great talent as a mechanic, having several inventions in the Coast Survey to his credit and having supervised the construction of the Survey's tide-predicting machine.
6. Ibid., pp. 196, 200, 201; Rosalie M. Bradford to J. E. Hilgard, July 16, 1883, Records of the Coast Survey, Superintendent's File, Private Correspondence, 1881–85; Daniel Manning to F. M. Thorn, September 24, 1885, in ibid., Departments, Congress, Army & Navy . . . 1885; C. O. Boutelle to George Davidson, August 14, 1885, Davidson Papers; *New York Evening Post,* August 7, 1885.
7. B. A. Colonna to George Davidson, undated, received August 30; ibid., September 21, 1885, Davidson Papers; *Washington Evening Star,* September 14, 1885.
8. F. M. Thorn to Secretary of the Treasury, September 24, 1885, Alexander McCue to Daniel Manning, October 20, 1885, General Records, Treasury Department, Solicitor Correspondence, July 3, 1885–March 8, 1886; see also J. E. Hilgard to B. A. Colonna, August 10, 11, 1885, Superintendent's File, Assistants, E–K, 1885.
9. F. M. Thorn to Grover Cleveland, February 11, 1886, Grover Cleveland Papers, Library of Congress.
10. C. A. Schott to George Davidson, August 25, 1885, Davidson Papers.
11. G. A. Bartlett to George Davidson, February 14, 1889, in ibid.
12. F. M. Thorn to Secretary of the Treasury, March 18, 1886, Records of the Coast Survey, Superintendent's File, Departments, Congress, Army & Navy . . . 1886. See the order from the Executive Mansion, March 26, 1886, in ibid.
13. Definition of pendulum in *The Century Dictionary: An Encyclopedic Lexicon of the English Language,* IV (1890), 4371.
14. See the very valuable article by Victor F. Lenzen and Robert P. Multhauf,

"Development of Gravity Pendulums in the 19th Century," U.S. National Museum *Bulletin 240* (1965), pp. 301–48.

15. Norman Feather, *Mass, Length, and Time* (1959), pp. 182–84.
16. For the biographical detail in this paragraph, see C. S. Peirce to C. P. Patterson, March 24, 1874, April 30, 1875, September 6, 29, 1877, August 15, 1878, to F. M. Thorn, July 31, 1889, Records of the Coast Survey, Superintendent's File, Assistants P No. 1, 1866–75, H–Q, 1877, M–Q, 1878, 1889. For the science, see C. S. Peirce, "Measurements of Gravity at Initial Stations in America and Europe," *Report of the Superintendent of the U.S. Coast Survey . . . for the Fiscal Year Ending with June, 1876*, Appendix 15, pp. 202–337. C. S. Peirce, "On the Flexure of Pendulum Supports," *Report of the Superintendent of the U.S. Coast and Geodetic Survey . . . during the Fiscal Year Ending with June, 1881*, Appendix 14, pp. 359–441; see also Lenzen and Multhauf, "Development of Gravity Pendulums in the 19th Century," ibid., pp. 324–29.
17. Thorn Commission Report, p. 197; *Washington Post*, August 6, 1885; *Science*, VI (September 18, 1885), 254.
18. *Proceedings of the American Association for the Advancement of Science, Thirty-fourth Meeting, Held at Ann Arbor, Mich., August, 1885* (1886), p. 546.
19. D. C. Gilman to Superintendent of the Coast Survey, May 3, 1887, Records of the Coast Survey, Superintendent's File, Miscellaneous Correspondence, 1887.
20. C. S. Peirce to F. M. Thorn, September 14, 1885, in ibid., Superintendent's File, Assistants N–Q, 1885; Record and Hearings of the Joint Commission, p. 378.
21. B. A. Colonna to George Davidson, December 17, 1886, Davidson Papers. See also C. S. Peirce to F. M. Thorn, September 6, 1885, Records of the Coast Survey, Superintendent's File, Assistants N–Q, 1885.
22. F. M. Thorn to C. S. Peirce, January 4, March 3, 1887, Coast Survey Correspondence, C. S. Peirce Papers; see also C. S. Peirce to F. M. Thorn, November 30, 1887, Records of the Coast Survey, Superintendent's File, Assistants N–R, 1888.
23. For Schott on Peirce, see C. A. Schott to B. A. Colonna, August 14, 1885, Records of the Coast Survey, Superintendent's File, Assistants N–Q, 1885. F. M. Thorn to C. S. Peirce, March 3, 1887, Coast Survey Correspondence, C. S. Peirce Papers.
24. C. A. Schott to F. M. Thorn, August 4, 1885, Records of the Coast Survey, Superintendent's File, Assistants N–Q, 1885.
25. C. S. Peirce to F. M. Thorn, August 30, 1887, Records of the Coast Survey, Superintendent's File, Assistants N–Q, 1887; ibid., June 30, 1888, Assistants N–R, 1888.
26. "Report of a Conference on Gravity Determinations, Held at Washington, D.C. in May, 1882," *Report of the Superintendent of the U.S. Coast and Geodetic Survey . . . during the Fiscal Year Ending with June, 1882*, p. 507.
27. C. S. Peirce to F. M. Thorn, March 30, 1888, Records of the Coast Survey, Superintendent's File, Assistants N–R, 1888; C. S. Peirce to F. M. Thorn, January 30, July 31, 1889, in ibid., Assistants M–Q, 1889.
28. For the Coast Survey's treatment of its old or failing scientists, see *Report of the Superintendent of the U.S. Coast and Geodetic Survey . . . during the Fiscal Year Ending with June, 1884*, p. 14.

The personnel policy of the Cleveland administration was hard-headed and legalistic, whenever individual misfortune or disaster threatened to undermine economy of governmental expenditures. In 1887, W. B. Mapes, a member of a Coast Survey party on the Gulf coast of Florida, suffered a heart attack and died there. The family of the deceased asked for the return of his body at governmental expense to the East Coast for burial, but the government refused to assume the expense, despite lengthy correspondence involving even Cleveland. See L. W. Reily to F. M. Thorn, letters of September, October, and November 1887, Records of the Coast Survey, Superintendent's File, Miscellaneous Correspondence, 1887, under "R."

29. R. M. Bache to T. C. Mendenhall, October 1, 1889, Records of the Coast Survey, Superintendent's File, Assistants A–Z, 1889–97.

30. B. A. Colonna to George Davidson, July 2, 1888, Davidson Papers.

31. F. M. Thorn to B. A. Colonna, September 12, 1885, Records of the Coast Survey, Superintendent's File, Assistants R–Z, under "Winston," 1885; F. M. Thorn to George Davidson, January 4, 1886, Davidson Papers; Daniel Manning to F. M. Thorn, January 5, 1886, Records of the Coast Survey, Superintendent's File, Departments, Congress, Army & Navy . . . 1886.

32. M. J. Durham to Daniel Manning, February 19, 1886, General Records of the Treasury Department, 1st Comptroller Correspondence, May 1884–May 1886; see also C. H. Boyd to B. A. Colonna, April 15, 1886, Records of the Coast Survey, Superintendent's File, Assistants A–C, 1887.

33. See the pamphlet *Laws and Regulations Relating to the Coast and Geodetic Survey of the United States* (1881), Article 72d, p. 38, in Records of the Coast Survey, Superintendent's File, Miscellaneous Papers, Superintendent's Office, 1890, vol. I.

34. *Report of the Superintendent of the U.S. Coast and Geodetic Survey . . . during the Fiscal Year Ending with June, 1888,* p. 144; Records of the Coast Survey, Superintendent's File, Office, 1868–87, under "Disbursing Agent."

35. J. F. Pratt to B. A. Colonna, March 27, 1886, to F. M. Thorn, September 8, 1886, to B. A. Colonna, July 20, 1887, Outgoing Correspondence, J. F. Pratt Papers, University of Washington Library.

36. J. F. Pratt to G. A. Bartlett, December 29, 1885, to M. J. Durham, March 22, 1886, to F. M. Thorn, August 7, 1888, in ibid.

37. J. F. Pratt to C. H. Boyd, January 1, 1886, to B. A. Colonna, December 26, 1886, in ibid.

38. See the correspondence of Bache, Thorn, Manning, and McCue in Records of the Coast Survey, Superintendent's File, Departments, Congress, Army & Navy . . . 1886.

39. *Public Papers of Grover Cleveland, Governor* (1884), p. 167.

40. J. D. Richardson, ed., *A Compilation of the Messages and Papers of the Presidents,* IX (1897), 4932; F. M. Thorn to Grover Cleveland, December 14, 18, 1885, Cleveland Papers. There is a memorandum in the Record and Hearings of the Joint Commission, pp. 613–14, which answers to Thorn's description.

41. For the quotations of Colonna, see Record and Hearings of the Joint Commission, pp. 556, 598.

42. The quotation is from a circular of the Hydrographic Office of April 17, 1886, in Records of the Hydrographic Office, General Correspondence, 1886,

No. 1216A; see also J. R. Bartlett to G. H. Eldridge, April 3, 1886, in ibid., No. 982, to Editors of the *Marine Journal,* April 3, 1886, in ibid., No. 1002.

43. C. A. Schott to George Davidson, April 21, 1886, Davidson Papers; Simon Newcomb to O. C. Marsh, September 27, 1886, Marsh Papers.

44. For Thorn's account of the hiring of Glascock, see F. M. Thorn to Grover Cleveland, November 1, 1893, copy in Library and Information Services Division, National Oceanic and Atmospheric Administration. For Fagin, see F. M. Thorn to Grover Cleveland, November 3, 1886, Cleveland Papers.

45. For the tension in the Coast Survey at this time, see H. E. Coleman to C. S. Carrington, May 24, 1886, in ibid., to C. S. Fairchild, September 25, 1886, General Records, Treasury Department, Solicitor Correspondence, August 30, 1886–February 18, 1889.

46. *New York Evening Post,* March 8, 1886; F. M. Thorn to the Editor, *New York Evening Post,* March 15, 1886; *Washington Post,* April 16, 1886, p. 1.

47. "Limiting the Printing and Engraving for Geological Survey, the Coast and Geodetic Survey etc.," *House Report No. 2740, 49* Cong., 1st Sess., pp. 4, 6, 8, 10.

Only on the subject of subsistence payments did the Allison Commission become critical of the Coast Survey; it discouraged the practice without seriously grappling with the problem. Ibid., p. 13.

48. Ibid., pp. 66–68, 70, 77, 79.

49. For the three preceding quotations by congressmen, see (in order) *Congressional Record, 49* Cong., 1st Sess., June 24, 1886, Appendix, p. 450; ibid., June 25, 1886, pp. 6139, 6138.

50. Ibid., June 26, 1886, p. 6171; H. G. Wright to C. O. Boutelle, July 1, 1886, W. F. Smith to C. O. Boutelle, June 30, 1886, Records of the Coast Survey, Superintendent's File, Departments, Congress, Army & Navy . . . 1886, under "War Department."

51. *Washington Post,* October 17, 18, 1886.

52. *Hearings before the Committee on Naval Affairs, U.S. House of Representatives . . .* (1894), p. 44.

53. V. J. Fagin to F. M. Thorn, November 3, 1886, F. M. Thorn to Grover Cleveland, November 3, 1886, Cleveland Papers.

In October, Thorn admitted publicly (to the *Washington Post*) that parts of this report from the summer of 1885 were based on poor evidence. A. Hunter Dupree, *Science in the Federal Government,* p. 222.

54. B. A. Colonna to George Davidson, January 21, 1887, Davidson Papers; F. M. Thorn to C. S. Peirce, December 10, 1886, Coast Survey Correspondence, C. S. Peirce Papers; F. M. Thorn to Daniel Manning, January 5, 1887, as given in *Congressional Record, 49* Cong., 2nd Sess., pp. 1186–87.

55. *Congressional Record, 48* Cong., 1st Sess., March 4, April 23, 1884, pp. 1596, 3306.

56. Ibid., 49 Cong., 2nd Sess., January 31, 1887, p. 1188.

57. *Report of the Superintendent of the U.S. Coast and Geodetic Survey . . . during the Fiscal Year Ending with June, 1889,* p. 122.

For Colonna's activity, see the letters in Records of the Coast Survey, Office of the Assistant in Charge, Letters Sent, 1888, pp. 208–10; 1889, p. 30. See also H. S. Thompson to W. B. Morgan, January 15, 17, 1889, J. R.

Garrison to W. B. Morgan, January 15, 1889, Records of the Coast Survey, Superintendent's File, Departments, Congress, Army & Navy . . . vol. I, 1889.

58. *New York Times,* April 14, 1889, p. 20. Thorn meant by his lower-primate expression the horseplay that went on in the Coast Survey building before he came.

59. F. M. Thorn to O. H. Tittmann, January 31, 1903, Library and Information Services Division, National Oceanic and Atmospheric Administration.

60. *Congressional Record,* 50 Cong., 2nd Sess., February 19, 1889, p. 2044.

5: The Ordeal Renewed in the Nineties

1. For the changes in the pay of scientists and skilled workers, see T. C. Mendenhall to Secretary of the Treasury, March 23, 1892, in *House Ex. Doc. No. 180,* 52 Cong., 1st Sess. See also Records of the Coast Survey, Superintendent's File, Special Reports, Papers and Memoranda, 1859–98, vol. 2, under "Estimates, Appropriations, Expenditures."

    The revealing sentence from the Eleventh Census is in *Report of Manufacturing Industries in the United States at the Eleventh Census: 1890, Part II, Statistics of Cities* (1895), vol. 6, part 2, p. 784.

2. The two quotations in this paragraph are from Autobiographical Notes, pp. 136, 137, in the Thomas C. Mendenhall Papers, Niels Bohr Library, American Institute of Physics, New York City.

3. R. J. Wynne to T. C. Mendenhall, March 28, 1892, in ibid.

4. *Congressional Record,* 51 Cong., 1st Sess., June 11, 1890, p. 6043; 52 Cong., 1st Sess., May 10, 1892, p. 4153; 53 Cong., 2nd Sess., May 11, 1894, p. 4622.

5. Ibid., 51 Cong., 2nd Sess., February 5, 1891, p. 2207.

6. *Report of the Superintendent of the U.S. Coast and Geodetic Survey . . . during the Fiscal Year Ending with June, 1893,* part II, p. 350.

7. *Report of the Superintendent of the U.S. Coast and Geodetic Survey . . . during the Fiscal Year Ending with June, 1891,* part II, p. 654.

8. A. F. Rodgers to the Superintendent, October 1895, Records of the Coast Survey, Superintendent's File, Assistants R–Z, 1895.

9. E. F. Dickens to T. C. Mendenhall, November 7, 1893, in ibid., Assistants A–D, 1893.

10. H. W. Edmonds to G. R. Putnam, October 13, 1899, in ibid., Assistants G–Q, 1899.

11. J. F. Pratt to O. H. Tittmann, January 15, 1901, in ibid., Assistants O, P, Q, 1901. See also Pratt to Tittmann, November 28, 1901, in ibid.

12. T. C. Mendenhall, "Determinations of Gravity with the New Half-Second Pendulums of the Coast and Geodetic Survey at Stations on the Pacific Coast, in Alaska, and at the Base Stations, Washington, D.C., and Hoboken, N.J.," *Report of the Superintendent of the U.S. Coast and Geodetic Survey . . . during the Fiscal Year Ending with June, 1891,* part II, pp. 503–64.

13. *Hearings before the Committee on Naval Affairs, U.S. House of Representatives . . .* (1894), p. 154.

14. V. F. Lenzen to the author, November 30, 1973.

15. "An Unpublished Scientific Monograph by C. S. Peirce," *Transactions of the*

Charles S. Peirce Society: A Quarterly Journal in American Philosophy, V, no. 1 (Winter 1969), 3–24.
16. C. S. Peirce to T. C. Mendenhall, September 29, 1891, Mendenhall Papers.
17. "Report of a Conference on Gravity Determinations Held at Washington, D.C. in May, 1882," in *Report of the Superintendent of the U.S. Coast and Geodetic Survey . . . during the Fiscal Year Ending with June, 1883,* p. 512.
18. A. H. Cook, *Gravity and the Earth* (1969), p. 23.
19. For Holman, see *Congressional Record,* 52 Cong., 1st Sess., August 5, 1892, Appendix, p. 545, and ibid., 2nd Sess., January 31, 1893, p. 1010.
20. Ibid., 1st Sess., May 12, 1892, p. 4238, as cited in Daniel J. Kevles, *The Physicists,* p. 63.
21. *Congressional Record,* 52 Cong., 1st Sess., May 12, 1892, p. 4237, and May 19, 1892, p. 4437.
22. J. C. Counts to T. C. Mendenhall, March 17, 19, 1892, Records of the Coast Survey, Superintendent's File, Departments, Congress, Army & Navy . . . , under "House of Representatives," 1892; T. C. Mendenhall to Chairman of Subcommittee on the Sundry Civil Bill, March 18, 1892, in ibid., Special Reports, Papers and Memoranda, 1855–98, Superintendent's Office, vol. 2.
23. *Congressional Record,* 52 Cong., 1st Sess., August 5, 1892, Appendix, p. 545; ibid., May 24, 1892, pp. 4632, 4626; May 10, 1892, pp. 4146–47; and May 12, 1892, p. 4237.
24. T. C. Mendenhall to W. S. Holman, January 17, 1893, Records of the Coast Survey, Superintendent's File, Special Reports, Papers and Memoranda, 1855–98, Superintendent's Office, vol. 2.
25. For the complete discussion and vote, see *Congressional Record,* 53 Cong., 2nd Sess., March 15, 1894, pp. 2997–3017; for the preceding quotations in this paragraph, see ibid., p. 3006, and March 16, 1894, pp. 3015, 3016.
26. Diary, Saturday, May 19, 1894, Mendenhall Papers. W. S. Schley was prominent in the Spanish-American War.
27. *Hearings before the Committee on Naval Affairs, U.S. House of Representatives . . .* (1894), pp. 121, 97.
28. Ibid., p. 8.
29. Ibid., pp. 18–19. For the statement of the error in the Hydrographic Office surveying, see *Methods and Results of the Survey of the West Coast of Lower California by the Officers of the U.S.S. "Ranger" during the Season of 1889* (1892), p. 31.
30. *Hearings before the Committee on Naval Affairs, U.S. House of Representatives . . .* (1894), pp. 12, 14, 15, 20, 21.
31. Records of U.S. House of Representatives, Committee on Appropriations, 53 Cong., Petition of Members of the Faculty, University of Wisconsin, April 7, 1894, National Archives.
32. *Hearings before the Committee on Naval Affairs, U.S. House of Representatives . . .* (1894), pp. 159–63.
33. Autobiographical Notes, p. 147, Mendenhall Papers.
34. *Washington Post,* January 10, 1894.
35. *New York Tribune,* June 23, 1894.
36. T. C. Mendenhall to H. T. Thurber, June 23, 1894, Cleveland Papers; *Washington Post,* June 23, 1894; *Washington Evening Star,* June 23, 1894.

37. H. L. Whiting to W. W. Duffield, August 5, 1895, Records of the Coast Survey, Superintendent's File, Assistants R–Z, 1895.
38. *Washington Evening Star*, August 25, 1894; *New York Tribune*, September 5, 1894.
39. B. A. Colonna to George Davidson, December 5, 1896, Davidson Papers.
40. See the testimony of February 1, 1898, of H. S. Pritchett, Mendenhall's successor, in *Hearings before the Sub-Committee of the House Committee on Appropriations . . . Sundry Civil Appropriations Bill for 1899*, p. 61.
41. Grover Cleveland, "Second Annual Message," December 3, 1894, in J. D. Richardson, ed., *A Compilation of the Messages and Papers of the Presidents*, XIII, 5973; *House Report No. 1954*, 53 Cong., 3rd Sess., Appendix, pp. 27–29, or *Senate Report No. 1021*, in ibid.
42. W. W. Duffield to J. D. Sayers, January 2, 1895, *Hearings before the Subcommittee of the House Committee on Appropriations . . . Sundry Civil Appropriations Bill for 1896*, pp. 192–93; Martin Hensel to T. C. Mendenhall, February 18, 1895, Mendenhall Papers; *Congressional Record*, 53 Cong., 3rd Sess., February 28, 1895, pp. 2888–89.
43. *Congressional Record*, 53 Cong., 3rd Sess., February 25, 1895, pp. 2710–12.
44. B. A. Colonna to George Davidson, July 15, 1895, Davidson Papers.
45. On the shifting about of the assistants, see, for example, T. C. Mendenhall to George Davidson, June 30, 1895, in ibid., H. G. Ogden to T. C. Mendenhall, undated, but answered on July 17, 1895, Mendenhall Papers; G. A. Fairfield to H. S. Pritchett, December 20, 1897, Records of the Coast Survey, Superintendent's File, Assistants A–Z, 1889–97, Supplemental Volume; see passim in the same volume.
46. *Official Register of the United States*, I (1895), 112; Logan Carlisle to W. W. Duffield, June 16, 1896, J. W. Donn to H. S. Pritchett, December 14, 1897, Records of the Coast Survey, Superintendent's File, Miscellaneous Papers, Memoranda and Correspondence, 1889–99, Supplemental Volume.
47. G. G. Hubbard to W. W. Duffield, June 5, 1896, in ibid., Miscellaneous Correspondence, 1895, 1896, 1897; J. F. Moser to W. W. Duffield, May 21, 1897, in ibid., Departments, Congress, Army & Navy . . . 1896, 1897, under "Naval Officers."
48. *Congressional Record*, 54 Cong., 1st Sess., March 31, 1896, p. 3399, and ibid., February 28, 1896, p. 2276.
49. W. W. Duffield to O. H. Tittmann, October 19, 1897, in ibid., Miscellaneous Papers, Memoranda and Correspondence, 1889–99, Supplemental Volume; Transcript of Testimony, in ibid., Coast and Geodetic Survey, Assistants A–Z, 1889–97, Supplemental Volume.
50. For 55 pages on Duffield's complaints about the three men, see ibid., Miscellaneous Papers, Memoranda and Correspondence, 1889–99, Supplemental Volume.
51. O. H. Tittmann to Secretary of the Treasury, October 22, 1897, in ibid. Ever since Hassler's time the Coast Survey had maintained and communicated standards of capacity, mass, and length.
52. C. A. Schott to W. W. Duffield, October 20, 1897, in ibid. See also *List and Catalogue of the Publications Issued by the U.S. Coast and Geodetic Survey, 1816–1902*.

6: Confrontation of the Hydrographic Office and the House of Representatives in 1900

1. For the above quotations in their order, see C. D. Sigsbee to Talcott Williams, September 21, 1894, Records of the Hydrographic Office, Letters Sent and Received, 1894, No. 3030; T. H. Sherman to the Hydrographer, March 16, 1893, in ibid., 1893, No. 1033; Clipping of October, 1896, in ibid., 1896, No. 3256.
2. *Annual Report of the Secretary of the Navy for the Year 1985*, pp. 186–87.
3. R. E. Peary to C. D. Sigsbee, April 25, May 5, 1896, Records of the Hydrographic Office, Letters Sent and Received, 1896, No. 1337.
4. C. T. Hutchins to C. D. Sigsbee, January 15, June 25, 1894, C. D. Sigsbee to C. T. Hutchins, December 22, 1894, Records of the Hydrographic Office, Letters Sent and Received, 1894, Nos. 404a, 2305, 4365.
5. C. D. Sigsbee to G. P. Blow, April 12, 1894, in ibid., No. 1253.
6. G. J. Lydecker to J. M. Wilson, February 14, 1900, *Hearings before the Subcommittee of the House Committee on Appropriations . . . Sundry Civil Appropriations Bill for 1901*, p. 373.
7. *Report of the Superintendent of the Coast and Geodetic Survey . . . July 1, 1905, to June 30, 1906*, p. 213.
8. "Discussion on Precise Spirit Leveling," in *Transactions of the American Society of Civil Engineers*, XLV (1901), 147.
   Pritchett avoided trouble with the navy by agreeing to furnish charts with a Mercator projection, although the Coast Survey had always used another projection, called *polyconic*.
9. *Report of the Superintendent of the Coast and Geodetic Survey . . . July 1, 1898, to June 30, 1899*, p. 42.
10. *Report of the Superintendent of the Coast and Geodetic Survey . . . July 1, 1899, to June 30, 1900*, p. 243.
11. *U.S. Statutes at Large*, XXX, 1082.
12. Ibid., pp. 302, 374, 1029. For the backing by Long, see "Report of the Secretary of the Navy," *Annual Reports of the Navy Department for the Year 1899*, p. 61.
13. *Hearings before the Subcommittee of the House Committee on Appropriations . . . Sundry Civil Appropriations Bill for 1901*, pp. 531–40.
14. M. R. S. Mackenzie to the Secretary of the Navy, June 5, 1899, Records of the Hydrographic Office, Letters Sent and Received, 1899, No. 2291; H. S. Pritchett to the Hydrographer, June 10, 1899, Records of the Coast Survey, Superintendent's File, Departments, Congress, Army & Navy . . . 1899, under "Navy Department."
15. *Hearings before Subcommittee of the House Committee on Appropriations . . . Sundry Civil Appropriations Bill for 1901*, pp. 397–98.
16. Ibid., pp. 398, 400.
17. Ibid., pp. 401–406.
18. For the quotations in this paragraph, see ibid., pp. 404, 407; see also ibid., pp. 383–86, 391–94.
19. See, for example, Records of the Hydrographic Office, Letters Sent and Received, 1900, No. 1353.

20. For the quotations in the above paragraph, see ibid., C. C. Todd to Branch Hydrographic Office, Chicago, March 22, 1900, C. C. Todd to Branch Hydrographic Office, Philadelphia, March 21, 1900, No. 1006; C. C. Todd to Branch Office, Philadelphia, April 4, 1900, No. 1345; C. C. Todd to Branch Hydrographic Office, New York, April 25, 1900, No. 1723; C. C. Todd to Branch Hydrographic Office, Savannah, April 2, 1900, Letters Sent and Received, 1900, No. 1723; C. C. Todd to Branch Office, Duluth, April 30, 1900, No. 1723; C. C. Todd to Officer in Charge, Branch Hydrographic Office, Chicago, April 25, 1900, No. 1723.
21. *U.S. Statutes at Large,* XXXI, 118.
22. *Congressional Record,* 56 Cong., 1st Sess., February 14, 1900, p. 1790.
23. Ibid., April 19, 1900, p. 4443.
24. J. G. Cannon to A. E. Orr (no date), Records of the Hydrographic Office, Letters Sent and Received, 1900, No. 1723.
25. *Congressional Record,* 56 Cong., 1st Sess., April 19, 1900, pp. 4436, 4438–39.
26. Ibid., pp. 4427, 4431.
27. Ibid., p. 4429.
28. Ibid., May 4, 1900, p. 5135.
29. Ibid., pp. 5165, 5166.
30. Ibid., pp. 5139, 5140.
31. For this quotation and the one immediately following, see ibid., June 6, 1900, p. 6849.
32. J. G. Cannon to J. D. Long, April 21, 1900, as given in *Congressional Record,* 56 Cong., 1st Sess., p. 6851.
33. J. D. Long to J. G. Cannon, April 30, 1900, in ibid., C. C. Todd to Chief of the Bureau of Equipment, April 25, 1900, Records of the Hydrographic Office, Letters Sent and Received, 1900, No. 1781.
34. Memorandum, C. C. Todd to Chief of the Bureau of Equipment, April 25, 1900, in ibid.
35. J. G. Cannon to J. D. Long, May 14, 1900, J. D. Long to J. G. Cannon, May 15, 1900, *Congressional Record,* 56 Cong., 1st Sess., pp. 6849–50, 6852.

    Naval regulations forbade officers to combine for the purpose of influencing legislation; to influence legislation without the authority and approval of the Navy Department; or to publish and communicate information and criticism of acts and measures of any department of the government. Ibid., p. 6851.
36. Ibid., June 1, 1900, p. 6359.
37. Ibid., May 29, 1900, pp. 6226–28; June 6, 1900, pp. 6848, 6852.
38. Ibid., June 6, 1900, pp. 6849, 6850.
39. Ibid., pp. 6848, 6855, 6853. For this characterization of Burton, see Forrest Crissey, *Theodore E. Burton, American Statesman* (1956), p. 118.
40. *Congressional Record,* 56 Cong., 1st Sess., June 6, 1900, pp. 6855–56; June 7, 1900, pp. 6870–73, 6879–85.
41. *U.S. Statutes at Large,* XXXI, 689.
42. *New York Daily Tribune,* January 1, 1901.
43. T. E. Burton to J. D. Long, June 9, 1900, C. C. Todd to Secretary Long, June 13, 1900, Records of the Hydrographic Office, Letters Sent and Received, 1900, No. 2579.

44. *New York Daily Tribune,* January 1, 1901.
45. *Report of the Superintendent of the Coast and Geodetic Survey . . . July 1, 1900, to June 30, 1901,* pp. 11, 13.
46. *Annual Reports of the Navy Department for the Year 1903,* p. 365.
47. W. H. Moody to Secretary of Commerce and Labor, March 4, 1904, in *Hearings before the Subcommittee of the House Committee on Appropriations . . . Sundry Civil Appropriations Bill for 1905,* pp. 165–66.
48. *Report of the Superintendent of the Coast and Geodetic Survey . . . July 1, 1900, to June 30, 1901,* p. 12.

7: Reverberations in the Twentieth Century

1. *Congressional Record,* 57 Cong., 1st Sess., January 13, 16, 20, 22, 28, 1902, pp. 726, 758, 763, 765, 862, 1052; ibid., 2nd Sess., January 15, 17, 29, February 10, 1903, pp. 861, 929, 1446, 2008.
2. *Annual Report of the Director, United States Coast and Geodetic Survey . . . for the Fiscal Year Ended June 30, 1922,* p. 7.
3. *U.S. Statutes at Large,* XL, 87–88, 163.
4. *Hearings before the Subcommittee of the House Committee on Appropriations . . . Sundry Civil Appropriations Bill for 1921,* pp. 1810–20.
5. *Twenty-sixth Annual Report of the Secretary of Commerce, 1938,* p. xxviii.
6. *Hearings before the Joint Committee on Reorganization of the Administrative Branch of the Government* (1924), pp. 69, 330–31.
7. Ibid., pp. 152, 174, 175, 416.
8. Ibid., pp. 353–60, 387, 395, 674–75, 681–82, 371.
9. Ibid., pp. 429–69, 408.
10. See Marc L. Pinsel, *150 Years of Service on the Sea: A Pictorial History of the U.S. Naval Hydrographic Office from 1830 to 1980* (1981), pp. 39, 40, 43, 48, 54, 56.
11. Ibid., pp. 48, 50–51, 54, 56, 64, 68. See also (for this paragraph) the annual reports of the Hydrographic Office and its successor, the Oceanographic Office, for the years 1946, 1948, 1953, 1962–68.
12. For the two preceding sentences, see *Annual Report of the Director, United States Coast and Geodetic Survey . . . for the Fiscal Year Ended June 30, 1930,* p. 18, and *Annual Report of the Director, United States Coast and Geodetic Survey . . . for the Fiscal Year Ended June 30, 1928,* p. 7.
13. *Hearings before the Joint Committee on Reorganization of the Administrative Branch of the Government* (1924), p. 364; see also D. B. Wainwright, "Long Wire Sweep," *Report of the Superintendent of the Coast and Geodetic Survey . . . July 1, 1904, to June 30, 1905,* Appendix, pp. 285–87; *Annual Report of the Superintendent of the Coast and Geodetic Survey . . . for the Fiscal Year Ended June 30, 1912,* p. 5.
14. C. H. Swick, *Pendulum Gravity Measurements and Isostatic Reductions* (1942), pp. 1–12; *Thirty-ninth Annual Report of the Secretary of Commerce* (1951), pp. 44, 51–52.
15. See the annual reports of the Coast and Geodetic Survey for the years 1911, 1913, 1917, 1920, 1926, 1928, 1929, 1933, 1935, and 1966.
16. See the annual reports of the Department of Commerce for the years 1946, 1952, 1957, 1958, and 1964.

Essay on Sources

Manuscript Materials

A major location for research was Record Group 23, established in the National Archives to accommodate the historical materials on the Coast Survey. My page-by-page examination covered, first, some 230 volumes in the post–Civil War period, which are part of the "Superintendent's File, 1866–1905." The volumes in this "File" are listed and annotated in the impressive inventory of Coast Survey records by Nathan Reingold, entitled *Preliminary Inventory of the Records of the Coast and Geodetic Survey* (1958, reprinted in 1981). This same archivist and historian also wrote "Research Possibilities in the U.S. Coast and Geodetic Survey Records," in *Archives Internationales d'Histoire des Sciences,* 11 (1958), 337–46, where he classified the field records by number and scientific kind, and added to his commentary on these records and on the history of the Survey during the nineteenth century. I also went through, page by page, some 95 volumes in the Coast Survey records of the Office of Hydrography. The characteristic document in all the above volumes of Record Group 23 is the handwritten letter received.

Another important archival collection for my study was Record Group 37, which takes in the navy's Hydrographic Office. I read 100 volumes or boxes of the letters sent and received for 23 years, in the period 1870 to 1901. There is a good inventory of these records, entitled *Inventory of the Records of the Hydrographic Office* (1971). Also, there are some wonderful documents in three dark green boxes of the General Records of the Treasury Department (RG56), marked "Solicitor Correspondence, July 3, 1885–March 8, 1886," "Solicitor Correspondence, August 30, 1886–February 18, 1889," and "1st Comptroller Correspondence, May 1884–May 1886." Documents therein detail the malpractices of Superintendent Hilgard and the tumult of the Thorn regime.

The largest collection of private papers proved to be the most valuable: the George Davidson Papers in the Bancroft Library at Berkeley, California. Because he was dean of the Coast Survey scientists on the Pacific Coast and harbored the ambition to become superintendent, Davidson kept in touch with the Washington office. Letters to him from assistants in the national capital record many of the climactic events within the troubled organization. Unlike the Davidson Papers, the Thomas C. Mendenhall Papers (at the American Institute of Physics in New York City) do not have a large number of letters either received or sent. But Superintendent Mendenhall's Autobiographical Notes were very helpful for several crises; his Diaries are, for the most part, too brief. The outgoing letters from the John F. Pratt Papers (at the University of Washington Library, Seattle) give indispensable information on a talented engineer, who represented so well the long-serving, hard-working assistants of Coast Survey history. The Coast Survey Correspondence in the Charles S. Peirce Papers (Houghton Library, Harvard University) communicates the political activity of Peirce at Ann Arbor in August 1885, immediately after the Thorn commission had made its report. A helpful aid in using the Peirce Papers is the *Annotated Catalogue of the Papers of Charles S. Peirce* by Richard S. Robin, published in 1967. Several letters received in the Othniel C. Marsh Papers (Sterling Memorial Library, Yale University) add to our understanding of the beginnings of the Allison Commission. Letters from the Grover Cleveland Papers (in the Manuscript Division of the Library of Congress) show the personal interest which the president took in Coast Survey affairs. The Robert Lowry Letters (in the Library and Information Services Division of the National Oceanic and Atmospheric Administration, Rockville, Maryland) are 70 pages of typed copies of communications which Representative Lowry received when he asked for advice from scientists and administrators to prepare him for the sessions of the Allison Commission. Two letters each of Robert T. Lincoln, secretary of war, and Montgomery C. Meigs, quartermaster general (retired), are also connected with the origins of the Allison Commission. Even more important, they introduce the question of civil-military relations in the science and government of a democracy. The Lincoln-Meigs exchange is to be found in the Archives of the National Academy of Sciences: Records Series, 1863–1913.

Publications by Congress

In this period of legislative supremacy, the sessions of Congress and its committees chronicle the political endurance of bureaus, the ebb and flow of public and party opinion about government science, and the decisions of the elected officials. For finding out about the Coast Survey from the *Congressional Record,* reading is best for the seven years 1886, 1887, 1892, 1894, 1900, 1902, and 1903. The most significant talk in the *Record* concerning the Hydrographic Office is from February to June 1900, when Cannon and other House members spoke eloquently— and with outrage—against the political activity of that office. Concerning Cannon, no full and fair biography will appear until a biographer reads the daily *Record* for the 46 years that Cannon was in the House of Representatives.

A valuable and unexpected resource for research was the printed proceedings of the subcommittee of the House Committee on Appropriations when it held its annual hearings on the Sundry Civil Appropriations bill. The importance of the Sundry Civil bill was that for many years it carried the main expenditures for government science, and the heads of a dozen or more scientific agencies testified year after year before a House subcommittee on appropriations to plead their requests for money and to give opinions or information on many matters germane to this history. The publication of this series began in 1891, and they are most readily available in the Library of Congress or other government libraries of the Washington, D.C. area.

After 1922 and up to World War II, there were hearings on only one general appropriation bill, rather than several appropriation bills with slightly different names, and the scientists presented their requests when the departments to which they belonged came before the House Committee on Appropriations. Four congressional hearings are noteworthy, because they seriously considered the question of abolishing or changing radically the position of the Coast Survey in the government. From 1884 to 1886 there was the well-known Allison Commission, whose proceedings were printed as *Senate Misc. Doc. No. 82,* 49 Cong., 1st Sess. In the spring of 1894 the Government Printing Office published *Hearings before the Committee on Naval Affairs, U.S. House of Representatives . . . on the Bill H.R. 6338, to Abolish the Bureau in the Treasury Department Known as the Coast and Geodetic Survey, and Transfer the Work of Said Bureau to the Hydrographic Office in the Navy Department and the Geological Survey in the Department of the Interior.* At these 1894 hearings, Superintendent Mendenhall and other scientists had the opportunity to come to grips with a destructive congressional antagonist. Also, historians can consult the Thorn commission report of 1885 in these *Hearings.* This publication of the House Naval Affairs Committee is not a part of the federal series of public documents and therefore does not enjoy wide circulation; the Library of Congress has a copy.

In 1902 the House Committee on Interstate and Foreign Commerce published its *Hearings* of that year on the question of creating a Department of Commerce and of bringing the Coast Survey over from the Treasury; there is a copy in the library of the Department of Commerce. In 1924 a joint committee of Congress held hearings to consider the merger of the Hydrographic Office with the Coast Survey. The Library and Information Services Division of the National Oceanic and Atmospheric Administration (NOAA) has these *Hearings before the Joint Committee on the Reorganization of the Administrative Branch of the Government.* Three influential papers from Congress concerning the Hydrographic Office and the Coast Survey are the majority and minority reports (in 1886) of the Allison Commission (*House Report No. 2740,* 49 Cong., 1st Sess.) and the report of two "experts" working for the Dockery-Cockrell Commission (in 1895) that the Coast Survey should be transferred to the Hydrographic Office (*House Report No. 1954,* 53 Cong., 3rd Sess., or *Senate Report, No. 1021,* in ibid.).

For biographical information on senators and representatives, I used *Biographical Directory of the American Congress, 1774–1927,* one convenient number of a continuing series; *Dictionary of American Biography; Who's Who in America, 1897–1942* (1966); *Appleton's Cyclopaedia of American Biography* (1888); the *National Cyclopaedia of American Biography* (1898 and after); the *Twentieth Century Biographical Dictionary of Notable Americans* (1904); and *The Encyclopaedia of American Biography* (1915). One documentary source was that of wills—scores of them. I do not list individual biographies, but many of them are to be found in the revised edition of the *Harvard Guide to American History,* volume I (1974).

From the Executive Branch

The *Annual Reports* of the superintendent of the Coast Survey during the nineteenth century are bulky volumes in science and administration that are part of the congressional serial set of House and Senate documents. The numbers of the successive volumes in the congressional serial set are to be found in the *Checklist of United States Public Documents, 1789–1909,* volume I (3rd ed., 1911). Early in the twentieth century the *Annual Reports* lost their massive appearance and extensive scientific content. In 1933 they ceased to be part of the congressional serial set and were assimilated to the annual reports of the Department of Commerce, where they continued to be compiled for several decades. After 1956, there was no public circulation of separate annual reports of the Coast Survey, which had, in any event, become very abbreviated. Since June 1971, knowledge about the National Ocean Service and the National Geodetic Survey is communicated briefly in the annual reports of the Department of Commerce and its secretaries. From 1866 to 1932, the annual report of the Hydrographic Office and hydrographer appeared, along with reports of all other naval bureaus and offices, in the annual report of the Navy Department and its secretary. This comprehensive document is in the congressional serial set. After 1932, the annual report of the Navy Department did not include the presentations of its bureaus and offices, and ceased to be part of the congressional serial set; after 1948, there were no published and circulated departmental annual reports.

After the decline and demise of the Navy Department's annual report, the Hydrographic or Oceanographic Office annual reports were separates through 1969, when they too ceased publication. This defunct series must be sought in the Library of Congress, or in the Navy Department Library, or in the U.S. Naval Oceanographic Library (now in Bay St. Louis, Mississippi, but once in Greater Washington).

Concerning the departmental conflict between the navy and the Treasury, the navy went on the offensive in "Papers Relating to the Transfer of Maritime Services to the Navy Department as Recommended in the Report of the Secretary of the Navy," *Report of the Secretary of the Navy for the Year Ending June 30, 1882* (pp. 27–40, 236–398). These papers gave active naval officers the rare opportunity to express their opinions at book length on a current political question. The threatened agencies of the Treasury reacted with the sharpest kind of civilian criticism of the naval establishment. This criticism was delivered in the printed report of a special committee of the Lighthouse Board and in five other printed reports of the following Treasury officials: the chief of the Revenue Marine Division; the superintendent of the Coast and Geodetic Survey; the supervising surgeon general, Marine Hospital Service; the general superintendent, U.S. Life-Saving Service; and the supervising inspector general of steamboats. The Library of Congress has a bound volume of these six reports with the title *Reports in Regard to the Transfer of the Bureaus and Divisions of the Merchant Marine in the Treasury Department to the Navy Department* (1883). The letter of Superintendent Mendenhall to the secretary of the treasury on March 23, 1892, which justified the controversial reduction of the wages of skilled workmen in the Coast Survey, was published as *House Ex. Doc. No. 180* (52 Cong., 1st Sess.).

Newspapers and Periodicals

Research here was highly selective. Newspapers from Boston to Washington printed news about the Coast Survey during the two Cleveland administrations. Knowledge of important developments within the bureau and an understanding of the president's policy toward it would have been lost forever but for the occasional, brief articles which the Eastern press took pains with. The magazine *Science,* locally owned in the District of Columbia by Gardiner G. Hubbard and Alexander Graham Bell and with entree into the inner circles of the government, was helpful on a score of occasions for this history. Assistant Richard M. Bache, of the Coast Survey, wrote anonymously and in bombastic style against Samuel J. Randall, powerful member of Congress from Pennsylvania, in two articles entitled "The Late Attacks upon the Coast and Geodetic Survey," *The United Service Magazine: A Monthly Review of Military and Naval Affairs* (XI [October, November 1884], 345–64, 530–59).

Science

Through 1911, the appendices of its annual reports are the main repository of published Coast Survey science. An abstract of the report itself and an alphabetical index of persons, topics, and places help the reader to enter each annual volume. For the whole nineteenth-century series there is the valuable bibliographical aid, *List and Catalogue of the Publications Issued by the U.S. Coast and Geodetic Survey, 1816–1902,* to be found in the Library and Information Services Division, NOAA. Part I of this aid lists annual reports and their appendices, tide tables, notices to mariners and coast pilots, and the successive Survey catalogues of available charts and maps; Part II—the "catalogue" of this bibliographical aid—is actually a 100-page index of the scientific appendices in the *annual reports* (separate publications are also indexed); author, subject matter, and geographical location provide the bold-type headings for this useful index. Through this *List and Catalogue* the student comes easily to the most original scientists of the Coast Survey and their work: to Ferrel on tidal research, to Peirce on the flexure of pendulum supports, to Pillsbury on the Gulf Stream, to Mitchell on the circulation of the sea in New York Harbor, to Sigsbee on deep-sea sounding, and to Schott on geodesy. Examples of Coast Survey mapping are best observed in Peter J. Guthorn, *United States Coastal Charts, 1783–1861* (1984).

Among Coast Survey scientists of the nineteenth century, Charles S. Peirce has attracted the most attention in the hundred years since. For explanation and perspective concerning Peirce's work with gravity pendulums I am obligated to the late Victor F. Lenzen and Robert P. Multhauf for their joint article, "Development of Gravity Pendulums in the 19th Century," in U.S. National Museum *Bulletin 240* (1965), pp. 301–48. In my search for knowledge of the science and history of pendulum swinging I was also fortunate in finding Norman Feather, *Mass, Length, and Time* (1955), and Alan H. Cook, *Gravity and the Earth* (1969). Clarence H. Swick, in his *Modern Methods for Measuring the Intensity of Gravity* (1921), has much to say about developments in gravity studies since Peirce's time. Professor Lenzen summarized and interpreted the last work of Peirce for the Coast Survey in "An Unpublished Scientific Monograph by C. S. Peirce," *Trans-*

actions of the Charles S. Peirce Society: A Quarterly Journal in American Philosophy (V, no. 1 [Winter 1969], 3–24). See also Victor F. Lenzen, "Charles S. Peirce as Mathematical Geodesist," in ibid. (VIII, no. 2 [Spring 1972], 90–105), and "Charles S. Peirce as Astronomer," in Edward C. Moore and Richard S. Robin (eds.), Studies in the Philosophy of Charles Sanders Peirce (1964). For the recent Dictionary of Scientific Biography (X [1974], 478–81, 482–88), Carolyn Eisele has written the biographies of Superintendent Benjamin Peirce, father, and Assistant Charles S. Peirce, son; see also Carolyn Eisele, "Charles S. Peirce, Nineteenth-century Man of Science," Scripta Mathematica (XXIV, no. 4 [December 1959], 305–24), and "The Scientist-Philosopher C. S. Peirce at the Smithsonian," in Journal of the History of Ideas (18 [1957], 537–47). Readers will soon have a new, full edition of Peirce's writings to consult for biographical and scientific information. In 1982, Writings of Charles S. Peirce: A Chronological Edition, Volume I, 1857–1866 appeared, followed in 1984 by Volume 2, 1867–1871, in 1986 by Volume 3, 1872–1876, and in 1989 by Volume 4, 1879–1884. The leading editors have been (in alphabetical order) Max H. Fisch, Christian J. W. Kloesel, and Edward C. Moore.

Harold L. Burstyn wrote the life of William Ferrel for the Dictionary of Scientific Biography (IV [1971], 590–93). Further accounts of Coast Survey scientists, in the Biographical Memoirs of the National Academy of Sciences, supplement the lives of the first three superintendents in the Dictionary of Scientific Biography and recognize the accomplishments of three other members of the bureau. The citations from this biographical series of the National Academy are "William Ferrel" and "Julius Erasmus Hilgard," in volume III (1895); "Charles Anthony Schott," in volume VIII (1919); "Thomas Corwin Mendenhall," in volume XVI (1934); "George Davidson," in volume XVIII (1936); and "Henry Mitchell," in volume XX (1939).

The best statements on the science of the Hydrographic Office during the nineteenth century are to be found in the reports of Hydrographer John R. Bartlett, submitted annually to the Navy Department in the years 1883 to 1887. Characteristic publications of the Hydrographic Office include Steam-Lanes Across the Atlantic (1873), which is a republication of a Maury paper from the 1850s, without his name; Lieutenant Commander Henry H. Gorringe, Coasts and Islands of the Mediterranean Sea, parts I, II, III (1875–79); and Lieutenant George L. Dyer, The Use of Oil to Lessen the Dangerous Effect of Heavy Seas (1886). See also Everett Hayden, "The Pilot Chart of the North Atlantic Ocean," Journal of the Franklin Institute (CXXV [April 1888], 1–28).

In seeking to understand and interpret the geodesy and oceanography of government bureaus, I needed the help of past and present scientists. A U.S. Air Force publication, Geodesy for the Layman (1959), edited by Captain Richard K. Burkard, furnished lucid and convincing explanations of geodetic terms and concepts. In learning the traditions and practices of nineteenth-century geodesy, I drew on Alexander R. Clarke, Geodesy (1880), and on James H. Gore, Geodesy (1891). For the contemporary science, I studied Guy Bomford, Geodesy (1962), and Weikko A. Heiskanen, The Earth and Its Gravity Field (1958). In tidal theory and its application to tidal measurements, I used Henry A. Marmer, The Tide (1926), and George H. Darwin, The Tides and Kindred Phenomena in the Solar System (1898). Marmer also communicated to me the contribution of Henry Mitchell to the knowledge of tidal currents. Henry M. Stommel, in his authoritative *The Gulf Stream. A Physical and Dynamical Description* (1965), warmly praised Lieutenant John E. Pillsbury and his observations in the Gulf Stream.

Two books helped orient me in the technology of oceanic research: C. Wyville Thomson, *The Depth of the Sea . . . Dredging Cruises of H. M. S. S. Porcupine* (1874), and John Murray and Johan Hjort, *The Depths of the Ocean: A General Account of the Oceanography Based Largely on the Scientific Researches of the Norwegian Steamer Michael Sars in the North Atlantic* (1912). In their *Essentials of Astronomy* (1966), Lloyd Motz and Anneta Duveen provided excellent diagrams for the better understanding of astronomical terms. Anita McConnell's *No Sea Too Deep: The History of Oceanographic Instruments* (1982) is clear and full, for the nineteenth century, about what the maritime nations were doing in the technology of underwater exploration.

History

There has been plenty of writing on the history of the Coast Survey. An early, worthwhile effort came on an anniversary of the first field work and bears the title *Centennial Celebration of the United States Coast and Geodetic Survey, April 5 and 6, 1916;* it has good summaries and interpretations of nineteenth-century Coast Survey science as seen by twentieth-century experts in the bureau. Next, in 1923, came Gustavus A. Weber's *The Coast and Geodetic Survey: Its History, Activities, and Organization;* through laws, facts, and bibliography, this booklet, a release of the Brookings Institution, gives anyone a good start in the institutional understanding of the bureau. In his book of 1957, *Science in the Federal Government: A History of Policies and Activities to 1940,* A. Hunter Dupree has two sections on the origins of the Coast Survey in Jeffersonian and Jacksonian times, and in the same year was the 90-page sesquicentennial publication of the Department of Commerce by A. Joseph Wraight and Elliott B. Roberts, entitled *The Coast and Geodetic Survey, 1807–1957: 150 Years of History.* In 1963, Victor F. Lenzen brought out a little book with the title *Benjamin Peirce and the U.S. Coast Survey,* which is solid on what Peirce did for science when he headed the Coast Survey. A summarial chapter, "Putting the Nation on the Map: The Coast and Geodetic Survey," can be found in Roy Popkin, *The Environmental Science Services Administration* (1967). Robert C. Ingersoll wrote an article, "The Effect of the Coast Survey on 19th Century American Science," for *Synthesis: The University Journal in the History and Philosophy of Science* (2, no. 4 [1975], 22–32). Carolyn Eisele did the Coast Survey article for the revised edition (in 1976) of the *Dictionary of American History* (II, 87–88), and Daniel J. Kevles has a number of knowledgeable pages on the nineteenth-century Coast Survey in Chapters IV and V of his *The Physicists: The History of a Scientific Community in Modern America* (1979). Peter J. Guthorn's volume on coastal charts to 1861 has half a dozen integrated pages on many features and topics of the antebellum Coast Survey. (This account is marred, however, by printing errors, even to the extent of blank spaces in the text.)

Sometimes, biography furnished me with institutional knowledge. Several items on Charles S. Peirce which contribute in this way have already been cited. Both of the first two superintendents have had biographers: Florian Cajori, *The Chequered Career of Ferdinand Rudolph Hassler, First Superintendent of the United States Coast Survey: A Chapter in the History of Science in America* (1929), and Merle

M. Odgers, *Alexander D. Bache, Scientist and Educator, 1806–1867* (1947). There are two full-length studies of George Davidson, which include the contribution of the Coast Survey to scientific knowledge of the Pacific Coast: Oscar Lewis, *George Davidson, Pioneer West Coast Scientist* (1954), and William F. King's doctoral dissertation of 1973 at Claremont Graduate School, "George Davidson: Pacific Coast Scientist for the U.S. Coast and Geodetic Survey, 1845–1895" (University Microfilms Order No. 74-965). Again, Nathan Reingold has knowledge to communicate on the Coast Survey, this time through two articles on Bache, "Alexander Dallas Bache: Science and Technology in the American Idiom," *Technology and Culture* (XI [April 1970], 163–77) and his "Alexander Dallas Bache" in *Dictionary of Scientific Biography* (I [1970], 363–65). Despite the number of works or articles by talented persons, there was plenty of room for a monograph study over a 40-year period, which this history has aimed to be.

The first significant historical work on the Hydrographic Office is the volume by Lieutenant Walter A. Hughes, *Founding and Development of the U.S. Hydrographic Office,* published in 1887 by the Government Printing Office. This book can be called *official history,* for it was prepared under the direction of Commander John R. Bartlett, the hydrographer of the navy, to help him in his campaign to acquire control of all coastal surveying, and it is a reasonable speculation that officialdom was responsible for the exclusion of Lieutenant Commander Henry H. Gorringe, the important surveyor and compiler. Nevertheless, there is solid information here, and a copy may be found in the library of the U.S. Naval Oceanographic Office, Bay St. Louis, Mississippi.

Recently (1982), Marc F. Pinsel brought out *150 Years of Service on the Seas: A Pictorial History of the U.S. Naval Oceanographic Office from 1830 to 1980, Volume I (1830–1946).* Pinsel has three chapters on science and scientists, military and civilian, and one chapter on administrative history, with many portraits of naval leaders and plates of Hydrographic Office charts. In the governmental relations of the late nineteenth-century Office, civilian names are almost completely absent. The biography by Frances L. Williams, *Matthew Fontaine Maury: Scientist of the Sea* (1963), tells all about the antebellum Hydrographic Office and Maury's part in it. I used Leon B. Richardson's biography, *William E. Chandler, Republican* (1940), for communicating the activity and temperament of this secretary of the navy. Richardson says nothing about Chandler's attempted coup during the Arthur administration, but Charles O. Paullin knows about Chandler's deed and declares briefly against it; see *Paullin's History of Naval Administration, 1775–1911: A Collection of Articles from the U.S. Naval Institute Proceedings* (1968). Paullin provides what was needed on the political and scientific affairs of the Navy Department to give the Hydrographic Office its larger administrative setting.

Two general histories helped me to verify or enlarge the perspectives of my writing and to include scientific aspects of the Hydrographic Office and the Coast Survey, which might otherwise have been overlooked by me. I mean Margaret Deacon, *Scientists and the Sea, 1650–1900: A Study of Marine Science* (1971), and Susan Schlee, *The Edge of an Unfamiliar World: A History of Oceanography* (1971). Oscar Kraines in his *Congress and the Challenge of Big Government* (1958), which studied some of the classic congressional investigations of economy and efficiency within the Executive branch, supported the transfer of the Coast Survey to the navy, as urged by the Dockery-Cockrell Commission. The grave weakness of

Kraines' advocacy is his failure to consider the science of the issue: Would the progress of knowledge have been advanced or retarded by the abolition of an independent Coast Survey?

The relation of the military to civilian government during the last two centuries is best presented in Volker R. Berghahn, *Militarism: The History of an International Debate, 1861–1979* (1982). Berghahn gives the origin and meaning of the word in Europe and England, and places the idea in a constitutional and political setting, both in the United States and abroad. Clarence G. Lasby's "Science and the Military," in David D. Van Tassel and Michael G. Hall, eds., *Science and Society in the United States* (1966, pp. 251–82), furnished me with ideology and events in the connection of the military with science during the nineteenth century. Howard Plotkin's "Astronomers versus the Navy: The Revolt of American Astronomers over the Management of the United States Naval Observatory, 1877–1902," in *Proceedings of the American Philosophical Society* (122 [December 1978], 385–89), surveys the long and active relationship within the Observatory between civilians and the Navy Department, and the strength and weakness of the Observatory, which naval officers have always directed.

On party history, I found that Joel H. Silbey's book, *A Respectable Minority: The Democratic Party in the Civil War Era, 1860–1868* (1971), was congruent with my conception of the party from 1870 to 1900. Knowledge as an issue between the parties had yet to arise in the period of Professor Silbey's study. No comparable volume exists for the Republicans; the scholarly literature concentrates on economic affairs and their effects. On science and the first Cleveland administration, there is Thomas G. Manning, "Peirce, the Coast Survey, and the Politics of Cleveland Democracy," in *Transactions of the Charles S. Peirce Society* (XI, no. 3 [Summer 1975], 187–94).

Index

Adams, Robert: House member with Hayden in Yellowstone country, 57
Agassiz, Alexander: Cleveland thought of as superintendent, 87
Airy, George B.: consulted by C. S. Peirce in England, 76
Alaska: Seward insisted Survey enter, 41; navy published directory of, 42; Coast Survey worked first in Alexander Archipelago, 104; decision of Great Britain and the United States to establish boundary between Canada and Alaska, 105; in Panhandle, Americans did coastline, 105; Canadians did interior between watercourses, 105; surveyors of Coast Survey and Canada marked ground for north and south boundary on one hundred and forty-first meridian, Mount St. Elias to Arctic Ocean, 105; discovery of gold in Klondike, 106; 30,000 miners entered Yukon River basin, 106; Congress appropriated money for survey of Yukon River, 106
Alaska Boundary Tribunal: Coast Survey provided maps for, 106
Albany (N.Y.): C. S. Peirce swung pendulum, 77
Aleutian Islands: Coast Survey passed through into Bering Sea, 106; Dutch Harbor center of operations for Americans, 106

Alexander, W. D.: surveyor general of Hawaiian Islands, 135
Alger, R. A.: secretary of war, would not move against Superintendent Duffield, 126
Allegheny (Pa.): C. S. Peirce swung pendulum, 77
Allison Commission: presided over by, senator from Iowa, 52; barred spoilsmen from Coast Survey, 52; fought reduction of Coast Survey budget, 52; established, 1884, 61; duties anticipated, 61; renewed March 1, 1886, 67; Schott, Mitchell, and Colonna appeared before, 88; Mitchell testified that surveying must be repeated, as sands and shoals shifted, 88; majority findings, 91; stood with scientists, 91; minority, H. A. Herbert and J. T. Morgan, opposed to geodesy, 92; Allison agreed to support Coast Survey salaries, 95
American Academy of Arts and Sciences: spoke against Chandler plan, 58
American Association for the Advancement of Science: sent resolutions to government on gravity research, 78
American Journal of Science: praised work of Hydrographic Office near Puerto Rico, 37–38
American Philosophical Society: spoke against Chandler plan, 58

despite presence of naval officers there, 12–13

Davis, C. H.: admiral who helped found Hydrographic Office, 28

Dawes, H. L.: respected weather service for helping people go about their business, 49

Dayton, A. G.: would cancel powers of Coast Survey in new empire, 142

Denby, Edwin: secretary of the navy, described Hydrographic publications, 155

Dennis, W. H.: removal of opened way for Superintendent Duffield's son, Will Ward Jr., 124

Dewey, George: directed naval surveying on Mexican coast, 30

Dickinson, D. M.: advised Cleveland on Duffield, 122

Dingley, Nelson: defended growth of government expenses, 102

District of Columbia: topographical surveying by Coast Survey, 104

Dockery-Cockrell Commission: congressional body looking into efficiency of executive, 114; Enloe proposal that this commission consider transfer of Coast Survey defeated, 114; led to hearings by House committee on naval affairs, 115

Dole, S. B.: Hawaiian government of joined Coast Survey, 135

Donn, J. W.: dismissed by Duffield, 125

Donnelly, Ignatius: explained glacial mantle as tail of comet, 54

Duffield, W. W.: background, 122; as superintendent, bullied into approving reduction of Survey expenditures, including own salary, 123; purges by in Survey, 124, 125; attacked Tittmann, Pratt, and Schott, 126; spoilsmen Griffin, King, Renfro dominated Duffield administration, 124

Duffield, W. W., Jr.: place made for in Survey office, 123

Dumont, J. A.: inspector general of Steamboat Service, accused navy of being aristocratic, and a threat to liberty and equality, 45

Durham, M. J.: sneered at tinsel and ornament on government buildings, 48; treasury accountant in Coast Survey during Thorn's regime, 85–86

Dyer, G. L.: for Hydrographic Office published *Use of Oil to Lessen the Dangerous Effect of Heavy Seas*, 34

Ebensburgh, (Pa.): Peirce swung pendulum there, 77

Economy: Democratic principle concerning public expenditures, 46; Randall said that $150,000 could be saved on Survey budget, 45; historic forces behind rise of movement, 47–48; call for retrenchment and reform, 48; Democrats called powers of taxation "steals," 48; associated expenditure for science with fringe groups in society, with aristocrats, capitalists, and esthetes, 50; exception to the general attitude, Democrat Randall favored geology over geodesy, 55; Herbert, big navy man, 55; Holman defended Geological Survey, which hired his son, 55; Lowry, a Democrat, defended Coast Survey, 57; parties collaborated in behalf of western mapping, 56; yet abiding significance of partisan dialectic, 96, 127–28

Edison, Thomas A.: approved Sigsbee publication, 38

Edmunds, G. F.: legislated Coast Survey onto Lake Champlain, 4

Eimbeck, William: would not take orders from Davidson, 12

Eldridge, G. H.: bought Survey charts, and lessened topographical detail, 89

Eleventh Census: higher earnings of plate workers in District of Columbia, 101

Eliot, C. W.: reviewed second volume of *Atlantic Coast Pilot*, 15

Elkins, S. B.: Republican, anti-science, 55

Endicott, W. C.: secretary of war, supported C. O. Boutelle, 71

Engineers Club, Philadelphia: supported Coast Survey, 58

Enloe, B. A.: accused Mendenhall of neglecting workers and favoring scientists, 112; proposed dividing Coast Survey between navy and interior departments, 113

Environmental Science Services Administration: Coast Survey in, 161

Etruria: ship's officers praised Great Circle Chart, 35

Everhart, J. B.: drew House applause for Coast Survey, 93

Fagin, V. J.: protégé of Congressman Butterworth, 89; knocked down waiter, 89; harassed field assistants, 89; spread misinformation, 89; hit one of tidal scien-